Living with
It Daily
Meditations for People
with Chronic Pain

Living with It Daily

*Meditations for People
with Chronic Pain*

Patricia D. Nielsen

A DELL TRADE PAPERBACK

A DELL TRADE PAPERBACK

Published by
Dell Publishing
a division of
Bantam Doubleday Dell Publishing Group, Inc.
1540 Broadway
New York, New York 10036

Library of Congress Cataloging in Publication Data

Nielsen, Patricia D.
Living with it daily : meditations for people with chronic pain /
Patricia D. Nielsen.
p.   cm.
Includes index.
ISBN 0-440-50555-0
1. Chronic pain—Patients—Prayer books and devotions—
English.   2. Chronically ill—Prayer books and devotions—
English.   3. Pain—Religious aspects.   I. Title.
BL625.9.C47N54   1994

291.4′3—dc20   93-46867
                                                            CIP

Printed in the United States of America
Published simultaneously in Canada
September 1994
10   9   8   7   6   5   4   3   2   1
FFG

To those with chronic pain
who yearn for healing
in their lives

and

to Tom, Erik, and Sonja
for their love and patience
through all the hills and valleys
of my sojourn

Acknowledgments

I have many people to thank for their support, encouragement, and practical help in the completion of this book. I am grateful to these individuals for their support:

Jeanne Cavelos, my editor at Dell Publishing, who originated the idea for this book and has given me creative liberty and needed editing suggestions.

Laura S. Hitchcock, Ph.D., executive director of the National Chronic Pain Outreach Association, who wrote the beautiful foreword to this book.

John W. Nielsen, D. Phil. Oxon, who gave me helpful suggestions, optimism, and confidence.

Shari Friedel and my husband, Tom Nielsen, who made many entries into the computer.

Pain support group members and other friends with chronic pain, Sharon Legmann, Kelli Marquardt, Anne Stephens, and Priscilla McGrath, who offered kind words of encouragement.

Pastors McBride and Nelson, who have been spiritual examples and advisors. Willard and June Meier, my parents, who have given me tireless caring, listening, and assistance.

John and Elizabeth Nielsen, my father- and mother-in-law, who gave thoughtful support and guidance.

Penney Cowen, executive director of the American

Chronic Pain Association, who introduced me to the concept of pain management.

Drs. J. Parsow and R. Gentry, who have been exceedingly patient with me.

And I especially thank my physical therapist, Dave Nannen, who has never given up trying to help me function better and have less pain.

Foreword

Chronic pain is a devastating public health problem that affects as many as one in ten Americans (at least twenty-five million people). As our population ages and more and more people suffer on-the-job injuries, some experts are labeling it an epidemic. Chronic pain disables more people than either cancer or heart disease, yet little attention has been paid to it by the medical profession and even fewer dollars have been spent on research.

Unlike acute pain, which goes away quickly, chronic pain often lasts for years and gets progressively worse over time. Traditional treatment methods often fail to bring relief, leaving the person with a ''life sentence'' of unrelenting pain. The most common types of chronic pain are back pain, headaches, and arthritis pain. Other common types include neck pain, sciatica, fibromyalgia, myofascial pain, neuropathy, and neuralgia. Many illnesses or conditions also can produce chronic pain in some patients; some examples: diabetes, endometriosis, osteoporosis, scoliosis, and lupus. Chronic pain brings a burden of depression, anxiety, fear, frustration, fatigue, isolation, and lowered self-esteem—it can shatter productive lives.

Like Patti Nielsen, the author of *Living with It Daily,* I have firsthand experience with chronic pain, having lived with it daily for the past seven years. I am a licensed psychologist and have worked professionally with chronic pain patients for many years. When I was injured and later developed chronic pain, I found that I, too, had developed many of the difficulties in coping with pain that I used to discuss with patients who consulted me in my private office or whom I met in the local support group I led. Having chronic pain meant that I had to face the same difficult and varied tasks my patients do. I had to learn to adapt to a chronic medical condition that holds no promise of improving over time. I had to accept that I could never again be the healthy athletic person I had been all my life prior to the accident. Maintaining my sense of dignity and self-worth as well as my sense of humor despite the limitations that chronic pain brings has been an ongoing struggle for me, as it is for all of us whose chronic pain is severe enough to alter our lives substantially.

For the past eight years, I have been the executive director of a nonprofit organization that serves as a clearinghouse for information about chronic pain, the National Chronic Pain Outreach Assocation (NCPOA). I came to know Patti Nielsen when she sent us an article for possible publication in our newsletter. The topic of the article was how affirmations and visualizations can help people cope with chronic pain. I was struck by the modesty with which Patti described herself and her many accomplishments as a hospital nurse, nursing manager, patient educator, and writer whose articles have been published in magazines and nursing journals.

Living with It Daily is a self-help book about finding ways to heal the many hurts that accompany chronic pain. Sorely needed and long overdue, this book will be welcomed by many people with chronic pain as well as by their loved ones and friends. It is the first self-help book about chronic pain that emphasizes the role of affirmations in our daily lives. Patti teaches us that affirmations can be used to empower us to make positive changes in the many aspects of our lives that are affected by chronic pain—the physical, emotional, and spiritual. Affirmations are tools that can help change negative thoughts into positive ones, ineffective coping strategies into effective ones, and feelings of guilt and despair into feelings of hope and encouragement. In short, affirmations can heal us and, in doing so, help us become emotionally healthy enough to realize that we can live productive lives in spite of chronic pain and that we are not our pain.

Using affirmations to heal ourselves does not imply that we will no longer suffer from chronic pain—at least not most of us, unfortunately. Nor am I suggesting that using the affirmations to improve the quality of our daily lives means abandoning all efforts at exploring new medical treatments that may reduce our pain, should they become available. But they can help us with the daily reality of living with chronic pain.

In *Living with It Daily,* Patti writes knowingly about what it is like to live with chronic pain. She seems to speak to each of us personally about all the hardships of living with chronic pain—the uncertainty, the negative emotions, the adjustments our pain forces us to make. At the same time, her book teaches us new skills to help us cope with our pain more effectively. Patti realizes the importance of hope and comfort and guides us gently and honestly toward making positive changes in our lives, as only a person who has not yet reached her own final destination can. In my view, the book addresses all of the major issues that affect the daily lives of people with chronic pain. These include coping with depression, the importance of learning to accept oneself, pace oneself, and set one's priorities appropriately; how chronic pain affects relationships, and perhaps most important of all, the ''Why me?'' question. How can we accept what has happened to us through no fault of our own? How can we find the support, comfort, and hope we all need to help us carry on with our lives, even at the darkest of times when we think we would be better off ending our lives?

In her own personal journey, Patti Nielsen has come to realize the power and importance of spiritual strength. Patti describes the way "spiritual power" has helped bring her comfort, support, hope, guidance, and, ultimately, healing. And through her affirmations, she helps to guide us on our own spiritual journeys.

I know that Patti "speaks the truth" because I recognize myself and the daily challenges I face in my own struggle to live a productive, satisfying life on virtually every page of her book. May you be as comforted, encouraged, and inspired as I am by this wonderful book.

Laura S. Hitchcock, Ph.D.
Executive Director
The National Chronic Pain Outreach Association
Bethesda, Maryland
November 1993

Introduction

Perhaps in the beginning we were told to "just learn to live with it." Undoubtedly, we were not ready to hear those words. How could we accept a life sentence of enduring pain? We felt that the pronouncement was unfair, and became angry and depressed. Searching for someone to blame was natural, but only made us feel more miserable. Our close companions became anger, depression, lowered self-esteem, and negative thoughts.

In time, we faced the reality of our pain. We felt not only the heavy load of physical pain, but also the burden of emotional and spiritual pain. Were endurance and survival the only things left in life?

This book is meant to be both comforting and instructive on the means by which you can live successfully with chronic pain. You can take comfort in knowing that others have had the same thoughts and felt the same feelings. I know how you feel. Because I have chronic pain, I understand your struggles, for they are mine also. In these pages, you will find support during whichever particular stage of the coping process you are in.

Acceptance of ourselves as changed persons with pain is not where this book stops. The daily meditations will help lead you toward a life that, even with disappointments and setbacks, is moving in the direction of greater peace, more joy, better relationships, and further spiritual growth. Spirituality, not religious doctrine, is spoken of. If God,

Higher Power, or Great Spirit has negative connotations for you, please substitute your own words for your source of strength. If a particular page does not appeal to you when you are reading it, please use the index to find a more suitable one to reflect your mood and the problems you're facing.

This book may be shared with family and friends to further their insights about chronic pain. Many topics also could be used for discussion in a pain support group.

Through my own personal experience with pain, I know that all is not lost and that hope can be reclaimed. May you find the courage and strength in these pages to help you reclaim your own life.

Perhaps you have felt alone and have wanted to give up. Perhaps you feel that way now. Grab hold of the hope you find in this book. Though it is sometimes hard, don't turn your back on life. Use this book to move forward in your journey into finding peace again, in spite of the pain.

PATTI NIELSEN

JANUARY

January 1 ❧ Hope

Come, my friends, 'tis not too late to seek
a newer world.
—Alfred, Lord Tennyson

No, it's not too late. I once thought it was. I thought it was too late to have a fresh start—I'd tried so many times before. I thought it was too late to hope—I'd hoped enough, seeing hopes vanish. I thought it was too late to change—I couldn't seem to break free of old habits.

It's never too late to seek a newer world. For us, this new world may contain pain with which we never thought we could cope, but with newly discovered resources, we do. We don't want to just endure day in and day out, settling for less than is meant for us, but to live at the peak performance that we can.

There is a newer world—of believing in ourselves to do what is healthy and right for us, of proceeding in the direction of our hopes, of being as functional as we can be, and of changing our attitudes from submission to pain to managing it more successfully.

This newer world is a world that we can learn to fit into more easily, a place where we can have moments, hours, or days of peace and a home that is much more comfortable to live in.

'Tis not too late.

FOR TODAY: **I believe that a newer world awaits me and I am willing to be shown what I must do to find it.**

January 2 ∽ Pain Stories, Emotions

We cannot afford to forget any experience,
not even the most painful.
—Dag Hammarskjöld

I marvel at what someone else's pain story does to me. I listen for what the person says: when the pain began, what treatments were tried, how it has affected the person's life, the conflicts that have arisen, and the general effects on his or her well-being.

At the same time, I listen for what the person is not saying—the feelings of anger, resentment, impatience, fear, or emotions that their manner, body language, or eyes reveal. I don't always notice when it is hard for me to meet someone else's eyes, but I see it clearly when someone else cannot meet mine.

I feel that I am not alone with my pain when I hear someone else's pain story. Either I recognize my growth in coping with pain or I see my need for growth.

We can share our stories with each other. Others know about us and our experience because we have a common bond. We know that we are safe exposing our inner selves to them, and there is comfort in doing so.

FOR TODAY: **Experiences are different but emotions are very much the same. I can share what I have learned with another person who has pain also. It may be the beginning of a new friendship.**

January 3 ∾ Attitude

*I don't think, then, of all the misery, but of
the beauty that still remains.*
—Anne Frank

Some of us have lost days, weeks, months, and years to
chronic pain. We have found ourselves fighting the pain
one day by proving that we could do old activities in the
same way, only to find ourselves flat in bed the next. We
had tried to conquer pain by brute force. We might spend
months trying to regain our lost level of function or be so
afraid of trying that we spend too much time in bed. Some
of us have spent years chasing an elusive goal: to be free
of pain. Today we can accept the pain and balance our
physical, intellectual, and spiritual lives. Maybe it is time
to get back on the exercise bike or offer to walk with a
friend. Learning might be one of our intellectual pursuits,
so we first look at our interests or those we'd like to develop. Spiritually, we can make our God a more personal
one and spend time relating our concerns, asking for forgiveness and direction, and being grateful for even small
joys.

This life has quality, it has some stillness and silence,
and it has beauty.

FOR TODAY: **My attitude today is good. If it becomes unbalanced, I will wait for balance to return. I am proud
of my persistence in being willing to start over when I
have slid backward.**

January 4   Failure, Peace

If you set a physical goal, then you may fail,
but if you make peace of mind your goal,
you can achieve it.
—Bernie Siegel, M.D.

I tried it again. And again. The treatment had worked so well once. Why couldn't it help me now? I was to call the doctor's office and report how I felt. Trying to assume some of the blame, I said, "I just don't get the same effect. Maybe when I first tried it, I had so much hope that all those endorphins were released. Maybe I overdid my activity. But last time it helped so much."

"Maybe you've just reached a plateau," I was told. "Maybe it isn't going to work for you anymore."

I was discouraged. Secretly I had wanted a quick fix, and like the surgeries, the drugs, the acupuncture—all of the things that had once helped—it now failed me. I didn't like to entertain the thought that this last treatment I had tried would not help, even though I had waited a year to see an effect.

One by one, analgesic methods have failed. Does my pain reroute? Does it hide? Whatever it does, I need to let go of what once worked but no longer is effective. I feel remorse, but in accepting that these particular methods are now inadequate, I strive to gain some peace of mind.

FOR TODAY: **I am never a failure even when treatments fail. I can mourn one more loss. Maybe the scientific community will have answers. If not now, then someday. I will have peace of mind in knowing that my life holds goodness and that pain need not rob me of all that I value.**

January 5 ∾ Moderation

> *One of the best things we can do for those*
> *in pain is to encourage them to slow down,*
> *focus more on being than doing, and adjust*
> *to a more limited energy span.*
> —Tim Hansel

"No," I argue with my pain. "I can't stop now. Leo called and wants me to drop something by his office. Erik wants something at the store. The children need to go to the dentist. The relatives are coming from California, and I need to go through that stack of magazines and that pile of papers. Oh, and my family is tired of hot dogs and hamburgers. I really should fix something better."

And I argue some more. "I just have to get this done. I just have to get this done. I can't stop now."

Sooner or later I stop. But this time I don't stop for a couple of hours. I stop for days because I've pushed too hard for too long. I stop running errands, I stop caring about who's coming when, and I stop doing anything that's not necessary. The only thing I don't stop is the pain. I can't argue about all the things I want to do any longer, because it really has me this time.

How could I have changed? Moderation. Will I ever learn to adapt? Yes, if I'm willing to focus more on being who I am and accepting what I can do at any particular time.

FOR TODAY: **I seek balance and moderation. It's not second nature yet, but I'm learning not only to listen to my body but to cooperate with it.**

January 6 ❧ Blaming Ourselves

Pleasure is oft a visitant; but pain clings
cruelly to us.
—John Keats

A health professional listened to a person with chronic pain complain about how much pain he still had, in spite of his efforts at pain management. He was trying to have a good attitude, was exercising and substituting distracting activities for his obsession with pain. He felt angry and depressed, expecting total pain relief.

The professional helped him see that, although he was working hard and persistently, his pain was complex and it was still the center of his life. He was told that blaming himself only made the problem worse. The man lowered his expectations and was pleased at how much more he could accomplish. He was less disappointed when the pain returned.

Like our bodies, the mind has its limits, too, but we are blessed that it can change our perspective on pain. Stress and negative emotions seem to interfere with our efforts toward pain control, but they are part of our humanness and can lead us to growth, maturity, and wisdom.

With less self-blame, we can direct our minds to other things as we try to modify our pain and live more richly.

FOR TODAY: **I will use my mind to live well, even though I may doubt that the pain will allow it. If necessary I will change my present expectations and strive for patience to acquire wisdom.**

> *Sometimes it's worse to win a fight*
> *than to lose.*
> *—Billie Holiday*

I don't know much about my pain. There was a time when I asked for copies of X rays, office reports, and history and physical reports to try to piece together on my own the puzzle of my pain. No doctor seemed to be able to do it, so I tried, but my efforts didn't work. I was mystified, too. The other night I heard a person with chronic pain say, "If I only knew what was wrong with me, I'd find somebody to fix it."

Many of us have a pain problem that cannot be "fixed," and some of us have had worse pain after having tried a treatment or surgical procedure. We blame the doctors and then wonder why they have trouble dealing with us. We may have proven to the physician that such methods didn't work, but we, not the doctor, are the losers if we harbor resentments.

We need to stop fighting the medical profession and treat the relationship that we have with our doctors respectfully. We need to know what the reasonable expectations are for improvement, but we also need to know that, for the most part, it is up to us to handle our pain and be responsible for our own lives.

Doctors can't solve everything, such as retraining us for a job or solving our family problems, but they can give us suggestions as to people and techniques that may help. How we live our lives is up to us. Self-responsibility places less dependence on the medical community and puts more decision making in our hands.

FOR TODAY: Hope is not gone when I can't be "fixed." It is the beginning of a new chapter for me and the discovery of how to manage my pain.

January 8 ❧ Doubt

All the religious thinkers were doubters.
—*Isaac Bashevis Singer*

If great theologians and philosophers through the ages have experienced doubt, why should I be any different? We doubt if God exists, and then we doubt if He cares. We do so because we feel His absence and wonder if He caused our affliction. Doubts are not a denial of, but a necessary ingredient of faith, a faith forged in honest questioning.

Though the force of pain, doubt, and uncertainty threaten to strangle and confuse my spirit, they prompt me to ask questions about God, life, and death that I may not, up to this time, have asked.

I have the opportunity to deepen my faith, to trust more fully, and to help with a spiritual vision for the world's good by my actions and being. All of this is possible after I have wrestled with doubt.

I do not approve of the pain, though I accept that I have it. Doubts lead me to a spiritual reconstruction of a physically painful life, one in which strength is needed, beyond what I alone can give. Doubts lead me to risk faith, to trust that God is for me, not against me, and to believe that this Spirit did not cause my pain, but stays near and loves me through it.

FOR TODAY: **I won't be ashamed of feeling doubt. It may be the pathway to finding a power greater than my own.**

January 9 ❧ Decisions

Circumstances are like clouds, continually
gathering and bursting.
—John Keats

My life used to come to a standstill during a flare-up of chronic pain. I became depressed, immobilized myself, canceled plans, retreated into isolation, and had others "pick up the pieces" of my responsibilities.

Now I know that when my pain is severe, I need time to rest, recover, and gain strength. Having time alone and having extra help satisfies these needs, but I need to prioritize and pace myself to avoid escalating the pain and causing an even greater relapse. By not scheduling too many things at once, I'll be able to recover gradually.

It's a fine line between knowing when to avoid situations that increase my pain and when to risk the consequences. I ask myself how important some event is to me or to my family, and then ask myself what the possible negative effects of participating would be and how I may avoid them. Sometimes extra planning is all that's needed.

Avoiding activities due to pain becomes unhealthy when it becomes a way of life. Then pain has gotten too much control and I am giving up too much of my life to it.

FOR TODAY: **Making decisions that affect my pain level can be very hard. I will weigh the pros and cons when it comes to making up my mind but will aim for participating as fully as I can.**

> *And is not the chief good of money the*
> *being*
> *free from the thinking of it?*
> *It seems so to me.*
> —*Elizabeth Barrett Browning*

Money can help us but it won't cure chronic pain. One of
the Grimm brothers' fairy tales tells of three men with a
magical healing salve who offered to cut off body parts in
order to demonstrate to an innkeeper how well the salve
worked. Overnight, the severed parts were stolen from the
platter by a cat. Horrified, the innkeeper's daughter substi-
tuted a hand from a hanged thief, eyes from a cat, and a
heart from a pig.

Unfortunately, when the magical healing salve adhered
these foreign parts to the men, they acted respectively like
a thief, a cat, and a pig. After threatening to set the inn on
fire, the men were given a large amount of money. Still,
they knew it could never compensate for their losses.

Those of us who have received a financial settlement
have a similar realization. In our case, money can never
make up for the losses brought on by chronic pain; money
will neither cure the pain nor remove the anger some feel
toward people whose neglect contributed to their pain.

If money is less important and less effective, what can it
do for us? It can help us to help ourselves. Paying off bills,
helping us to further a worthy cause, enabling us to express affection and show gratitude, or providing us with
education and training for possible new careers are just
some of the ways money can help us. Perhaps we need to
invest in something that may help us stay in good physical
condition, such as a treadmill for rainy days. Money may

not make us happy, but it can be a means used for good ends.

FOR TODAY: **I'll use my money thoughtfully and not be afraid to use it for something that may help me help myself.**

January 11 ❧ Myths

Life is what happens to us while we are
making other plans.
—Thomas la Mance

Myths and misconceptions regarding chronic pain abound.
Some of these are:

- If you seek help from a psychologist trained in pain
  management, the pain must be in your head.
- The right drug or surgery will cure chronic pain.
- "You don't look like you're in pain. It must not
  hurt much."
- Prolonged periods of time in bed will help, just as
  when you're sick.
- It's impossible to be happy in spite of the pain.
- The pain affects only you and no one else.
- If the cause could be found, so could a cure.

Perhaps we have heard or thought these statements. It
may have taken us a long time to realize chronic pain's
realities. We may have resisted, believing that a cure could
be found if only we searched long enough. Prejudices may
have kept us from realizing that our perspectives on pain
and our reactions to stress could have some effect or
blinded us to how pain has affected others. Finally, as in
the last misconception, planning how to fix our pain can
rob us of today's happiness. We can absorb only those
realities that we are ready for. This is part of the process
of coming to terms with chronic pain. Others may share
these ideas we have clung to, reinforcing the illusions.
Now we know these ideas for what they are—myths and
not truths.

We hear the whisperings of the myths, but we no longer have to listen. Reality speaks louder, and heeding its call brings us closer to acceptance and the peace that is never realized in myth.

FOR TODAY: **Reality takes all my attention. I'll meet its challenges with confidence today.**

January 12 ∾ Anger

The battle, sir, is not to the strong alone;
it is to the vigilant.
—Patrick Henry

There's so much to be angry about. We're angry at pain's effect on our work, our finances, our future, and on our role in the family. We're angry at health care professionals who can't help enough and at our medical bills that pile high for things that haven't worked. We're angry at ourselves for doing all the things we can to help ourselves and, still, we have pain.

We can use anger to our advantage because of the energy we can get from it. It signals that something is wrong, and by identifying the source of our anger we can make decisions that will give us a sense of taking charge.

We can list the different issues and the options we have. If our work and earning power has been affected, we can list what jobs we might be retrained for or the ways we might modify our work environment. If we cannot work, we look at volunteer activities or hobbies to do at home.

There is a channel for this energy; all we have to do is find it. We can mobilize the energy of anger and take on the challenges before us until the challenges turn into accomplishments. If the energy from the fury has been expended and we are still angry, we have to let our anger go. We can find someone who needs our kindness and extend it to them. Small, compassionate acts may extinguish the hot flame of anger.

FOR TODAY: I can recognize anger and try to find its source, using renewed energy to find solutions to my problems. I need to not dwell on my anger but to find someone who needs compassion, too.

January 13 ∾ Assertiveness

Not everything that is faced can be changed
but nothing can be changed until it is faced.
—James Baldwin

How do we learn to be assertive if this does not come naturally? We can want this for ourselves, and we can learn and practice. Our goal is not to bully others—that's aggressiveness. Rather, our goal is to state our needs in a positive, courteous way that allows us to take care of ourselves. It sounds simple, but often it is not. We with chronic pain often suffer from low self-esteem. We are not all that we want to be and feel ashamed at having to ask for what seems to be ''special favors,'' even though they are not.

We have to get past such ideas, even acting as if we feel assertive when we don't. As we become less uncomfortable with stating our needs, doing so will come more naturally.

If we cannot express ourselves, we not only put another blow to our self-esteem, but the resentment can make us tense and increase our pain. We owe it to ourselves to say ''I'd like to . . .'' ''I need to . . .'' ''I'd appreciate it if . . .''

If we meet resistance, we firmly say, ''This is what I need.'' Perhaps there are compromises to be made, but if there are none, we stay on course, clarify if necessary, and repeat ourselves. We realize that no one else can take care of us but ourselves. Part of this care is to be assertive about our needs.

FOR TODAY: **I will speak honestly, rather than expecting others to read my mind. I will say what I mean and mean what I say in a kind, nonaggressive way.**

In my greatest emptiness, God can fill me;
in my largest sorrow, He can bring joy.
In overwhelming isolation, He can bring
me companionship.
—*Patti Nielsen*

We feel as if we have nowhere to turn in trying to cope with our chronic pain. We're tired of hearing "But you look so good" when we feel like we're dying inside; we're tired of being limited by pain; and we're tired of saying prayers for healing that go unanswered. We're tired of asking why this has happened to us, but we can't stop asking.

We ask why a loving God doesn't remove pain and suffering—once an abstract question but now a very personal one. We search for meaning for our pain with the hope of making some peace with it. We search for knowledge and understanding of God, whom we alternately implore and denounce.

In response to the question, "Why has this happened to me?" we can cling to any positive answers, such as, "I can use pain's lessons to be compassionate to others," but if no answer appears, we finally have to let the question go. Disasters happen, even to us. If there is a "why," we may never know it.

The more important question is, "Now that this has happened to me, what do I need to do?" God isn't against me. He'll help me rebuild my life and surround me with His love. The pain will never keep Him from me because He is there in the midst of it, hurting with me. When I rely on this perception, He is as close to me as my pain is.

FOR TODAY: What now, God? I don't approve of the pain, but show me what to do from now on and help me learn to trust in Your plans for ultimate good.

January 15 ❧ Acceptance

*Realities are always defeating ideals, but
ideals have a way of taking vengeance upon
the facts which momentarily imprison them.*
—Reinhold Niebuhr

I read a story about a man whose pain had gotten so bad
that even lifting a glass of milk was unbearable. Here was
a man who had once prided himself on his physical condition and took on the heaviest jobs at work to get even
stronger. A simple slip off a curb caused an injury that
made him feel weak and helpless.

What turned his life around was a change of attitude.
One of the most important lessons he learned was to stop
trying to prove that he could master his body overnight.
Once he acknowledged this, he attempted to recover at a
slower pace.

I have sometimes felt that I was in a race against myself.
This man learned that by trying to be in better harmony
with himself, other people, nature, and his physical limitations, he made inch-by-inch progress in spite of setbacks
and mistakes. It happened on both a physical and mental/
emotional level.

Today he goes canoeing, works, does volunteer service,
and even went bicycling across his state, accomplishing
the trip in only one week. He is an inspiration, not only for
what he has achieved, but for how he has persisted and
worked toward his ideals, learning from his mistakes along
the way.

FOR TODAY: **I am not the only one who has setbacks and
makes mistakes. I can learn from those who have had
them, too, but did not give up.**

January 16 ∿ Feelings

Any system approaching perfect self-control
also approaches perfect self-frustration.
—Alan Watts

I have a whole array of emotions when I think of how I feel about chronic pain. Some of these seem to fall into a rebellious category, some into a passive, depressed category, and some into a category whereby I am motivated to contest the pain and its impact on my life.

When the pain encircles me, I feel annoyed, angry, frustrated, outraged, disgusted, and impatient. If I feel passive and depressed, I can feel alone, abandoned, deprived, grief-stricken, trapped, gloomy, pitiful, or numb. When I accept my pain as a challenge that I can surmount, at least partially, I feel brave, energetic, able, and undaunted. What is so surprising is the frequency at which my feelings about chronic pain change.

Some emotions as diverse as feeling outraged or undaunted can lead me to accomplish what I might not otherwise have had the energy for. Others, such as passivity, help me step back and save my emotional energy.

I can't stay perfectly composed all the time, and experiencing a variety of feelings is a natural feature of chronic pain. I don't need to surrender to negative emotions because I know that they won't last forever, providing that I put pain into its proper perspective of being a facet and not the entirety of my life.

FOR TODAY: **I can acknowledge my negative feelings without judging myself. Sometimes the sooner I accept them the sooner they are transformed into a positive insight or action.**

> *The Straight Road—to live for others in*
> *order to save one's soul. The Broad—to live*
> *for others in order to save one's self-esteem.*
> —Dag Hammarskjöld

Either on a conscious or subconscious level, almost everyone with chronic pain feels guilty. It is a hard matter for us to discuss. Some of us gradually accumulate layers of guilt; some have guilt placed on them; and some even create their own guilt.

For example, a child with migraines feels guilty missing school; a teenager who has chronic pain from a car accident feels guilty for having to go home early from a date; a worker feels guilty for not asking for help while lifting; and a parent feels guilty for being angry with the children when they are too noisy.

There is also the family and friends' guilt: parents who accuse their child of "faking it" before finding out the child's diagnosis, the spouse who wonders if he or she is fostering a sick role by helping out, and the friend who feels guilty for changing the subject when pain is brought up.

The trouble with guilt is that it can escalate out of proportion, especially when we assume things that may be entirely false. It is of some comfort to know that others with pain experience guilt, too, and that this common problem can be handled. We can begin by saying "Ease up on yourself" when an excess of guilt creeps up on us, and say it whenever we need to, as well as asking close ones to verbalize how they feel about us and the lifestyle changes that have occurred. We can let them know that we are striving for greater independence but that we may need their assistance to achieve this goal.

Guilt separates, but communication can bind us together.

FOR TODAY: If I am being too hard on myself, I will repeat "Ease up on yourself" as often as I need to.

January 18 ∾ Faith, Severe Pain

Only one thing is needful, and faith
expects victory.
—Sören Kierkegaard

While affirmative thinking is good, the benefits are short-lived for me, compared to having a faith that says, ''There is a spiritual presence that abides with me and always will.'' It is easy to have faith when the pain level is low and the range of physical abilities is high. However, when we're in greater pain, either we can be drawn to God for sustenance or we can deny spiritual comfort.

Times of great pain show me what I instinctively want —to at least survive. I wait, sometimes for a long time, to be able to do more than hang on. Sometimes all I can do is to trust that the intense pain won't last forever. The intensity subsides for a moment, only to return in full fury. The moment comes again and remains awhile longer. Finally the pain eases.

During the dark night of pitiless pain, I see only a small shadow of hope that it will subside. Though God's presence seems distant, I have faith that it will comfort me. In time, I feel the peace that comes from trusting that I am not alone and hopeless. When a release finally comes, I realize that through it all, my mind and spirit have been kept sheltered and secure.

FOR TODAY: **God, give me a faith that withstands the fury of pain.**

> *. . . it is one thing to see the Lord of Peace*
> *from a wooded ridge . . . and another to*
> *tread the road that leads to it.*
> —*St. Augustine*

We need to be proud of our accomplishments, no matter how small.

One day I was proud of having bought a dozen pairs of socks. It sounds bizarre, but at the end of the day I felt as if I were a responsible, goal-achieving individual.

My son had complained for quite a while that he never had any socks (despite the fact that often there seemed to be hidden sock treasures in the couch or under his bed). He was right, though. Usually the ones I found had holes in them. But buying new socks meant an extra trip across town at a time when getting groceries at a store six blocks away was all I could physically handle.

One week I put a lot of preparation into a party and had little energy to spare. It struck me that I had tried to stretch my limitations for guests but had little consideration for my son's needs.

I finally did it. I paced myself one day and finally bought my son, and other members of the family, a total of twelve pairs of socks. I didn't suffer because I prioritized, and best of all, I didn't think, "If you only knew how I hurt when I do things for you. . . ."

My son didn't say, "Mom, that was wonderful what you did for me." But instead he said, "Oh, new socks," in a nonchalant tone. I only smiled at his lack of gratitude. I didn't expect greater appreciation. I was only thankful that

I had finally gotten the job done. Accomplishment, how-ever small, is its own reward.

FOR TODAY: **Our families may not appreciate the effort and pain it requires to do certain things, but we can be happy about the responsibilities we can still handle.**

January 20 ❧ Goals

> *The secret of success is consistency*
> *of purpose.*
> —Benjamin Disraeli

"I've only added one new exercise this week, but I'm making progress toward being able to do all my prescribed ones," my friend said. Once depressed and despondent, her eyes now sparkled as she talked about committing herself to a goal and moving toward its accomplishment.

Goals help us move from a state of existing to accomplishment. We have reasons for looking forward to tomorrow. Since many of us have felt like failures for not being able to conquer our pain, we can feel successful at being able to do something to enhance our lives.

We must be careful not to be unrealistic about our goals, thereby sabotaging our efforts and damaging our self-confidence. "I want to be able to add three new water exercises this month" is better than "I want to swim like an Olympic athlete."

While exercise and weight loss are common goals, we can try to include ones that focus on leisure activities. For example: "I'll join the family in walking the dog once a week." And there can be some long-term goals. For example: "Next year I'd like to have enough money to visit my brother." We can choose some that can be started now, for example: "I'll see if there is a part-time job that I can handle."

However limited we are, we can accomplish a small goal and build on it.

FOR TODAY: I won't put off setting a goal another day. I'll choose a reasonable goal and begin now to take small steps in realizing it.

January 21 ❧ Labels

He that respects himself is safe from others;
he wears a coat of mail that none
can pierce.
—Henry Wordsworth Longfellow

She's the one with the back pain, he's the one with the hip pain, she's the pharmacist, he's the teacher, she's the Baptist, he's the Buddhist. Such classifications assign labels to people on the basis of observation or prejudice, but labels do not tell us much about another person's true individuality.

Chronic pain may be both our diagnosis and our label. To different people, this can mean different things. Some may consider people with chronic pain complainers or malingerers; others may consider the same people courageous and strong. Still others assign no label because they have had no exposure to or knowledge of any stigmas that may be attached to persons with chronic pain.

We can't change someone's preconceived idea, but we can live as well as we can to avoid portraying a negative stereotype.

FOR TODAY: **I am more than my pain. I will let the best of me show today.**

January 22 ❧ Limitations

Solitude either sours or teaches
self-dependence.
—John Fowles

I wonder why I ignore an intuitive thought. When I dismiss it, my failure to follow my intuition causes me hardship in common, ordinary events and in my experience with pain. The thought crosses my mind as I leave the house that I might have forgotten to turn off the coffeemaker, but I ignore it. When I return, I find burned coffee and a very hot pot. I wonder why I didn't listen to myself.

With my pain, I'll disregard a thought that says, "You're walking too far" or "You're doing too much," in favor of attempting to make progress or to finish what I set out to do. Later I realize that I should have heeded my intuition, and I pay for my actions with more pain.

In an age of scientific explanation and theoretical rationalization, we can easily lose sight of one of our greatest learning tools: our intuitive awareness. There is an art and skill to be found in listening to ourselves, in following the melody we hear.

FOR TODAY: **My intuitive thoughts are the best indicator of when I'm nearing my limits. I'll tune in to them today.**

January 23 ∾ Distraction

Leave no stone unturned.
—Euripides

Sometimes leaving the house offers distraction. A trip takes my mind off my pain. A recent vacation to a new state did this. There were new foods to try, new scenery to gaze at, new people to meet, and historical places to visit.

But usually I can't leave town. Being around people sometimes helps me, so if I'm not up to conversation, I go to a place where there are happy people. Often this involves being around young people. I can go to the park and watch the smiles on the children's faces as they go up and down on the teeter-totter. One day I took a walk in the halls of the local high school as the last bell rang. I noticed that just observing young people talking, shouting, and laughing lifted my spirits.

But even at home I can enter another life through books. Adventure, mystery, romance, travel, and interesting biographies allow me to gain entrance to a world apart from my pain. My well-being depends on not dwelling on the pain.

For today: I do not need great amounts of money, nor do I need to travel far to practice distraction. For a while, my mind can concentrate on something else, something happy.

January 24 ਚ Fatigue

Do not peer too far.
—Pindar

Fatigue robs me of my energy. It is particularly noticeable if I have an acute illness or an acute pain along with my chronic pain. My energy reserves go down and I need more rest. On those days I can't accomplish as much. When I feel fatigued, I need to be patient and concentrate on the priorities of the day. Can something wait until tomorrow?

Trying to think of what might help, I consider what will nurture my body, mind, and soul. Maybe it's a hot bath, a relaxation tape, or a "Help me" prayer.

When I am sick or fatigued, just getting through the day in a pure survival sense is my goal. I feel unbalanced but I trust that the acute problem will pass.

I need to recuperate before I can progress. Treating myself well and being patient with how long it takes to recover from an acute injury or illness will enable me to return to my former lifestyle and make what further progress in my physical self that I can. For now, my resting time is productive time.

FOR TODAY: I hope that tomorrow will be better. If I get adequate rest today, I am more confident that it will be.

January 25 ∾ Affirmations, Feelings

Many people are living in an emotional jail
without realizing it.
—Virginia Satir

An affirmation makes a positive statement about ourselves. Some examples are: "I am doing the best I can," "I know what's important to me," and "I live one day at a time." We say them, even when we are hesitant or doubtful, because we need the self-encouragement. At the same time, an affirmation can be a stepping-stone toward some goal for self-improvement.

Affirmations should provide encouragement, not discouragement. Sometimes we try a particular affirmation and feel as if we've failed if it doesn't bring the desired result, such as a change in attitude.

In those cases, we need a different course of action. What if we say the affirmation, "I have what I need today," but inside we want to scream, "What I need is to get rid of this pain!"? What if we try to visualize ourselves happy in a group of people, when we really can't see anything but wanting to stay in bed feeling sorry for ourselves?

In those times we need to acknowledge our feelings that won't go away, no matter how positive we try to be. Maybe we need to make an honest phone call; maybe we need to start a journal; or maybe we need to have coffee with a friend.

We can't ignore the feelings, but with the help of others we again can believe in ourselves and the good within us. Then we can say an affirmation such as, "I have the strength to do what I need to do,'' and believe we can.

FOR TODAY: **If I feel like a hypocrite when I tell myself to think positive things, it's not a failing. I just need to talk about what's bothering me first.**

Your entire education has deprived you of
this capacity because it was preparing you
for the future, instead of showing you how
to be alive now.
—*Alan Watts*

I am good at keeping a problem a problem by analyzing it too much. The more I look at its dimensions, the more angles I see. The more angles I see, the more trouble I find. On it goes, until the problem has been magnified into a crisis of epic proportions!

Sometimes I need to turn away from the problem that is bothering me. When no solution is apparent, focusing all my attention on it only exaggerates it and aggravates me further.

I need to step back and take a reprieve, even if it is only a short one. I can begin with rest, meditation, or a walk. Perhaps a quiet notice of other matters, the observance of something that brings me peace of mind, or an increased mindfulness of other people will give me perspective.

When I shift my attention away from the problem and onto the present moment, the solution may come unexpectedly. It may not be perfect, but somewhere there is an answer. That I can trust.

FOR TODAY: **I will slow down my racing thoughts, bring my mind back to the matters at hand, and seek a workable balance between thought and action.**

January 27 ❧ Blame, Pain

*In a word, each man is questioned by life;
and he can only answer to life by answering
for his own life; to life he can only respond
by being responsible.*
—Viktor Frankl

I have been known to blame my pain on things that my physical self had nothing to do with. For instance, ever since I was a child, I've had a habit of losing or misplacing things. I can't count the number of times since then that I've had to retrieve my purse from a store's dressing room, grocery cart, or bench, not to mention the times I couldn't find it in the house!

Sometime during the course of my pain experience, I began to blame my carelessness on my discomfort. I'd think, "Anybody would lose things if they had pain on their mind, like I do."

When I find myself blaming the pain, I take a serious look at my accusations. Am I being fair? If I frequently have pain on my mind, what can I do for more comfort or greater distraction? I can own responsibility for my actions and determine how to fill my thoughts with something other than pain.

FOR TODAY: **I want to see my faults as they are, rather than inappropriately blaming the pain. I want to be able to see what to do about my human frailties and be patient with myself along the way.**

> *When you're feeling afraid, if you ask*
> *someone for a hug, for some love, the fear*
> *will quiet down.*
> —Bernie Siegel, M.D.

My daughter came into our bedroom to tell me that she couldn't get to sleep. "When I close my eyes, it's all dark, but I see them—the red eyes. I'm scared because my imagination thinks they belong to wolves."

I sat beside her and said, "It's scary, isn't it? But do you know what? It isn't always going to be this way." After I gave her a hug, she looked hopeful. Twenty minutes later she was asleep.

When I first learned that my pain had crossed the line from acute to chronic, I was very afraid. I wanted to hear that it wasn't always going to be this way. No one could tell me that the pain would go away, but like my little girl, the fear has diminished because of people that care—family, friends, and others with chronic pain. I can do more than coexist with the pain. I can live more fully than I had once imagined and love more deeply than I had once thought possible.

FOR TODAY: **It isn't always easy to lean on someone else, but it lessens my load. I can give and receive a hug today if I need one.**

January 29 ✿ Loneliness

If I shall be like him, who shall be like me?
—Anonymous

My pen pal lives alone and is unable to work outside her small, city apartment. She is looking for a volunteer activity. Because her social contacts are few, depression comes easily and she has found little to distract her mind from the pain. While our correspondence helps fill her need for companionship, I get the sense that not only does she lack companionship, but she is not a friend to herself.

Being alone, with few social outlets, can be very hard. Until we develop our own interests, we may watch others leading busy lives, while ours only seems to drag on.

If loneliness is our problem, we might need to initiate contact with someone or learn new ways to spend time alone. We may start by asking ourselves more about our likes and dislikes. What is our favorite movie, food, color, holiday, style, or leisure activity? Perhaps we are lonely because we've never paused to learn about our distinctiveness. We are worth getting acquainted with.

For today: **There is someone who will appreciate my company today. Maybe it is I.**

January 30 ∾ Living in the Present Moment

Life is but a day at most.
—Robert Burns

Living in the present moment means that we can make plans for the future but, without worry about tomorrow, we can devote most of our attention to things that are happening today. Some say that it is helpful to set up a routine for the day, whether we have outside employment or not. We learn to compensate for what we are unable to do on a particular day by finding something we can do, even if it is not ambitious by most standards.

We can ask ourselves, "What are my limitations today?" and then work around them. This helps us feel that we have some say about our lives.

When my pain is worse and I can't do as much, I worry about precious time I'm wasting. This adds to my stress and can defeat me. The best thing that I can do is strive for more patience, for the willingness to persevere, and for the ability to resume my tasks as soon as possible.

I often get tired of being patient with pain, but my quality of life suffers when I refuse to be patient.

For today: **I can live in today but enjoy planning for tomorrow. With patience, I can do both.**

January 31 ∾ Guilt

If God should punish men according to what
they deserve, He would not leave on the
back of the earth so much as a beast.
—From the Koran

Many people, at least for a time, feel that their pain has been sent to them as a punishment from God. One nurse relates, "One busy day at the hospital, I was assigned to a lady dying of cancer. She appeared comatose and near death, so I hadn't asked her if she needed anything for pain. Hours later, something prompted me to ask her and the woman moved her head to indicate 'Yes.' I felt awful for not asking her earlier."

The nurse went on: "I gave her an injection and proceeded to the next room to help lift a patient back to bed. It was there that I hurt myself. As the weeks and months went by, what I thought was an acute back strain turned into chronic pain. I felt that God was punishing me for neglecting the patient with cancer that fateful day by giving me chronic pain."

In her alienation, how could she pray to a vengeful God who was out to strike her down, to make her feel, possibly for the rest of her life, a fraction of the pain intensity that her patient did?

It took time before she could come to God with this terrible burden. The guilt grew until it spilled over into her relationships with family, friends, and her work.

Finally she humbly sought the grace of a forgiving God and was not disappointed. She came to believe that her injury was not God-given but that through the darkness of adversity, He had illuminated her spiritual need to be accepted again as a child of a God who loved her unconditionally. She now looks with new compassion at others in pain.

FOR TODAY: **God, help me see that You are for me and not against me.**

FEBRUARY

February 1 ∞ Love, Honesty

There is only one happiness in life, to love
and be loved.
—George Sand

If I need to ask for help, I need to trust that the people I love have the honesty to say no and know me well enough to believe that I won't be crushed if they say it. Often I wonder if the friend or family member would like to say no when he or she says yes, but ungrounded suspicions reveal my own mistrust of the person I ask for help. Letting others answer honestly is all I can do. Then I am free to be appreciative rather than apprehensive.

Sometimes we don't reveal that we need help because we feel "less than" and ashamed of our dependence. Sometimes our pride gets in the way and we deny to ourselves that we need a little help because we want so desperately to manage things alone. Our need for independence may be strong, but if we don't let others help, we may become overly dependent—the very thing we don't want.

FOR TODAY: I can trust loved ones to be honest with me when I ask for help. I'll make a request in order to prevent greater pain and to stay as self-sufficient as possible in the long run.

February 2 ❧ Denial

People only see what they are prepared
to see.
—Ralph Waldo Emerson

There was a young football player in my state who became mentally ill. He had never had a problem before. Then one day during college, a psychotic outburst led to his assaulting and injuring another person. He was given psychiatric care and medication as part of his rehabilitation.

Months later several stressors hit him at once. At the same time, he neglected to take his medication. One evening he became violent and, in an altercation with police, was shot and critically injured. He recovered but was paralyzed from the waist down.

One can't help but wonder why he didn't take the medication that would have prevented the tragedy. Perhaps he didn't like the drug's side effects. Perhaps he didn't want to accept that he was mentally ill. Perhaps he didn't want to be different. Perhaps he didn't think any harm would come from skipping a few days' medication.

The young man denied his condition and denied the need to take responsibility for it. I've done it, too, and I sometimes still do. I, too, don't like to be different and I, too, miscalculate the consequences of my actions. In denial, I bypass preventive measures, such as pacing myself, and am likely to increase my pain. In denial, I am the loser, but in acceptance and responsibility, I am the winner.

FOR TODAY: I don't have to like chronic pain to accept it and to take responsibility for myself. Denial disregards consequences, and although it may bring a few false minutes of peace, the additional amount of pain it may cause is not worth it.

February 3 ❧ Depression

Depression: despair, despondency, sorrow,
unhappiness, gloom, dejection, melancholy,
misery, discouragement, hopelessness,
darkness, bleakness
—*From* Webster's New World Thesaurus

We walk on an unsteady path, hovering at the edge of the precipice, fearing that a wrong step may plunge us into the abyss. It is with hesitating steps that we walk with pain, frightened that our depression may cause us to deprive ourselves of living—if not through suicide, then through submitting to a life that is no life, a mere existence of basic survival, waiting for the end where there is no pain.

When we are depressed, hopeless, and all is bleak, taking even a few steps requires tremendous effort. Time is meaningless, and the future seems mournful.

I need a Companion on my path, a God who will not allow me to plunge into the abyss, a God who will keep me from danger and who will lead me forward from my present experience to a future worth living. He is ready and available. I am ready for help.

FOR TODAY: **Help me to keep walking, God, and to start trusting that a new future is being created even now. Help me to trust that You are my Companion. Help me to know that I can rest in Your strength.**

February 4 ❧ Envy

*Our envy always lasts longer than the
happiness of those we envy.*
—François, duc de la Rochefoucauld

I am more troubled when I envy what others who are free
of pain have than when I accept my life as it is. Envy only
makes me feel alone and different. In envy, I want to retreat from those "normal" people who have no ongoing
pain or physical limitations and, like a hurt animal, be by
myself and nurse my wounds.

What I don't know is what other kinds of pain these
"normal people" are experiencing. Their pain can be as
hidden as mine. Someone who appears happy may, in reality, be struggling with a willful teenager or be trying to
decide if a troubled marriage is worth salvaging.

Underneath envy is a deep sadness over chronic pain.
Sadness and remorse can drive out the realization of what
we do have and what we can be thankful for. It also can
put up a wall between us and the people we want to know
better or whom we care about. Alone, we become jealous,
concentrating on what we can't do, and thereby we become more miserable.

Time spent in jealousy is less time we have to feel alive,
energetic, and purposeful. Jealousy and envy rob us of
gratitude. We can make a gratitude list for ourselves every
day, if that's what we need to appreciate what we have and
who we are. We'll be surprised at how our list will grow
when we make this conscious effort.

FOR TODAY: **I won't compare myself with someone else
today. I'll acknowledge what I have lost, but I'll accept
the life I have as one with dignity and merit.**

February 5 ❧ Listening

> *When a man is wrapped up in himself,*
> *he makes a pretty small package.*
> —*John Ruskin*

Others remind me when I am too wrapped up in myself and my pain. My children remind me of my preoccupation by saying, "I told you that last week. You must not have been listening—again." Often I have to tell myself consciously to pay attention, listen, observe what is happening, be mindful of the person I'm with and not be so absorbed in my own thoughts.

In order to do this, I need to trust that my needs will be met, that the details of living with pain will be worked out, and that the love I put into life helps me as much or more than it helps others.

Wrapped up in myself, I'm a small package. Unfolded, I present others with the larger, more useful gift of my listening and caring.

FOR TODAY: **Sometimes my concentration is broken by preoccupation with pain. The cares of today will be taken care of, so I can stop being obsessed with problems. I can show my love and try to prevent my lack of listening from becoming a habit.**

February 6 ∾ Understanding

*I think too many of us are hiding ourselves
from each other.*
—Mary Anderson

"The person who gave me a ride wanted to stop and have a bite to eat after the lecture we attended. I said that I was hurting and wanted to go home, but he said he'd eat fast. Instead of going to a fast food restaurant and having something 'to go,' he stopped at a diner. He ordered a burger and fries, and he didn't realize that every time he stabbed a french fry into the ketchup, he was torturing me," said a friend.

Do we "not make waves" and go along, even if we have to pay the consequences? Or do we follow up our statement of need with an emphatic "I have to do this" and risk argument? Do we feel that it is more socially acceptable if we agree to be uncomfortable for the sake of not imposing and feeling our separateness?

Unfortunately, there is no one easy answer. Each situation is different and may call for a different response. The important thing to remember is that although it may seem as if our options are all no-win solutions, we do have choices.

Ideally, we would like to take care of our needs and act in cooperative agreement with the needs of others. If this is not possible, we may have to assert our needs or compromise. Avoiding resentment over an increase in pain is worth at least the attempt.

For today: **I need to define my boundaries and remember that others are not likely to understand how important it is to respect those boundaries.**

February 7 ∾ Change

> *The best way out is always through.*
> —Robert Frost

What does a rabbit do when it's afraid of being seen? It freezes. It doesn't fight, it doesn't run. It remains alert and motionless until danger comes too close.

I'm tempted to do the same at times, to be paralyzed by fear and hide behind my pain rather than go in a new direction. The rabbit and I may stay safe for the moment, but eventually we'll have to run and take the risk of moving.

Change can scare me. Whether it's a new job, working on a relationship, trying a new pain management skill, or undergoing therapy, I initially freeze and am afraid to go on. Like the rabbit, when I feel a need to change, I run helter-skelter in fear rather than straight toward a goal. First I need to overcome the inertia and the fear.

Gradually I learn or discover that I can relax about change. I can ease into it rather than run from it. I can build on the strength that I've brought from my past and set small goals, then larger goals, until the change is complete and I have accomplished what I set out to do.

FOR TODAY: **Change is necessary and inevitable. I do best when I don't run from it but gently take risks and live one day at a time.**

*The only kind of dignity which is genuine is
that which is not diminished by the
indifference of others.*
—*Dag Hammarskjöld*

The pain is real. One can't tell one's amount of pain from
a lab test or X ray. Because it can't be quantified, some
think we are "faking it."

It is particularly disheartening when we encounter dis-
belief from a health professional. A friend of mine who
now regularly works out with weights at a local YMCA
was once told, "You know, you'll probably always be in a
wheelchair." Years later she is proof of the results of her
persistence in spite of such devastating statements. "There
are times when all I can do is the kind of exercise that a
person in a wheelchair can do," she confesses, "but I've
always had the vision before me of a return to a more
active life. I now am able to do more then I ever
dreamed."

Another health professional once dropped this woman's
leg to see if she was really in pain. That act caused such
excruciating pain that she never went back to that professional again. "If you're not satisfied with your care, it is
all right to search until you find someone you trust," she
says.

Our pain is a fact. Other people's assessments are opinions and some are far from fact. We need not adopt defeating opinions.

**For today: I believe in my ability to be as functional as
I can be.**

February 9 ❧ Asking for Help

> *Everything is so dangerous that nothing is*
> *really very frightening.*
> —Gertrude Stein

"I just spent the whole weekend in bed because I couldn't bring myself to ask someone to help me move a heavy box at work. It makes me feel so inferior when I have to ask," my friend said, "but I really paid for it by lifting it myself."

We often have to make a conscious effort to weigh the benefits against the consequences of the actions we take. There is always the danger of making that split-second decision to do something unwise. More than once I have argued with myself.

"I should ask for help," I have said.

"But I feel foolish, asking someone to help me with such a little thing. They'll think I can't carry my own weight," I rationalized.

"On the other hand, I'll probably have an extreme flareup of pain that will ruin tomorrow's plans if I do it myself. I won't take the chance," I reminded myself.

"Who can help me?" I finally asked.

In this instance, the initial feeling of humiliation over needing to ask for help turned into the humility of making the request for assistance. I got the task done and saved myself added pain. Asking wasn't so difficult after all.

FOR TODAY: **Sometimes I need more help than at other times. If this is one of those days when I do, I will put pride aside and ask.**

February 10 ❧ Bad and Good Days

Thank heavens, the sun has gone in, and I
don't have to go out and enjoy it.
—Logan Pearsall Smith

I don't know anyone who is genuinely happy all the time. There is freedom in realizing that we don't always have to be cheerful but that our humanness includes occasions when we are unappreciative, unhappy, and disgruntled. Realizing this is a relief to people suffering from chronic pain who try to deny their feelings in order to convince themselves that they are doing fine.

Some of the mental techniques of pain management encourage positive thinking, taking our focus off of what we can't do, doing enjoyable things, and so on. These can be useful, but at times even trying to feel good about the day that lies before us can be difficult.

We are similar to other people, in spite of individual circumstances and differences. As the ancient poet Virgil wrote, "We cannot do all things." Neither can we be happy all the time.

Others feel sad, ungrateful, and irritated, just as we do. Perhaps we are fatigued and too tired to be happy. Even though it may not be true every day, the next time the sun comes up again, we may be excited about going out to enjoy it. We learn not to take our best days for granted. Today may be one of them, and we can have the willingness to believe that it will be.

FOR TODAY: **I'll accept how I feel today and know that much of my growth happens through difficult days. I'll accept that I don't have to be happy all the time but can let happiness ebb and flow naturally. I'll accept that today may be the best day and work to make it so.**

February 11 ∾ Commitment

Who has not set out towards some distant
Spain, some momentous goal, or some
glorious realization, only to learn at last
that he must settle for much less?
—Martin Luther King, Jr.

I once had a commitment: to be cured of chronic pain. Since it was unattainable, I have a new commitment: to live as well as I can with the pain. So much living remains to be experienced. There is so much learning left to do, so many projects still to accomplish, so much love to show, and so much foolishness to laugh at.

Today I forget that my zest has been sporadic. Only a short time ago my longings and ambitions were stifled by pain. I felt alien to the world; instead of being a part of it, I felt little happiness, passion, or striving. There was only endurance, with no thought of enthusiasm.

There are days that dawn like that, but I embrace the better ones—the days when the flowers of joy thrive and when I can root out the weeds of self-defeat. The soil of opportunity waits and people who care encourage the shoots of patience and generosity. I have only to add my commitment to growth.

I don't overestimate the power of pain, but I also don't undervalue my resources. The sunshine of faith blesses it all.

FOR TODAY: I will be alert to the glimpses of my growth that I see today and find supportive people to help me live an abundant life.

February 12 ❧ Exercise, Limitations

Time, that aged nurse
Rock'd me to patience.
—*John Keats*

I have to work at my limits the way an athlete does. Both of us have to explore our boundaries over an extended period of time, patiently but persistently. Athletes want to improve their strength, flexibility, endurance, and performance, and that is what I want for myself, also.

I have to fight a body image that defines me as more limited than I am, that assigns me a body deterred by pain instead of challenged by it. My body needs to bend, squat, stretch, and walk so that my muscles, joints, blood vessels, and nerves don't degenerate from disuse. I need full-body conditioning so that all parts of my body are involved. I can't concentrate exclusively on the area that hurts, as many areas of my body work in conjunction with each other.

There are days when my body reacts to certain activities entirely differently than usual. I can discover no reason for this, but I simply cannot do what I did. My determinism drops off sharply. Yet I have to work with my body and start from where I am at the moment—not from where I think I should be.

Only I can take the responsibility for learning what my limitations are and for being in the best physical condition that these limitations allow. I get deterred by pain but press on. The time I've spent with pain has taught me patience.

FOR TODAY: There is some form of exercise that I can do that can help spare my body from disuse. Whether I am a team player or a wheelchair athlete, there is something I can do.

*Faith is the opening of all sides and at
every level of one's life to the divine inflow.*
—*Martin Luther King, Jr.*

Chronic pain is a severe attack on the faith. Dietrich
Bonhoeffer says that the lamentation Psalms don't deny
that suffering happens, nor do they try to deceive us with
pious words. Instead, the Psalms complain to God.
Bonhoeffer points out that "there is always struggle, anxiety, doubt."

Still, in the depths of despair, it is my personal God
whom I address. There comes a time when people can't
help and when I want God to comfort me by bringing
good blessings to my life, as I believe He has done in the
past.

Out of this attack on my faith comes trust. I trust that
He will be with me through whatever happens and that He
wants me to have all the necessities of physical life. I trust
that He'll give me the courage I need for facing the struggles, anxieties, and doubts that swirl around me in the
whirlwind of pain.

Out of my complaint comes hope and trust, and my requests go to God in confidence and love. My mortal life
opens to the divine, and I relax.

FOR TODAY: **God, help me with the struggles, anxieties,
and doubts that my pain evokes.**

February 14 ❧ Love

> *If you would be loved, love and be lovable.*
> —Ben Franklin

How do we love when we feel unlovable, when pain makes it difficult to smile, let alone love? We feel as if we can barely do the tasks at hand, much less do special things for others to show our love.

What we are able to do in one day is all we are capable of, and we need not feel guilty if we are incapable of doing more. Many small expressions of love may be open to us. Our presence or availability to someone can itself be an act of love. We can start with the small things and add acts of kindness as we are able.

A squeeze of the hand or a "How was your day?" takes effort when pain overshadows love, but it may be the first step toward freeing our thoughts from pain's curse. From the smallest expressions, we can offer more of ourselves—the letter we've wanted to write, the phone call we've wanted to make, or the gift we've wanted to give.

The smallest things cause us to reach out with love and enable us to be lovable.

FOR TODAY: **Small tokens of kindness can lead to a wealth of love. I'll offer courtesy and respect to someone today.**

February 15 ✢ Affirmations

> *Suffering relates not only to the pain*
> *sensation itself but to the individual's*
> *feelings, thoughts and behavior which result*
> *from the pain.*
> —Neville Shone

Positive thoughts and an optimistic attitude can make us feel in better control of our pain. Thinking positively takes conscious and persistent effort at times, but it helps us to be our best: individuals who are not defeated by pain.

Following is a list of thoughts that have been transformed from negative thoughts to positive affirmations:

Negative Thought	Positive Affirmation
If only this hadn't happened . . .	I am free, I release the past.
I'm not interested in sex anymore.	I lovingly accept my sexuality.
How will I pay the bills?	Whatever I need will be there for me.
I can't get anything done.	I am decisive, but also open to new ideas of how to do things.
I'm very anxious.	I relax and trust.

We aim for the greatest good, and affirmations can point the way.

FOR TODAY: What negative thought is bothering me the most today? I will seek to turn it into a positive affirmation.

February 16 ❧ Asking for Help; Children; Guilt

Patience is sorrow's salve.
—Winston Churchill

In an ideal world, there would be no pain, children would be perfect, and parents would always show unconditional, unfailing love. It is surprising that we expect these things, even when we know that we do not live in an ideal world.

We with chronic pain often worry about the effect our pain will have on our children when they grow older. What will they remember of us? Because we have needed their help, will they only remember the duties of the home and not the conversations and good times?

Someone once told me, "You're not doing them any favors if you don't have them help around the house." Those words helped relieve the guilt I felt for needing their assistance. Children need responsibilities to feel wanted and needed at home; we need not feel guilty, even if it is pain that makes their help more necessary.

We can envision them as adults who take the initiative to be good workers. In this way, asking them to help won't be so guilt-provoking.

FOR TODAY: **I will ask my children to help me. If I have none, I'll remember not to deprive someone else of the good feeling that comes when he or she is able to help me in some way. I may not always need the same level of support.**

February 17 ❧ Dependence

No one can build security upon the
nobleness of another person.
—Willa Cather

Being in pain can bring back images from the past of being sick at home and getting extra attention, being fixed favorite foods, staying on the couch, and having little expected of us. Perhaps some of these acts from childhood carried over, so that when we first had pain, we got similar treatment from those around us. They may have offered to do things for us that we were capable of doing. When the pain stayed on, unfortunately, so may have some of our dependency.

Needing people in our lives is natural and healthy. A close relationship is a wonderful thing. But love is quite different from an overdependence on someone. We may start demanding more than is necessary from others who may be unable to make healthy choices for themselves because we cling to them.

We need an independent identity, and if the pain has altered that identity, we need to do some rethinking as to how we like to spend our time, who we are deep inside, and what responsibilities are ours to carry out.

We may still be dependent on others for certain tasks or to help meet expenses, but such ''healthy'' dependence can provide opportunities to practice healthy independence, also.

FOR TODAY: I won't sit idly by while someone does things for me. I'll accept the help I need but also do as much as I can.

February 18   Direction

We are always getting ready to live,
but never living.
—Ralph Waldo Emerson

One of the hardest things for me to accept has been uncertainty. I always needed to know where, how, and when I was arriving. Now I don't know. I don't know if I'll get better or worse with time. I don't know if some new treatment will be developed. I don't know if I'll always have the imperfect but fairly healthy attitude toward chronic pain that I have today. I just don't know.

I do know that there are things that can't be forced. The direction of my life seems to be one of them. I used to put off my life, waiting to see where I was going. I was so obsessed about my purpose in life that I lost touch with the moment. My children would ask me, "Remember when we told you . . . ?" and I'd shrug it off with, "I must have forgotten." But they knew better and said, "No, you weren't even listening," as if that's the least I could do. I delayed my responses to many people and activities.

When I am uncertain, there is one thing I need to do: slow down and listen to those around me and to that still, small voice that gives direction.

Simplify. Do small tasks. Enjoy simple things. Retreat from noise. Listen. Direction will come.

FOR TODAY: I can keep my mind on the details of today and listen for the direction I should move in. I can live in today rather than put off living any longer.

February 19 ❧ Feeling Abandoned by God

*My God, my God, why hast thou forsaken
me? Why art thou so far from helping me,
from the words of my groaning? O my God,
I cry by day, but thou dost not answer; and
by night, but find no rest.*
—Psalm 22:1–2
The Bible, Revised Standard Version

When I need to feel God's presence the most, it can seem farther away than it has ever been. I quit praying because I can't pray with only positive words. I have been afraid that God would get angry with me for pointing out that He has not taken away my pain.

Since time began, people have been asking why God has forsaken them. Like me, they blamed God, themselves, and other people for the suffering they have gone through and for the anguish that they could scarcely endure.

As many before me have discovered, perhaps it is not God who has withdrawn Himself from me, but maybe it is I who have moved away from God. Originally, when I found myself not getting relief from pain—the thing that I have wanted more than anything in the world—I distanced myself from the Supreme Being who seemingly didn't help or care about me.

I've come to understand that God can and does help me. The pain may stay but my life can be redirected. My questions may remain unanswered, but I can move on. And God can help me accomplish a life of beauty and worth again.

FOR TODAY: God, I don't ask You to prove Yourself and Your power to me, but to help me facilitate what is necessary for me to do today.

February 20 ❧ Anger

*Quarrels would not last long if the fault was
only on one side.*
—François, duc de la Rochefoucauld

In times of anger, it is difficult not to have a burst of temper, engage in furious argument, or succumb to self-pity and sulking. We feel that our anger is justified by what someone else has said or done, and we seethe with a desire to retaliate.

We must consider alternatives. Resentment and self-righteousness can hurt us more than the one with whom we are angry. Preoccupied by resentment, we lose our use-fulness to others and pain levels rise.

When we are tempted to utter hateful words, we should step back and think. If we are being criticized, we can consider if there is any truth in what was said, or whether we have had any part in causing the situation. Having done this first, we can calmly present our viewpoint to the other person.

Whatever the cause, we want to still the disturbance within us. We don't need the ravages of anger to make us feel worse. Responses can be expressed calmly and chan-neled constructively.

FOR TODAY: **I will try to be more tolerant of others to-day, saving me from resentment and unhappiness.**

February 21 ❧ Expectations, Relationships

> *I think self-awareness is probably the most*
> *important thing towards being a champion.*
> —Billie Jean King

Self-examination takes a lot of work. Being honest with ourselves about our motives and taking a look at our behavior takes courage. It is much easier to find fault with our partners than with ourselves. It is easy to list their weaknesses while being blind to our own. We need to start looking at situations from the other side.

With chronic pain, we expect more of everything from our spouses—more support, more caring, and more physical help. There may be emptiness inside that we unconsciously expect our spouses to fill.

We need to look at our part if we have problems in these areas. Are we courteous at home? Have we demanded help rather than asking in a gentle way? Have we insisted that our spouses help us according to our timetable rather than theirs? Have they already given as much support as they can? Might we find other caring people to supplement what our spouses are doing? What apologies do we need to make? What do we need to discuss? How can we fill the emptiness without being dependent on our spouses? Our answers may lead to compromise, cooperation, and understanding.

FOR TODAY: If love is patient, kind, courteous, and unselfish, which of these areas do I need to improve on?

> *You may have habits that weaken you. The*
> *secret of change is to focus all your energy,*
> *not on fighting the old, but on building the*
> *new.*
> —Socrates

Pain affects not only us, but the ones closest to us, too. We need to be aware of this, so we can take action aimed at fostering better relationships.

For the married person, this means realizing that one's marriage is vulnerable to the effects of chronic pain. Effects such as a loss of recreational activities, a change in roles, and a change in the couple's financial picture are only some of the things that can cause problems. A spouse may say that the partner with chronic pain is not the same person he or she married, that the person is more irritable, withdrawn, or anxious than before.

We may not like ourselves as well, either. We may have fallen into the role of a "sick person," by which pain and a long-lasting dependence on others have lowered our self-esteem. If we think of ourselves as well and capable, we may be able to build on our strengths and become capable of first doing a few things and then progressing to doing more.

A good relationship with others depends, in part, on the relationship we have with ourselves. We can help develop this primary relationship by not giving up on ourselves, by encouraging our own independence, by keeping as active as possible, and by putting our heart and soul into overcoming our helplessness.

Using our inner resources, we must act on our own behalf, because our lives and relationships are too valuable to sell out to pain.

For today: My self-esteem grows when I am engaged in worthwhile pursuits. One of these pursuits is to think kindly of myself and my efforts, so that I can pass this love on to others and better my relationships.

February 23 ❧ Fear

Be not afraid of life. Believe that life is
worth living and your belief will
help create the fact.
—William James

There are four antidotes for fear that help me to not be afraid of life, of pain, and of the future.

The first antidote is the ability to examine and face my fears. It does no good to repeat to myself, like the cowardly lion in the *Wizard of Oz,* that I'm not afraid, if indeed I am. When I face them, I can distinguish which of my fears are real and which are imaginary.

The second is the kind of courage that affirms that life is worth living. It takes a sort of creative will to carve out a place for myself, in spite of pain and uncertainty.

The third is love. It releases me from fear and harmonizes my life.

The fourth antidote is faith. Inadequate for the task of coping with pain, I fall back on faith in a personal God who has not left me defenseless in the vast universe in which I live.

Fear is paralyzing. Facing it, gathering courage, giving and receiving love, and having faith frees me from its crippling effects.

FOR TODAY: **With my antidotes, fear does not have the final word. I'll do what it takes to keep fear at bay and trust that God will sustain me today.**

February 24 ❧ Friends

A friend is a person with whom I may be
sincere. Before him I may think aloud.
—*Ralph Waldo Emerson*

Since I have to be selective about how I expend my energy, I am selective about spending time with friends. A friend is someone who will listen to me attentively, is free to disagree with me without fear of rejection, one whom I can be close to without servitude, and someone whose enthusiasm brings joy into my life.

I have been guilty of delaying contact with friends because of my desire to wait until I felt better. It was a red-letter day when I had friends over, in spite of severe pain. That simple get-together prevented me from sinking into self-pity.

Friends help me to rediscover humor, but they are more than providers of entertainment. They teach me about gratitude for friendship and the importance of my presence to them. I prize the emotional bond between us that has once again been claimed.

For today: **I will reach out to a friend. I will enjoy the comfort and camaraderie that our friendship gives.**

> *The greatest danger, that of losing one's*
> *own self, may pass off quietly as if it were*
> *nothing; every other loss, that of an arm, a*
> *leg, five dollars, is sure to be noticed.*
> —Sören Kierkegaard

I don't wear a cast, I don't walk with crutches, and I smile a lot when I'm in public. People who do not live with me are not likely to know I have chronic pain.

They are not likely to know the extent of my grief, either, unless they are one of a chosen few to whom I can "bare my soul." My grief over having pain is largely a personal matter, and even when I think that I've moved past it, something triggers it.

I know the feeling of "losing one's own self" while appearing happy on the outside. That self that I knew before my pain began has, to outsiders, "passed off quietly," but I know the losses that I have experienced.

I grieve the losses of a physically comfortable life, of coworkers, and of some of my future aspirations. We need to grieve, and it is normal to do so. It is only in the process of grieving for our losses that we can finally come to acceptance.

Grief enables us to complete the process of mourning our lost self and of forming an idea of who we are in terms of our new reality. It helps us become ready to live a life of letting go of the past and of dreaming new dreams.

FOR TODAY: I will give myself permission to go through grief in order to make peace with myself and my past life, and I will allow hope to lead me forward.

February 26 ❧ Growth

Only in growth, reform and change,
paradoxically enough, is true security
to be found.
—Anne Morrow Lindbergh

Anger at our pain can be the motivation that we need to take steps toward managing the pain, providing we direct our anger at the pain itself and not at innocent people around us.

The anger can give us the determination that we will not let the pain overcome us and that we can take whatever steps are needed to live a quality life. Some people write a letter to their pain and feel that it is a cleansing experience. Just because we have accepted that our pain is a fact in our lives doesn't mean that we don't ever get angry at it.

Sometimes we are in the kind of mood that undercuts our motivation, and we are too depressed to be angry. Sometimes the pain lowers our spirits, no matter what we try to do. In those instances, it helps to remember that we will have more cheerful days again, that medical research offers prospects of hope, and that we can do something involving physical and mental activity to lift us up.

Anger and depression are natural reactions, but even if they push us down, we can and will get up again.

FOR TODAY: **Pain may gain an advantage over me, but I won't let it knock me down.**

February 27 ❧ Honesty, Love

I've heard it [hope] in the chillest land
And on the strongest sea.
Yet never, in extremity,
It asked a crumb of me.
                    —*Emily Dickinson*

I called my friend with cancer one day to ask how she was feeling. Many times I had turned to her for emotional support, so she must have assumed I had a problem to discuss. "I'm no better than I was a week ago," she said. "I'm sorry that I have nothing to give today, but I'm so tired and weak," she apologized. Quickly I assured her that I was only concerned about her well-being and expected nothing in return. We talked for as long as her energy allowed.

Once, I felt she was the only friend I could be honest with regarding the anger, fear, depression, and grief surrounding me, because she was with me from the very beginning of my pain. Immediately after my second injury, while in moderately severe pain, I asked if I could see her because I had an ominous feeling that this injury was more serious, as indeed it was. I will always be grateful to her for being willing to come to my aid with her calm presence and comforting words. As time went on during my pilgrimage with pain, I could always admit my anxieties to her and be offered her consolation and hope. Admitting my impatience, I received empathy and encouragement.

My friend did not delude me into thinking she was well during our last telephone conversation. I was grateful for her honesty because it enabled me to return my own love and support to her. I could care deeply about her world when she had no strength to come to mine.

Motivated by her example, I can be truthful with myself and others. She faced her illness and, to the best of her ability, took care of her own needs. Even though I am still learning, my friend has passed this lesson on honesty and self-care to me.

FOR TODAY: **I can reach out with love to someone, whether it is to give or to receive support and understanding. Love and honesty are freeing and hopeful.**

February 28 ∾ Depression

As long as I have a want, I have a reason
for living.
—George Bernard Shaw

It's not wrong to feel depressed, nor is it an indication of a personal failing. Depression is not a moral issue. Sometimes we are just a breath away from depression. It happens to me most often if (1) I am reminded of something I once could do but now can't, (2) I am extra tired and weighed down by my responsibilities, (3) I feel financially burdened, or (4) my pain is worse.

I once knew no way out of this black hole. Especially when my suffering is great, depression is my natural and normal reaction. There are, however, tools I can use. I can focus on what I can do instead of what I can't. I can entertain the thought of visiting someone worse off than I. I can break up my responsibilities into smaller tasks. I can take a realistic look at my finances and make a plan. I can ''ride out the storm'' during times of worse pain and use whatever pain management techniques I need, such as distraction, relaxation, visualization, meditation, resetting goals, or exercising.

If depression is prolonged, I may need professional assistance. There is no reason for me to avoid seeking help.

FOR TODAY: **Because I value self-care, there is much that I can do to help myself, but I will seek professional assistance if necessary. I don't need to let my depression be prolonged.**

February 29 ∾ Abilities

Live all you can; it's a mistake not to. It doesn't so much matter what you do in particular, so long as you have had your life. If you haven't had that, what have you had?
—William James

What does it mean to have had our lives? What do we do when we start to believe that pain has claimed more than its share of our lives? Perhaps we have lost a skill, but maybe there is a talent that is awaiting our discovery. Maybe it doesn't have monetary value but is of value to others, like an ability to listen to them.

Perhaps we have been forced to slow down our lifestyles enough to appreciate the simpler pleasures of life and the people around us. Perhaps we have coped better with our hectic ones.

It is healthy to grieve our losses, but there may be gifts and undiscovered abilities awaiting us. What door has closed? Has it had to do with our employment and our finances? Does the door have a crack to see out of yet? Have we gotten closer to another person and treasured life as we become aware of its gifts? Can we see someone besides ourselves who is in need of comfort?

Do we recognize life's frailty and so value our time? Do we take less for granted and appreciate something more? Have we exercised our minds, spoken from our hearts, and developed ways to solve problems that once made us helpless? Some doors seem locked to me, but the crack that I see out of is getting wider. I must continue to look and be willing to walk out when it is time.

FOR TODAY: My eyes need to be open to my abilities. When I have discovered one thing, I will search for more. My gratitude will lead me to do the best I can with those abilities I've been given.

MARCH

March 1 ❧ Doctors

*Vitality shows in not only the ability to
persist, but in the ability to start over.*
—F. Scott Fitzgerald

The pain and disappointment was evident in her voice. After a vacation trip, her pain had gotten out of control. "We took the wrong car and I knew that, but I really wanted to go," she said. "I haven't had a major flare-up like this for a long time, so I was totally unprepared for what my doctor said when I came to him.

"All I got was his gruff 'Your chart is two inches thick. What do you *want*?' I honestly could not think of what it was that I wanted. All I knew is that I wanted help," she said. "Somewhere along the line, he's gotten to the point of not wanting to deal with me. That day I felt like saying, 'Don't you have any other patients with chronic pain?' I didn't say it because I was afraid I'd cry. It's devastating when your doctor gives up on you," she went on. "You really feel alone."

What do we want? We want to learn how to live with chronic pain. Many doctors don't know what to say or where to begin to tell us how to help ourselves. Because they have so little to offer, some don't want to see us. In their frustration, words may sound rude and insensitive.

We need to ask our doctors, "Who can teach me pain management? What can I do to help myself? How can I be as functional as possible?" That's what we need help with, and we have the right to ask.

FOR TODAY: **My mind is open to learning how to live with this pain. I hope to find the right teachers.**

March 2 ❧ Alternative Therapies

*Theirs is not to reason why; theirs is but to
do or die.*
—Alfred, Lord Tennyson

Patients in this age want to know what's wrong with them
and what can be done. Waiting rooms provide many helpful pamphlets, and the media can educate us on a variety
of subjects. We, in our quest for knowledge, are no different from others with chronic medical conditions, but
sometimes we feel that the information we need is not as
readily available.

We may have heard that alternative therapies can com-
plement the medical care we receive, but we may know
very little about these therapies.

It is up to us to seek answers to our questions and help
educate ourselves. Libraries, health professionals, and others with chronic pain can be of help.

This Latin phrase is one of the most important warnings
given to physicians: *Primum non nocere,* meaning ''First,
do no harm.'' In other words, the treatment should not
make a person worse.

Some forms of pain relief or relaxation may be only
temporary, such as a deep massage, but there are times
when we are happy to take relief where it can be found.
We ourselves must remember the phrase *Primum non
nocere* and strive not to risk an alternative therapy that is
apt to make us feel worse.

FOR TODAY: **If I want to try an alternative therapy, I will
seek advice and proceed with caution.**

March 3 ∞ Learning and Unlearning

*Virtue and learning have intrinsic value but
if they are not polished, they certainly will
lose a great deal of their lustre.*
—Earl of Chesterfield

Learning how to cope with chronic pain is like learning a new language. I have had to unlearn as much as I have had to relearn.

I've had to unlearn that the pain is always a warning signal. Most of the time, my chronic pain just is, and over-protecting myself with inactivity makes it worse. Un-learning that I should place "mind over matter" means that I need to acknowledge the pain and not charge reck-lessly ahead. I've had to unlearn that just because the pain can slow me down doesn't mean I'm sick and in need of constant attention from others who inquire how I feel.

Learning to be as happy, fulfilled, and useful as I can be, in spite of the pain, is an ongoing process. I still have things to learn and unlearn, and there are days when I want to shut this book of knowledge, to close my mind on it all.

I keep at it, though. The new language I'm learning is getting easier and I can think in new ways more naturally. I rehearse and rehearse because I want to make the most of what I have.

FOR TODAY: **I'll keep learning about coping so I can be more comfortable with living with pain.**

March 4   ∞   Limitations

> *Just keeping yourself maintained consumes*
> *much of the time, attention, and energy you*
> *would otherwise devote to life's*
> *"optional" activities.*
> —Cheri Register

What are my abilities and limitations today? I need to know the answer in order to live more comfortably. Notice the word "today." What applied yesterday may not apply today, and what applies today may not apply tomorrow. I want to challenge my limitations but do so slowly and gently.

At one time when my pain was more severe, noise was almost unbearable. I needed to excuse myself from family gatherings when the noise level became too great for me. Today, this day, it doesn't bother me. I can anticipate that tomorrow's limitations will be similar to today's, but I won't make absolute predictions.

My sense of comfort depends a great deal on knowing what my limitations are for the present. Questions I might ask myself include: How long can I work? How long can I shop? How long can I sit? How long can I exercise?

Pacing myself comes easier when I know how long the pain will allow me to do each activity. Slowly and cautiously I try to reach beyond today's limitations.

FOR TODAY: It takes more for me to accept or gently test my limitations than just knowing what they are, but asking myself "What can I do today?" is a good place to start.

March 5 ∾ Attitude

Find your happiness in yourself.
—Albert Camus

It has been said that appearance isn't everything, but it is first impressions that can make the difference. For example, a person carefully plans what he or she needs for the important "first look" that employers give to interviewees.

Perhaps we have not paid as much attention to our appearance since our pain began. If we don't feel good, we may not care whether we look good. We may not feel that we deserve to spend money on a wardrobe, having spent money on doctor bills. The mirror may reflect a person who does not accept his or her looks and someone who is not happy on the inside, either.

We can improve our attitude about ourselves by working on the inside and the outside. We can consider what is possible for us. Externally, we can start by dressing well, taking care of our skin, nails, and hair as if we wanted to make a good first impression on a stranger. Soon we may look and feel so good on the outside that we start feeling better on the inside. Our total appearance will radiate the good feelings we have.

FOR TODAY: **I have "inside" and "outside" work to do. I'll begin today to make any changes I need in order to look and feel good.**

March 6 ∾ Honesty

> *Lying in ambush deep down inside him,*
> *however, was an extremely compelling,*
> *extremely tender weakness: he had an*
> *absolute need to be loved and admired.*
> —Nikos Kazantzakis

Needing to be loved and admired may lead me to try to please someone in an excessive way. This may take the form of trying to protect someone else's feelings through some form of dishonesty. I convince myself that it is more important that others not feel disappointed, awkward, or uncomfortable than it is for me to take preventive steps in order to avoid added pain.

After we've lied to ourselves, we lie to others. "Yes, I can do whatever you want to do today," "No, it's no problem—really," we say. Many of the things we say yes to, when we really want to say no, are worthy endeavors and good causes. Still, we must realize that if we push ourselves too far, we'll be of no help to anyone.

Let us not be too hard on ourselves if we have ignored personal consequences while saying yes, when we really meant no. In time, we will be more comfortable being honest regarding our needs.

FOR TODAY: **I live a lie and make myself miserable if I distort reality to please someone else. Instead, I will try to be true to myself.**

March 7 ❧ Hope

> *Hope is the thing with feathers—*
> *That perches in the soul—*
> *And sings the tune without the words—*
> *And never stops—at all—*
> *—Emily Dickinson*

I can't stop hoping. I think that if I did, I would die. Some of my hopes have needed to be tempered; some have needed to be made more realistic; and some I have had to give up. But hope goes on.

I hope that my pain gets less and doesn't get worse. I hope my body gains more function instead of deteriorating. And I hope that I can be useful in some ways and not be a burden in all ways. I hope that I can have a happy life in spite of the pain. I hope modern science can unlock the secrets of chronic pain and find a way to provide relief.

While I hope, I work. I exercise my body to prevent deterioration. I think of how to be helpful to others so I feel self-worth. I try to change my thoughts to focus on something positive when I look back at what I perceive to have been a stressful day.

Hope is life-sustaining. Though the future can't be predicted, I want to keep my hopes alive. I live partially because of my hopes.

FOR TODAY: **I hope rather than merely wish that my pain problem either improves or does not get worse, and the hope that sings in my soul never stops at all.**

March 8 ❧ Acceptance

> *As you begin to work on a goal that you*
> *have chosen you have a focus for both your*
> *energy and your attention. Your pain will no*
> *longer be the center of your life.*
> —Penney Cowen

A member of our chronic pain support group said she was finally relieved when she was told that there was nothing left to try to cure her pain. She was relieved because she didn't have to have her expectations let down again. She wouldn't have to chase any more cures, she could stop throwing money into treatments that did her no good, and she could attend to other things in her life.

Accepting my pain doesn't mean that I have resigned myself to wallowing in it. There is still much to be done, even though I am finished with the search for a complete cure. There are less dramatic but important actions I can take, like understanding my wants and needs, selecting priorities, learning to be assertive, and attaining personally selected goals.

For now, the pain is a given; it is a fact. How I feel about its impact is up to me. Without acceptance I am like a boxer fighting an opponent but swinging only at air. I can fight the pain and lose, or I can accept the pain and win back a new life.

FOR TODAY: **Acceptance doesn't mean passivity; it takes courage and growth. Acceptance helps me make a good life for myself.**

March 9 ❧ Meditation

> *In my periods of retreat, perhaps I can learn*
> *something to carry back into my worldly life.*
> —Anne Morrow Lindbergh

Meditation helps to clear our minds and free us of the demands of our thoughts. Through meditation, we put ourselves in a state of nondoing, away from being driven to do more. While it is a good feeling to have accomplishments to look back on and future events to look forward to, meditation isn't a means to take us anywhere. Instead, it helps us to be content where we are.

I do not need to be a mystic or someone who must drop out of the mainstream of life to practice meditation. I need only the desire to give my body, mind, and soul the nourishment that comes from just being, the yearning to calm my mind and quiet my heart, the eagerness to find an inner balance that will remain in the midst of pain, and the willingness to see it as not another demand but an adventure into myself.

In meditation, I concentrate on my breathing and let the thoughts come without judging them, only remembering that I do not have to act on them. In its simplest form, being aware of my breathing can revive and rejuvenate me.

Even if my pain interrupts me, I visualize my breath coming from the pain itself. The inhalation breath fills my painful area, and the exhalation breath removes the unease and pain.

Meditation teaches me how to be with my body as it is and not as I would have it be.

FOR TODAY: **Meditation gives me a greater sense of wholeness. I can practice it today.**

When we cannot act as we wish, we must
act as we can.
—*William Wordsworth*

"I can't believe it happened again!" she exclaimed. "It all comes back so clearly now that the pain is severe. It was stupid of me to lift that peat moss, but I've done stupid things before and bounced back. Now I don't know what's going to happen. You don't think it's all in my head, do you?" she asked.

"No," I reassured her caringly. "You wouldn't be hurting this badly. It's going to take time to recover."

What do you say to someone who makes that split-second decision that creates severe pain? What do we all need when we have "done something stupid"? We don't need judgment and self-condemnation but compassion, encouragement, and support.

If it is someone with chronic pain who has made a mistake, we can offer the person what we ourselves would like to hear—a message of comfort, hope, and the reassurance that the acute episode will not last forever. If it has happened to us, we can tell ourselves that, after some healing, we will be able to begin again and learn from the mistake.

Most of all, we remember that the pain "is not all in our heads." It is real, and it is one of our biggest challenges.

FOR TODAY: **By being careful and respecting my limitations, I hope to prevent many accidents and mistakes, but when they happen, I know that understanding and support are needed.**

March 11 ∾ Worry

'Tain't worthwhile to wear a day all out
before it comes.
—Sarah Orne Jewett

Worry can wreak havoc on my pain. The first thing I have to do is step back out of the future, back into the present. I have to ask myself, "What would I be doing if I weren't worrying?" If it's listening to someone, I do it. If it's doing routine, everyday tasks, I do them. And I preface my acts with, "I will get through this. I can do what's in front of me."

It's not easy to "turn off" worry. Often we put worrying aside, only to have it return a short time later. We feel anxious about things that cannot be resolved until some future time, and it is hard to refrain from worrying. It affects our ability to concentrate on things at hand.

A friend said, "I have to wait five more days to find out whether I'm going to lose my job. Every time I think about it, I tell myself to wait and worry about it tomorrow. I feel like Scarlett O'Hara in *Gone With the Wind,* but it helps!"

People can advise us, direct us, counsel us, and empathize with us, but we must work out our own ways of handling worry. We find solutions in paying attention to the day's responsibilities, asking for direction, or postponing worrisome thoughts. Discoveries are ours to uncover but we can rest first. Our worries may not materialize.

FOR TODAY: I can take a deep breath and believe that I will be able to cope with whatever happens next.

March 12 ❧ Attitude

The greatest discovery of my generation is that human beings, by changing the inner attitudes of their minds, can change the outer aspects of their lives.
—William James

Chronic pain causes a paradox: it complicates my life, but it also simplifies some decisions. I need to think twice about doing things I once took for granted, and this complicates things for me. Simultaneously, the pain causes me to decide how best to use my energy, and that results in simplification.

My life isn't as black and white as I once thought it was. Making time for relaxation, contemplation, and stretching exercises first seemed to complicate my already rushed day. Now I see how much they positively affect my well-being.

A ray of sunshine passes through a prism, and the light no longer only illuminates the darkness but instead turns into dancing colors of pink, yellow, and green. The light first hits one wall, then another, changing direction and color as I touch the prism. My touch affects the movement of the light.

Chronic pain complicates my life, to be sure, but I can still enjoy simple pleasures and practice needed disciplines that simplify my decisions. Like the prism, it depends on my personal touch.

FOR TODAY: **I want to see color in my life and not just black and white. I will simplify my life to see with greater clarity.**

> *Why is life so tragic, so like a little strip of*
> *pavement over an abyss? I look down; I feel*
> *giddy; I wonder how I am ever to walk*
> *to the end.*
> —*Virginia Woolf*

I never thought it would be this way. First, I did not think that chronic pain could be the fate of a strong-willed, goal-oriented person like myself, who never allowed anything to slow her down. I never, ever thought it could happen to me. Once it did, I couldn't believe that pain could cause so much disruption. I never imagined that it would invade so many territories: relationships, self-esteem, spiritual life, and social activities, to mention but a few. I never dreamed that it would cause my emotions to roller coaster—riding high on a less painful day, only to crash down with the severe pain of the next.

It is hard to describe our pain, to articulate such feelings, but we all know them. There are dark days when we grope for answers to the questions of where to go from here, and how. Our eyes strain to adjust to this darkness.

An outsider can't fully enter into another person's pain. I don't know the pain of mental illness, and I don't know the various sufferings of the world, but I can relate to more of them than I did.

Faith, hope, and love are the streaks of light that lead me on through the darkness, through the times when I repeat, "I never thought it would be this way," and then add, "How can I go on?"

FOR TODAY: **My approach to life improves with deeper faith, more hope, and greater love. I'll lean on these principles today.**

March 14 ❧ Enthusiasm, Recovery

Things do not change, we do.
—Henry David Thoreau

We know how sluggish we feel when we are depressed and how energetic we feel when we are excited. In recovering from the negative effects of chronic pain, we have reason to be excited. The pain hasn't changed, but we have. With acceptance and an open mind, we feel the need to take back the parts of our lives that we've neglected. We regain the desire to try old things in a new way and to try some things that are entirely new.

"I'm not able to work or go to school at this time, but I'm so excited about learning how to use our new computer," someone said. "I've really got to slow down today, though, because I can't stay away from it and that's making my pain worse," she added as she recognized her limitation.

We must be careful that euphoria does not keep us from taking care of ourselves, forcing us to a point where we can hardly move. For some, a pain flare-up is worth it because they have had a chance to do something special, regardless of the consequences. For others, the euphoria-turned-incapacitation isn't worth the price. We are the only ones who can decide.

What we want most is to have the feeling of exaltation without having to pay for it later.

FOR TODAY: **I can be enthusiastic today and still practice moderation.**

March 15 ❧ Exercise

> *. . . I was taught that the way of progress*
> *is neither swift nor easy.*
> —Marie Curie

Physical fitness is defined as the ability to adapt to the demands and stresses of physical effort. For one reason or another, some of us have lost much of the ability we once had. Our bodies have been likened to wonderful machines, but many of us long for a new one, because ours does not serve us well.

There are ways of working with our bodies to get as much good as we can from our bones, joints, and ligaments, as well as our hearts and lungs. Regardless of what part of our body hurts, we all need to stretch and strengthen our muscles each day. Exercise helps us achieve greater mobility, better circulation, and increased muscle tone. It decreases pain for certain conditions and helps our general feeling of well-being.

In spite of all the benefits, there is an argument going on in my head. "But I'm afraid of reinjury," one voice tells me. "Go slow and do it anyway," another voice replies. "What's the use?" the first voice says. "You want to reach your potential," the other replies. "But I don't have time," the original voice protests. "Make time," the other insists.

Exercise is a priority for me. I don't let the excuses reduce me to inactivity.

FOR TODAY: **I can stretch some today. Exercise will move to my must-do list.**

March 16 ∾ Stress, Worry Over What Others Think

> *We're all of us sentenced to solitary*
> *confinement inside our own skins, for life.*
> —Tennessee Williams

We recognize that stress can increase our pain, but we don't want to ''live life in a bubble,'' either. What is the proper balance as far as stress is concerned?

Because of the effect of stress on chronic pain, we first need to know something about how we react. What stresses one person may motivate and stimulate another. We need to learn the warning signs of unhealthy stress, such as worsening pain in our bodies, fatigue, and emotional distress.

After we have learned the particular stresses that affect our pain, it is up to us to take necessary action. For instance, if a noisy party increases our pain, we may need to remove ourselves from the situation for at least a period of time. If sitting too long bothers us, we may have to stand and stretch periodically.

We may worry what others think when we make such decisions, but no one else feels our pain or experiences our stress. We will be more happy with ourselves for preventing pain from getting out of control.

FOR TODAY: **I will be in tune with my body and my emotions. It is I alone who must take care of myself.**

March 17 ∾ Prayer

Be not afraid to pray, to pray is right. Pray
if thou canst, with hope, but even pray,
though hope be weak, or sick with long
delay. Pray in the darkness if there
be no light.
—Hartley Coleridge

I used to pray to God, "Please take away this pain." No answer. Then I'd get angry and ask, "Is that too much to ask?" No answer. Fearing that I had been too demanding, I'd rephrase it and implore, "Please take away this pain so I can be a better person and accomplish better things." No answer. "I've got it," I thought. "If it be Thy will," I'd pray, sure that that was the way to get through to God. Still, no answer. Without patience, I would quip, "Why not?" I still heard no answer.

Today I may not understand this silence, but I believe that God has uses for me now, in spite of my pain. I live, touch, listen, **see,** speak, taste, smell, move, make, create, smile, and laugh. The pain stays, but God offers me help to accommodate to it. I have faith that, though I can't comprehend the "why," I am given versatility, adaptability, helpfulness, and value. My questions are less adamant; my actions, more productive.

FOR TODAY: **There comes a time when I quit asking why this has happened and ask how I should now live. God, please disclose this to me and make my aims conform to Yours.**

March 18 ❧ Morning

That man who does not believe that each
day contains an earlier, more sacred and
auroral hour than he has yet profaned, has
despaired of life, and is pursuing a
descending and darkening way.
—Henry David Thoreau

Thoreau believed that each new day contains a sacrosanct, holy element and if we fail to have a hopeful expectation at each day's dawn, we despair of life and take ourselves down a dark, dreary road. He went on to say that he believed that all memorable events happen in the morning and in the optimism of a morning mood. He felt that a positively expectant attitude is the way to affect the quality of the day.

For us with chronic pain, morning can bring a mixed reaction. Stretching, I test my body and see what level of pain I start the day with. My comment to myself no longer is "Another awful day of pain," but, instead, an acknowledgment of its presence and a thought regarding its intensity. Then I think of what is ahead of me in the way of responsibilities—old challenges and new questions, such as "What do I need to know so that I can perform this task more easily?"

I can't say that each morning finds me saying, "Hello, morning. What a beautiful day; I couldn't feel better." I do know, though, that in working with my pain, the morning hours are my best and most productive time. I need to take advantage of the physical energy, the emotional brightness, and the mental confidence that I feel in the dawning of a new day.

FOR TODAY: I am reinvigorated today. I will make the most of my "best hours," whether they are in the morning, afternoon, or evening—hours that hold the expectation of a beautiful day.

March 19 ⤞ Inactivity

> *If we all did the things we are capable of*
> *doing, we would literally astound ourselves.*
> —*Thomas A. Edison*

To regain the energy I need, I rest, because activity can hurt and I want to avoid added pain.

But prolonged avoidance of activity spells negative consequences for me. Muscles get weak; my mental outlook becomes depressed; and my social and recreational outlets diminish. I can't afford excessive rest, which complicates my pain.

I don't want to watch the world pass by without striving to be part of it. There is much to be interested in, occupied by, involved in, and entangled with. Life has possibility, and I am attracted to the opportunity to live it fully. I won't give up easily.

FOR TODAY: **Too much rest can be detrimental to me. There are many interests that can offer me challenge and excitement. I am eager to be occupied with them.**

March 20 ❧ Success

Never let success hide its emptiness from
you, achievement its nothingness, toil its
desolation. And so keep alive the incentive
to push on further, that pain in the soul
which drives us beyond ourselves.
Whither? That I don't know. That I don't
ask to know.
—Dag Hammarskjöld

Many of us have felt that we are stuck with a flawed life
because of a defect in our bodies. We're tempted to think
that our lives were ones of perfection and ease before our
pain started, though we know that such was not the case.
We see failure rather than success before us, and we see
dreams of achievement, accomplishment, and good fortune
vanish.

While people with money or power are often referred to
as successful, Webster's New World Thesaurus lists other
synonyms for that word, such as "unbeaten, strong, and
triumphant."

In this sense, we are all successful. We are not perfect,
and we don't feel strong at all times, but our affirmation
that our life, even with pain, is worth living enables us to
lead lives of triumph. We develop a love of life through
embracing our best moments and being unbeaten by our
worst ones.

A person's success is not due to the perfect management of a life with pain but to being an imperfect cham-
pion over the bondage of discouragement and desperation.
At times, we give in to such despondent feelings, but that
does not diminish our success. Mourning our lost abilities
and feeling sad about our changed self is part of the pro-

cess of healing. But we must keep the intention to envision ourselves as unbeaten, strong, and triumphant.

FOR TODAY: I'll live and love my life today and take pride in the success that I have, but I will not feel guilty if this day requires time for grieving.

March 21 ❧ Balance

Take the course opposite to custom and you
will almost always do well.
—Jean Jacques Rousseau

It takes many of us a long time to discover what constitutes balance in our lives. One of the Grimm brothers' fairy tales tells of three sisters who wanted to marry a shepherd. He was encouraged to watch how the three young women ate cheese. The first ate the cheese with the rind on; the second cut off the rind, but cut away much of the good cheese; and the third cut neither too much nor too little. The third was chosen, and as in most fairy tales, they lived happily ever after.

Finding a balance between two extremes can be difficult. We may not even like moderation! Like many in our society, we may want to exercise hard on the weekends and take it easy the other five days. We may want to eat on the run, instead of eating nutritious, balanced meals. We may want to be stimulated to work longer and harder by an excess of caffeine, rather than striking a balance between work and play.

Our well-being may depend a great deal on balance. That makes excess less appealing, consistency more desirable, and balance worth the effort.

FOR TODAY: **I have to stay as healthy as possible, and moderation is critical. It matters to me and my pain, even if it is a course opposite to custom. As much as possible, I'll practice moderation in what I do.**

> *It is a funny thing about life; if you refuse*
> *to accept anything but the best you very*
> *often get it.*
> —W. Somerset Maugham

I remember being a child and having a favorite doll to hold.

I remember when I skinned my knee and someone helped me stand.

I remember when I got lost but found my way and watched the relief on my parents' faces.

I remember spending time on the hood of a pickup truck with my brother, watching the clouds move across the sky.

I remember after arguments, wanting to grow up fast, so I could do whatever I wanted to do.

We can connect with the best of the child that we were, even if chronic pain has blocked out many good memories. The child was the one who trusted that things would work out, the one who found happiness in everyday events and everyday people, the one who wanted to love and be loved, the one whose pity for another person was transformed into being helpful, and the one who admitted to being impatient while waiting to grow up.

As adults we can still trust; we have before. We can be happy; we remember when we were. We can love and be loved; it has occurred. We can help someone else; we've done it in the past. Even if childhood was unhappy, there is a childlike part of us that is awaiting our love and devotion, whenever we are willing to recognize and embrace it. We have more patience than we thought we had. We waited and we grew up. There were special moments then and they can happen now.

FOR TODAY: I can embrace the part of me that is really alive, energetic, creative, and fulfilled, and be a child at heart.

March 23 ∾ Control

Thus the current of destiny carries us along.
None but a madman would swim against the
stream and none but a fool would exert
himself to swim with it. The best way is to
float quietly with the tide.
—*William Cullen Bryant*

To be able to use and control our bodies seems like such a basic matter, until we are racked with chronic pain. Whether it interferes greatly or slightly with what we try to accomplish, or whether pain occurs sporadically and unpredictably or constantly, we are frustrated by our lack of control over our physical selves.

The inability to do what we want to do, when we want to do it, can cause us to try to control other things. Without knowing it, we may try to manipulate people to do things our way. We may try moving to a different geographic location, thinking that the change of scene will help. Or we may alter our home environment, thinking that a change in living conditions will do us good. We try to control people or things around us because we haven't been able to control our pain. Although some changes may be helpful and give us a sense of order in our lives, control can turn into our obsession. We might unconsciously feel that if we aren't in control of something, we will give up and die.

Using all of our energy to keep some semblance of control can wear us out. Admitting that we can't control our pain entirely begins an emotional healing process. We can use our energy not for controlling others and our environment, but for love, cooperation, creative endeavors, and finding workable solutions for coping with our pain.

FOR TODAY: I will relax and "go with the flow" today.

> *Pain alone was not the enemy; the real*
> *enemy is fear and resistance.*
> —*The Buddha*

We have a lot of time to decide how we will respond to pain. "Chronic" means "long-standing." One person says, "I think I have it for the duration." If this is our fate, how do we cope for the duration of our lives?

We bring to this experience the diversity of our personalities. One person may thrive on challenge and see chronic pain as an adversary to keep in check. Another person may lean toward the depressive side and allow pain to be a reason for giving in to self-defeat. Another person whose past history included frequent change, when accommodation was a fact of life, may adjust to pain quickly.

We consciously or unconsciously decide our responses to chronic pain through our prior coping mechanisms (or lack thereof), our adjustment ability to the new reality of pain, and our sense of community with others. Pain can pull people apart or, with work, bring us together.

Our future with pain depends a great deal on who we have been, who we are, and who we are willing to be. We can make the adjustments at any time. Even now we can begin.

FOR TODAY: **I have past and present resources to use in the long-term management of pain. I'm committed to coping as well as I can and to enlisting the help of whatever supportive community I have, whether it is large or small.**

> . . . *suffering . . . no matter how*
> *multiplied is always individual.*
> —Anne Morrow Lindbergh

Early in my pain experience, I heard that someone at work had asked where I had been, not having seen me for two months.

"She's taking an extended vacation," the person was told. Upon hearing this, I was shocked that someone had made such a false and insensitive statement. I felt angry.

"If that person were only in my place! How could anyone say that?" I demanded. Soon after I felt deeply hurt. It was my first encounter with the stigma of chronic pain. Most of us have experienced it in some way.

"But you look so good!" our neighbor tells us.

"Moves with ease from the exam table. Does not appear to be in pain," the doctor writes.

People don't understand us because chronic pain doesn't necessarily show on one's face and because nothing directs our attention to it, as a cast does to a broken leg. Perhaps our experiences will help us to be aware of another person's unidentifiable problem.

For example, a person who has had more than one open-heart surgery or lives with an aneurysm may look well outwardly, but may worry inwardly about the potential for sudden death.

We need to explain calmly, in terms that others can understand, the nature of our pain when we find ourselves confronted by misunderstanding. Anger at the other person only worsens our attitude. Let us focus on our own lives and practice empathy toward others, whether we know of their particular challenges or not.

FOR TODAY: **I will learn about chronic pain and how it affects me. My teachers will be people who understand.**

March 26 ❧ Negative Thoughts

*The mind is its own place, and in itself can
make a heaven of Hell, a hell of Heaven.*
—John Milton

Our thoughts can be distorted when we don't hold them up
to reality. Negative thoughts such as, "I'm a rotten parent
because I can't financially provide for my children as I'd
like," or "I'm hopeless and I will never be happy again,"
or "I'm letting everyone down," or "I shouldn't feel this
way," can make us believe that we are as worthless as we
feel. When we do this, we are discounting all the positive
things we have done and the positive qualities that we possess.

We need to list, on paper if necessary, the good things
we know about ourselves. We need to stop forecasting
gloom and stop telling ourselves that we shouldn't be unhappy, if that's how we feel. Real people have real feelings, and it is unreasonable to expect to feel cheerful and
confident at all times.

Depressing thoughts can distort the way things really
are. Such thoughts will pass eventually. If they persist, we
will find help to lift them.

FOR TODAY: **It is hard to erase my negative thoughts, but
I can find joy in some person or activity that will reduce the distortion of my pessimistic thinking. Using
the telephone or picking up a hobby may be just the
therapy I need.**

> *God does not die on the day when we cease*
> *to believe in a personal deity, but we die on*
> *the day when our lives cease to be illumined*
> *by the steady radiance, renewed daily, of a*
> *wonder, the source of which is beyond all*
> *reason.*
> —Dag Hammarskjöld

I used to bargain with God, having the idea that if I only said, did, or thought the right things, there was a chance that God would answer my prayers for relief of pain. "I won't let my job be so important next time," "I'll do whatever You want," "I'll be closer to You and think less about my plans." Silence, silence, silence. Was it that I didn't promise God enough, or was it that God wasn't listening? Was it that I wasn't sincere enough and knew that I'd forsake those promises if I got pain relief?

I believe that God listens and helps us through our pain, but I don't think He responds with a "yes" because we have bargained with Him. He wants our love but doesn't want to reward us for our resolutions by granting our wishes, even if they are honest.

I think God is better at removing the roadblocks that may aggravate pain, the things in our character that need revising to make living with chronic pain less difficult. He helps us with acceptance while helping us find healthy ways to cope.

I can find ways to become a stronger person who displays God's help, but I don't bargain. I just ask for His aid. I don't always feel helped, but I am grateful when it comes in some form. For me, just being able to share my concerns with God is comforting.

For today: Bargaining, for many, is a part of the grief process, on the way to acceptance. I bargain with God until my prayer life enlarges to include asking what God's will is for my life.

March 28 ❧ Being Human

> *It's great to be great, but it's greater*
> *to be human.*
> —Will Rogers

Fame and fortune don't happen to most of us. Most of our names will not be written in the history books for achieving distinction and eminence. Our successes may gain neither worldwide attention nor the envy of our community. Instead, our greatness may rest in our humanness.

It is human to be frustrated about the chronic nature of our pain, human to want to return to former abilities, human to make mistakes, and human to get discouraged. Emotions and errors are part of what makes us mortal.

Being human, though, is more than experiencing feelings and being wrong. In our humanness, humble successes can be major triumphs when we are in pain. Getting out of the house can be an achievement.

We may not achieve greatness in terms of making outstanding, worldly discoveries. We can, however, discover how to persist against discouragement and overcome many of the obstacles that pain presents. Our difficulties spur us on toward many successes that we can glory in.

FOR TODAY: **This day holds a measure of success for me. When I have pain, even the smallest act is a major accomplishment. I can take a moment and feel proud of my efforts.**

March 29 ❧ Anger

> *It's astonishing in this world how things*
> *don't turn out at all the way you expect*
> *them to!*
> —Agatha Christie

It's hard to keep on a steady emotional keel with chronic pain. Once I went for a walk on one of my favorite paths. At the end of it was a large cottonwood tree. I lay beneath it and listened to the sound of the rustling leaves and saw their bright green and silver colors glisten in the sun, being grateful that I had the time to enjoy the beauty of my favorite tree. For the moment I felt that my pain was secondary, that I would never allow it to cause me anguish again. Saying "never" was my downfall.

The next time I went back to the tree, my attitude was, unfortunately, much different. My pain had prevented me from pursuing a certain job and I was angry. The emotion robbed me of my capacity to appreciate my closeness to nature.

I need to be honest about how I feel, to God, to another person, or in writing. Anger is a natural emotion. It is how I handle it that matters.

FOR TODAY: **I want to grow in my ability to let fewer things anger me and to appreciate what's before me, even the beauty of nature. Since I will inevitably feel anger in this life, I will strive to express it appropriately and then release it.**

> *Believe, when you are most unhappy, that*
> *there is something for you to do in the*
> *world. So long as you can sweeten another's*
> *pain, life is not in vain.*
> —Helen Keller

The first time that it was suggested to me that I try mini-mizing my pain, I was offended. "You don't understand my pain," I thought. Then I heard someone say that their pain was "annoying." It made me think about the terms I used in association with my pain. When pain is mild, the word "annoying" acts to minimize my pain, but it also allows me to feel irritated by the limitations placed on me.

Of course, pain can be more intense on some days, but how I perceive it does influence how I think about it. The worse I feel about having the pain, the more angry or de-pressed I become and, often, the greater my pain grows.

Our thoughts alone won't make the pain go away, but they can help us put pain in perspective. We may find it within ourselves to make room for others who may need us, as Keller urged, to sweeten their pain.

FOR TODAY: I'll seek a balance between denying the pain and focusing on it too much. I will find someone who needs my concern and thoughtfulness.

March 31 ❧ Growth

There's a period of life where we swallow a
knowledge of ourselves and it becomes
either good or sour inside.
—Pearl Bailey

Difficult times and times of struggle can lead to growth. The first step may involve outgrowing old beliefs. Maybe it's an attitude that no longer "fits," such as "If only my _____ (pain, family, job, friends) were different, my life would be better." Growth is evidenced by the attitude "My life and the people around me are imperfect, but it is up to me to work on my own imperfections, not theirs."

Maybe we've grown spiritually, from asking "Why did God allow this to happen?" to affirming "I believe that God is not to blame and that He has compassion for me." Maybe our attitude has changed from "I want this pain to leave immediately" to "I have to take care of this day, whether I have pain or not."

I know that I've grown when I can say "What can I do about the problem now?" rather than "Who's to blame?" Growth uplifts my whole being while blame only stunts it.

Old beliefs can be challenged and new attitudes that foster responsibility and contentment can be found. So much potential exists when we are willing to grow.

FOR TODAY: **I am willing to look at myself first when I'm tempted to point the finger of blame. Bettering my life is up to me. I am patient enough to see beyond the pain to what I need to do with this one day.**

APRIL

April 1   Happiness

If something makes my heart bound like a
young calf, then I know I am standing in
front of happiness.
—Alan Watts

A newborn calf, first on its feet, looks gangly and stands precariously, as if about to fall. After a few hours, it gains its balance and bounds out of the barn, into the yard, eagerly running and touching the earth beneath its feet. It smells the fresh clover and feels the wind behind it as it hastens across the field. It is as if it runs to experience the world's delights, freed from its mother's womb. It is a wondrous sight to see.

Since our pain started, we perhaps have stopped expecting thrills and happiness. We may have been disappointed so often in our hopes for pain relief that we inadvertently shut our hearts and minds to protect ourselves from defeat.

We risk rejection when we care about someone; we risk disappointment if we want something; and we risk shattered dreams if we hope for something. The risks are worth taking. If we live our lives with the aim of avoiding disappointment, we may miss good times, enjoyable friendships, and watching dreams come true. We miss the joy and excellence that can give us reason for excitement.

If we really use our senses to see, taste, hear, and touch, we will find those things that make our hearts bound, as with the freedom of a newborn calf.

FOR TODAY: **I'll take a moment to think of something that I really love. I'll feel this thought with my whole being. I can't be happy all the time, but there are pleasures in today that I don't want to miss.**

April 2 ❧ Decisions

> *If our goal is peace, we're programmed for*
> *emotional stability no matter what happens.*
> —Marianne Williamson

I used to think I was a master at making decisions, but my confidence was shaken by chronic pain. I was sure that I was making the right decisions and that the surgeries and therapies would take away my pain. When the pain wasn't taken away, I didn't trust anyone—least of all myself. I became depressed and had trouble making simple decisions, such as what kind of pizza to order, what I should do with my day, or which shoes I should buy.

I had to start trusting my decisions again in order to discover what seemed to be the best choice for me. A friend had to remind me that whatever decision I made, large or small, I'd still be okay. I relearned that most decisions don't have life-or-death consequences. I can relax and decide to the best of my ability. I ask for guidance, trust the rhythm, and gently move with it.

FOR TODAY: **I will find a peaceful moment in which I can clear my mind of confusion so that I can make good decisions.**

April 3 ∿ Exercise

Whether you think you can or you think you can't, you are right.
—Henry Ford

Exercise can decrease some kinds of pain, but our philosophy must be to make steady progress through moderation rather than "no pain, no gain."

There are scientific reasons for exercise bringing about some pain relief. It is thought that exercise can stimulate the production of brain chemicals—endorphins, enkephalins, and serotonin. These chemicals raise pain tolerance and cause us to feel better.

We do need to use caution, because an excessively rigorous program that ignores a starting point and a plan of action could be injurious. A set of exercises specifically designed for us is the route to take. With the supervision of trained specialists, we are less likely to fail. After a period of time, we can follow the plan ourselves and individualize it, since our improved body awareness will enable us to "read our bodies" better than anyone else.

Sometimes it is helpful to do fewer exercises but to perform them twice daily. Doing so may develop our sense of success and improve our overall conditioning. According to pain management specialists, a slow and steady approach to the type of exercise that raises our heartbeats helps, too. Some suggest only a minute's increase every so often for such activities as biking, walking, and swimming.

Keeping a graph of our progress helps us see that we are gradually getting stronger and more functional. It can serve as our own reward. Scheduling a massage could be another way to congratulate ourselves for our persistent efforts.

"Go exercise" isn't enough. We need guidelines and helpful hints so we can work up to achieving our work, recreational, and social goals.

FOR TODAY: I'll exercise in order to be as functional as I can be.

April 4 ❧ Spring

We know that life is always in process, and
always on its way to greater good. We just
can't see that.
—Marianne Williamson

Spring comes to us with a day of sunshine, then a stormy one, a return to winter and frost, followed by tiny purple crocuses peeping up out of the still, waiting earth. Finally, warmth stays and the new growth of grass and violets spreads beneath our feet. Spring has been playful and teasing, but this time it stays.

One April day I wanted to feel excited, but I felt melancholy. I asked myself how I could feel sad at being shown such miracles, ones I had waited all winter to see. The answer was clear. It was because I wanted a miracle, too—complete and total pain relief. "I have waited longer than a winter," I complained. "Couldn't something miraculous happen to me?"

I have only this one life and it is sometimes a relief to express my complaints. I keep asking questions, even when no quick answer comes. Still, I am grateful when I comprehend that, in spite of my pain, there are elements of my life that bring me fulfillment and surprise. My heart is open to receive. In spring I can welcome the sunshine's warmth and the flowers' beauty and rejoice in the end of winter's ice and snow. My melancholy changes to thankfulness. That, too, I experience in spring.

FOR TODAY: **I am restless. Instead of focusing on miraculous cures, I'll make this day the beginning of a season of gratitude. I am grateful for the remarkable ways I live successfully with the pain.**

April 5 ❧ Dreams

Chance favors only the prepared mind.
—Louis Pasteur

I have a dream in my heart, and from it, I borrow timelessness. I don't know when or whether my fantasy will be realized, so as yet it remains a dream.

It is not now within reach and it may be unattainable, but it is still my dream. It is my fantasy before it becomes my goal and my gladness before it attains actualization.

As elusive as it is, it has power. It is an outlet for my frustration, a whisper in my stillness, a comfort for my pain, and nourishment for my spirit.

We need dreams to break up the monotony of our days. They may involve others or only ourselves; they may be shared or kept secret.

They are significant because they can keep us moving forward in hope, and they can give us some release from the rigors of problem and pain.

FOR TODAY: **When the pain closes down upon me, I can gaze upon my dreams. I need not think of how to pursue them today, but I am open to the possibility of doing so.**

April 6 ❧ Success

No bird soars too high, if he soars with his
own wings.
—William Blake

Just as others can't experience my pain, they can't truly
celebrate my overcoming it. Without knowing the struggle,
it is hard to understand the exhilaration of small but significant progress.

Success may take many forms: walking a little farther,
staying to visit someone a little longer, getting dressed a
little earlier, smiling a little more often, or pacing activities a little better. None of these changes happens without
work and struggle, and most do not occur overnight.

However, success may not always come from physical
progress. Instead, it may be found in our patience during
painful times, our determination to not let pain ruin plans,
or our tenaciousness in embracing a life that includes
skirmishes with pain.

Many lives have distinction. Though others may not
realize our contest with pain, we can rejoice over a cham-
pionship attained.

FOR TODAY: **Whether it is in progress or patience and
perseverance, I am grateful for victories over the negative effects of pain.**

April 7 ❧ Guilt

When we do the best we can, we never know
what miracle is wrought in our life, or in
the life of another!
—Helen Keller

If we say bitter words, neglect the needs of someone entrusted to our care, or affect someone by irresponsibility, it is natural to feel guilt. We can apologize to the persons harmed and make amends by changing our behavior. Having done this, we move on with our lives.

There is another kind of guilt we can experience about things over which we have no control. The man who can't play football with his son or the woman who has had to give up a high-paying position that she can no longer handle may feel that their families are deprived because of their limitations. Yet it is something over which they have no control. It is unhealthy guilt. This type of guilt limits the freedoms we do have—the freedom to affirm a quiet, honorable sense of who we are and what we can do.

If we are doing our best to stay involved with friends and family, to compensate for past wrongs and to do our best today, we need not fall into the deep well of unhealthy guilt.

FOR TODAY: I can ask for forgiveness for wrongs done and not be trapped by guilt over things that are out of my control.

April 8 ∿ Friends

*To accept oneself as one is may sound like a
simple thing, but simple things are always
the most difficult things to do.*
—Carl Jung

Most of us have been around people who make us feel
important to them, who love us as we are, and who radiate
happiness themselves. These are affirming people who instinctively know how to give us our own goodness by reflecting it through their being. They help us accept who we
are and who we strive to be, by finding delight in our
company and unconsciously mirroring the good in us,
while not needing to point out the bad.

You know this kind of friend by subtle indicators: a
look, touch, tone of voice, or forthright words. Other acts
of kindness are secondary to the understanding such people transmit. They give us their full attention, and they
reveal our goodness to us by giving of their time. They
allow us to grow at our own rate and in our own space,
and remind us that we are more than our pain.

They help us do what Carl Jung said is the most difficult
thing to do—to accept ourselves as we are.

FOR TODAY: **I like to see my goodness reflected in other
people's awareness. I enjoy my friends not only for who
they are but for reflecting the intrinsic goodness in me
that I see in their awareness and attention.**

April 9 ∾ Help

> *"If only's" are lonely.*
> *—Morgan Jennings*

Once, when I filled out yet another questionnaire at a doctor's office, there was a place for me to write in the doctors I had already seen. There were six or seven of them, and only when I saw the names on paper did it occur to me that I had, indeed, been doctor shopping. Most of us with chronic pain don't accept no for an answer. We want someone to cure us of our pain, and if we have to go to the ends of the earth, we will. Sooner or later, though, we can't travel any farther.

At some point we should seek a multidisciplinary approach to our pain in order to address our physical pain, vocational, social, and emotional issues; and training our bodies to be in the best condition possible. We'll want to become a partner in the health care process and not just a partaker. This might include asking the risks and benefits of anything new that we try. It may mean learning about pain support groups and organizations and about day-to-day management of pain.

I don't feel bad about my past doctor shopping. I'm just glad I don't have to do it anymore, since doctors aren't my only resource for this complex problem.

FOR TODAY: **Are my pain, the needs of my body, and emotional issues being addressed? If not, I'll find out how they can be.**

April 10 ∾ Living in the Present Moment

If you allow it, pain can destroy your life.
—Penney Cowen

The stress reduction speaker posed the question, "What would you do if you only had two more years to live?" He said that some people with life-threatening illnesses report that they begin to really live when they realize the brevity of their lives.

I am alive today, and I can make of today what I want, whether I like the terms set forth or not. It takes all my energy to live today, so I will not waste it on thinking about the past or projecting too far into the future.

I don't have to wait until my pain changes, or for the day when I have more money, or for the answer to why I have pain in order to start living. Today is the only reality I know, the only reality that really matters. I will use this day as a great blessing, and be grateful for the ability to take what comes, to allow for some possible unhappiness, and to let my heart sing in response to the day's goodness.

FOR TODAY: I can put aside worry because today, this valuable day, is what matters.

April 11 ☙ Pain

He has seen but half the universe who has
never been shown the house of pain.
—*Ralph Waldo Emerson*

I know about the house of pain. Not only has it been shown to me, but pain thinks it is the landlord of my house, which has many doors, some windows, and a number of full closets.

The doors are kept open to let people come and go, even though pain wants to keep them shut and selfishly craves all my attention. I clean and shine the windows to let the sun stream in, even though pain likes the drapes closed and the house dark. Old goods are discarded from closets to make room for the new, even though pain would have me keep the rags of helplessness and despair, fear and anxiety.

I won't allow pain to have the final say as to how this house is run. Sunshine of gladness, warmth of love, and the space for cheer is how I will decorate it.

If I cannot move from this house of pain, I will fill it with joy and sweep away the clutter of negativity that pain would have me keep.

FOR TODAY: **If I must exist in the house of pain, I will make it a home of love and cheer. I will work at this today.**

April 12 ∾ Humility

*The strength of the spirit prevents its being
used up.*
—Lao-tzu

One of the things that I've learned from chronic pain is that my body is not invincible. Rather, it is quite vulnerable. But for pain, I may never have recognized this or marveled at my body's complexity. Our society teaches us that anything is possible, if we push hard enough and try long enough. The media also repeatedly exposes us to the fit, trim, forever-young kind of bodies—the kind that never can be pictured unhappy, injured, or in pain.

With such delusion, it is no wonder that we've taken our bodies for granted until now. It is out of this process of learning about our vulnerability that we realize the gift of simply being alive. Attitudes change. Happiness can be considered less a goal than a gift gratefully accepted when it comes. Work can be thought of less as a moneymaker than an opportunity to share our usefulness. Pain can be less a curse, more a teacher.

Pain teaches me about the need I have to take care of my body. My vulnerability also can point out my need for spiritual growth, which in this imperfect body means to trust that a perfect Spirit cares and can lead me forward. I have the humility to see happiness, work, pain, and spiritual growth in a new way.

FOR TODAY: **The satisfaction of my demands is not the goal it once was. Demands for emotional security and** financial stability have been reduced to requests. I am gaining a humble spirit in my sojourn with pain, and I will use this humility to be sympathetic to my wants and needs, and kindhearted toward others.

April 13 ❧ Prayer

> *God does not sit on a throne above the*
> *clouds. He wrestles here on earth along*
> *with us.*
> —*Nikos Kazantzakis*

I asked my spiritual advisor, "Should I pray to be rid of chronic pain?" He said, "Absolutely, because God cares about your wants and needs."

I couldn't help thinking, "But God knows I want pain relief and nothing has happened. If I'm supposed to live with it, I'm not in favor of His will. It must mean being in pain for the rest of my life."

Then it occurred to me that perhaps I'd been assuming God's will wrongly. In the future, the pain may change or have fewer effects on my daily life. If it gets worse, I trust in God for strength. If the pain stays the same, I will live each day as it comes.

I'm not so disappointed by pain today. There are days when I can wake up in the morning and say, "Yes, the pain is still here. God, make it manageable today or take it away. Because I believe that Your will for me is good, use and guide me so that the pain does not overcome my spirit."

Even though my body is still in pain, I feel closer to God when my soul is satisfied in the midst of it.

FOR TODAY: **God, please reduce or alleviate my pain today. I'm not afraid to ask.**

The way to love anything is to realize it
might be lost.
—G. K. Chesterton

It happens less and less, but sometimes I look at my family with my "Blame Glasses" on. I have a million "if onlys." If only they wouldn't demand so much of me, I think. If only they wouldn't want to go places and do things, if only they'd do more for me. If only they wouldn't want to have people over, and if only they would just leave me alone.

Those "Blame Glasses" need a better focus, one totally opposite to the one they have. I need "Gratitude Glasses" when I look at my family. I am grateful that they want me involved in their lives, that they demand my time and energy so that it isn't wasted on my own depressed reflection, grateful that they want to explore life anew each day, grateful that I can ask them for help without being totally dependent, grateful that they want to share our home with others rather than hide me away, and above all, grateful that they don't just leave me alone.

FOR TODAY: **Chronic pain places a strain on family relationships, but isolation is not the answer. Things can sometimes get out of focus. I need to remember that I would not want the things I sometimes wish for and to be grateful for all that my family is to me.**

April 15 ❧ Peace, Escape

There can be no very black melancholy to
him who lives in the midst of nature and has
his senses still.
—Henry David Thoreau

Escaping city and town, I seek nature for some repose, for some example of peaceful living. I live near a wildlife refuge and every spring my family and I go out, before the birds and animals know that the opening date, April 15, has arrived. The wildlife is more easily observed, not having seen humans all winter, and I'm always impressed by the placid scenes I see. On this date there may be ducks quietly swimming, pelicans floating on the lake, a deer bounding down a path, birds calling back and forth to each other, and a muskrat parting the water. Although I know that unseen predators lurk in the refuge, too, everything seems to be moving and coexisting in perfect harmony and without struggle.

That's why I escape there when I struggle with my pain. The peace there affects me. All I see are the aspects of wildlife that symbolize harmony and order.

I return with hope that my life can get back "in sync" and be in harmony, too.

FOR TODAY: **I need a place to retreat to, a place that calms me. If I can't get there today, I will imagine one and experience a similar peace.**

You don't get to choose how you're going to die. Or when. You can only decide how you're going to live. Now.
—Joan Baez

A man who visualizes his cancer cells shrinking may still die. The woman with a history of heart disease who is watching her fat intake and exercising regularly may still be struck down by a heart attack. A man who has an optimistic attitude, faith, and the recognition of his pain triggers may still have an exacerbation of pain. All of these people may ask, "Why try? The worst is inevitable."

A worsening of chronic pain can leave us confused and upset. When the pain surprises us, a host of well-contained emotions rise up, like flames from smoldering embers.

The uncertainty of our pain can be, at the least, a major aggravation. It provokes the questions that we had thought we had put aside, such as "What went wrong?" "Why me?" and "What is this all about, anyway?" It makes us angry that we feel worse after having done "all the right things." The question "Why try?" comes back to haunt us.

We try because, instinctively, life is still worth it. We can handle this span of time and then the next, and the next. As our courage grows, so does our strength and our confidence that the exacerbation will not last forever.

FOR TODAY: **I may not be spared extra pain by doing what I believe will help, but I won't give up my courage.**

April 17 ❧ Anger, Apology

Every man has a right to be valued by his
best moment.
—Ralph Waldo Emerson

I don't overcome pain completely, but I cope with it to the extent that I can be happy in spite of it. I don't conquer it, but neither does it conquer me. In spite of my efforts, pain sometimes springs me a surprise. It might rush in like a hurricane at the worst times—during a vacation, a weekend, a holiday—the times when I want to experience it the least.

Sometimes it's hard to hold on against its force. I attempt to lash back in anger or pent-up frustration, but instead my response hits the ones I live with. They, too, are caught in the storm, but they see it originating from me, because it is I who hold the pain. Unfortunately, they can't see the combat inside. Full of regrets, I tell myself, "It's not their fault that they're caught in the tempest, too. They didn't ask to be here."

"I'm sorry. I'm having a bad day" doesn't seem to absolve me of the guilt over my short temper, avoidance, or irritability. To go into detail, however, seems excessive. They have heard long-winded apologies and explanations before and no longer encourage them.

Sometimes the less that is said, the better it is for everyone. A short apology is sufficient. Perhaps next time I won't impose my frustration on those around me or isolate myself to protect others from angry words. Perhaps next time I'll handle my pain in a healthier way.

FOR TODAY: All of us have days we are not proud of. I can only strive to be and do my best today.

April 18 ❧ The Past

> *This only is denied to God: the power to*
> *change the past.*
> —Agathon

In a university study, a doctor was once questioned about patients in extreme pain. The researchers wanted to know how they responded. Did the patients get closer to God or turn away from God?

The doctor said that there was no common response, but that those who dwelled too much on "Why am I suffering?" "What have I done?" became more bitter and despairing. The ones who responded with "This has happened. I trust God to help me get through this and rebuild my life" moved past their despair.

Which thought pattern do I follow?

It is easy to dwell on what I could have been or what I should have done. Recognizing loss is an important part of grieving. If I lose myself in grief, however, I may not realize my God-given potential for modifying old ways or finding new ways to move forward with my life.

The painful past does not give me answers, nor does it provide me with peace. I allow my spiritual life to substitute serenity and action for bitterness and despair.

FOR TODAY: I am not sure of the "Why?" but I know "Who can help?" is the question I must answer to get on with my life.

April 19 ✿ Acceptance

> *The goal of yesterday will be the starting
> point of tomorrow.*
> —Thomas Carlyle

I've had to quit fighting. Sometimes I feel an emptiness because of it. I fought doctors, employers, lawyers, therapists, and insurance companies. I thought I had a right to a pain-free life and if only all of these people would cooperate, I could get rid of my pain and get on with my life.

One day they all left. The doctors could do no more; my previous employer had no place for me; the psychologist released me; and the lawyer and insurance company reached a financial settlement.

There was nothing left to fight for. There was no victory over pain, and I was certainly no hero. What would give me the energy to go on if I had no one to fight?

I finally surrendered to the fact that I couldn't fight the pain, either. Although never giving it my approval, I have accepted it for two reasons: (1) it's a relief not to have to search for an answer that's not there, and (2) when I live in reality, I can concentrate on the positive things I want to do with my life.

FOR TODAY: **Living with chronic pain is a challenge. I'm a winner today if I do my best to meet the challenge.**

I want to inspire you to see that you can go
far beyond where you are right now.
—Virginia Satir

"They told me I couldn't work at construction jobs again, but now I am." "My daughter became a new person." "He's had nine surgeries, but he's doing much better." "I still have pain, but I tolerate it better and I can do more." "I was feeling so bad that I wanted to pack my bags and leave my family for good. Now they notice a big change in me."

Comments such as these are from people who, with help, improved their ability to manage their pain. Although I realize that each person is different, I want such good changes for myself. I want to be in a more fit condition, to give less attention to my pain, and to hurt less.

I accept where I am today. I need to remember that each day, even if I feel that I'm not making progress in being more active, I'll continue exercising my body and improving my mind. Hope of a better quality of life spurs me on.

FOR TODAY: I don't know what is possible and what is impossible for me. All I know is that I'm willing to take steps in the direction of hope.

April 21 ❧ Rewards

To travel well is better than to arrive.
—Alan Watts

We may take on commitments that require time and discipline but fail to commit to the one common denominator in the formula of all our activities—ourselves. Perhaps it is because we equate our other commitments with reward. We may think that if we work hard, our efforts will be appreciated. We may think that if we take time for our children now, they will grow up to be healthy, happy adults. We may think that if we eat properly, we will have less of a chance of getting cancer or heart disease.

Because pain is ongoing, we may feel that there is little reward for our commitment to meeting the pain, coping with it, and doing the things that may help, such as being active in spite of its constant presence.

There is satisfaction, though, in the feeling that we are standing up to the pain and conquering its debilitating effects. There is pride in making the effort to gain victory instead of succumbing to defeat. At times, there may be less pain. Finally, when we make the commitment to care for ourselves and to care about others without the thought of reward, there is the satisfaction of a life well lived.

FOR TODAY: **I'm willing to commit myself to creating the kind of life I can be proud of, without thought of any reward.**

April 22 ❧ Anger, Family

> *We feel and weigh soon enough what we*
> *suffer from others; but how much others*
> *suffer from us, of this we take no heed.*
> —*Thomas à Kempis*

There are times when we're irritable, in pain, fatigued, and frustrated. We've been pushing ourselves to the limit and no one seems to notice. Then it happens. Perhaps at work or at home we have too much to do, or we get six calls in one week from salesmen trying to sell us a new credit card line or siding for our house, or we agree to do someone a favor, even though we don't have time. Finally, one of our family members says, "It would be nice if you did something for us once." We finally lash out or we sulk.

Families often don't understand how much strain and effort is involved in maintaining as normal a lifestyle as we attempt to do. When we take care of ourselves by saying no to their demands, we appear selfish.

Sometimes we have to remove ourselves from a situation to defuse our hostility. Even a hot bath or a ten-minute rest can help. Resentment sours our relationships and keeps others at a distance. Anger-induced isolation is not what we need, but sometimes we do need a "time out."

We also need to be aware of what our families go through. We only know with certainty how chronic pain affects us; we know less about how pain and our behavior affect them. We hope that they don't judge us by our worst moments, when we are tired, in pain, and irritable. A forgiving spirit is needed on all sides then.

FOR TODAY: **I will look at my attitudes and take care of neglected needs, so I can be as caring as possible and promote peace within my family.**

April 23 ❧ Crisis

> *Philosophy is perfectly right in saying that*
> *life must be understood backward. But then*
> *one forgets the other clause—that it must be*
> *lived forward.*
> —Sören Kierkegaard

Just because we have chronic pain does not mean we are not free from crises. We may unconsciously think: "Chronic pain is bad enough; surely this is the worst that can happen to me." Whether it is our own crisis or that of someone else, problems sometimes arise that seem to have no solution and no way of escape. They dominate our thoughts so that we can think of nothing else. The crisis might take the form of a serious physical setback, a relationship breakup, divorce, serious illness, or sudden death of a family member.

One thing we can do is to repeat a phrase, verse, or philosophical line over and over until our minds become filled with its content, loosening the grip of our tormenting thoughts.

Another technique that helps is to think about what we would have done if the crisis had not happened and then do that thing, in order to remind ourselves that we can still function.

After the crisis passes, we can look back and see that we have tapped inner resources that we didn't know we had and that we have grown in our ability to deal with what happens to us without giving in to despair.

FOR TODAY: If I am in the middle of a crisis, I can repeat over and over "This, too, shall pass." I can do whatever task is before me, knowing that this, too, is healing.

April 24 ⤚ Humor

> *To be wildly enthusiastic or deadly serious—*
> *both are wrong. Both pass. One must keep*
> *ever a sense of humor.*
> *—Katherine Mansfield*

It is a well-known fact that children say some funny things. When my son was two years old, eating what was on his plate was not his idea of a good time. My husband came up with what he thought was a great idea, telling our child that the meat was "fireman's meat." It was a perfect suggestion for a boy whose toys included five fire trucks and whose favorite book was about a fire station. The meat was eaten immediately.

The next day after a long bike ride, my husband lifted our son down from the seat behind him, only to hear "I'm hungry. I want some fireman's chocolate!"

Finding humor in everyday events, funny things that have happened in the past, or in a comedian's monologue can help us put some perspective back into our lives. We see that days with chronic pain need not all be dark and that the lightness we need can come when we can see humor in everyday situations.

When we laugh, chuckle, or just smile, we can momentarily forget our pain. It is worthwhile to find something to laugh about.

FOR TODAY: **By joke, riddle, limerick, or ordinary conversation, I will try to find release in humor today.**

April 25 ❧ Joy

*We must constantly build dykes of courage
to hold back the flood of fear.*
—Martin Luther King, Jr.

Joy can be contagious. My friend says that nature is her particular source of joy. I smile as I hear her tell of the great horned owl she watched flying across the field and how she scrambled with binoculars to get a closer look.

She loves the wind, and, like a child, she enjoys the pleasure of blowing bubbles and seeing them sail through the air. Simplicity and wonder are components of her joy, but sometimes she must expend effort to extract it from heavy days of weariness and greater pain.

Joy can be influenced by the status of my pain or my temperament. I want joy to be less circumstantial. When I lower my expectations, joy can take the form of triumph over a difficult situation, or it can be staying power through defeat. It can be a quieting of the soul or the calm assurance that fear will not overcome me. Like birdwatching and seeing bubbles float into the air, there is simplicity and wonder in serenity, too.

FOR TODAY: **Freedom from turmoil and fear are my greatest joys. I'll let peace pervade me today.**

> *No one can make you feel inferior without*
> *your consent.*
> —*Eleanor Roosevelt*

The man has put in hundreds of hours of time into a prescribed form of treatment. In spite of this time investment,
his pain forces him to lie down for brief or longer periods
every hour. He once had to lie down on a sidewalk outside
his doctor's office while waiting for a ride and was told by
an office worker to get up. He had made sure he was in an
out-of-the-way spot. "Am I to lie in the street?" he
thought disgustedly. He felt once again that he was being
judged and misunderstood and that he was told to move
unnecessarily, since he was interfering with no one.

This was not the first, nor would it be the last time
someone was unable to comprehend this man's needs, but
he continued to do what he had to do in order to participate in life. At restaurants, churches, work, public meet-
ings, and concerts, he would look for a bench or two
chairs to semirecline across, or perhaps he'd use an aisle
or stairway. Doing so took courage, but he would not accept the life of a reclusive invalid.

We do what we have to do, and try not to be crippled by
other people's opinions. We trust ourselves to do what's
right, because only we know what's in our best interest.

For us with chronic pain, what others think affects us
but need not shame us.

**For today: I am willing to go to great lengths to stay
involved with life. My survival and very existence depend on it.**

April 27 ∾ Anger, Asking for Help

Anger is a short madness.
—Horace

Anger is a short madness, indeed, but it can carry with it a resentment that can linger indefinitely, if it is allowed to. Suppose, when we are unable to lift a box, we ask someone for help moving it and we get the reply, "I'll do it when I get around to it" or "Maybe I will and maybe I won't. I'll see how much time I have." We want to scream because we want it done now. We wouldn't be asking if we could do it ourselves. Mostly, we hate our dependence more than we hate the answer that makes us wait even longer.

Others may be picking up our share of the responsibilities, which angers them, as well. Unwilling to voice frustration, they may seek to have some control over us, because they know that they are powerless over the pain. Lack of control over the situation frustrates all parties involved.

On the other hand, perhaps we are impatient with ourselves and blame others who test our patience. Does what we need help with need to be done this minute? We want cooperation, but it may not come when we order it. Do we express our gratitude or quickly think of something else that we need help with? Instead, can we help the other person in turn?

If we are courteous and grateful, we have done all we can. If we still need help, we may need to enlist the assistance of someone else.

For today: Tolerance and patience are virtues that I often lack, but their development may help me when I become angry at someone else. I strive to be at peace.

April 28 ～ Pain Anniversary

Oh, I will think of things gone long ago
And weave them to a song.
—Euripides

How wonderful it is that we don't have to carry the accumulated hours, days, weeks, and years of chronic pain with us. On my first "pain anniversary," I felt the weight of all those time measurements pressing down on me. It seemed impossible that I had survived to that point, but I had no idea how I would continue to go on if the future held no relief.

For some, an anniversary date might be attached to the day an injury happened. For some, it might be the day the symptoms first occurred. For others, it might be the day that they were told that nothing could be done for the chronic pain.

The anniversary can be a date that we remember with feelings of loss and remorse, and these emotions can be very strong. Successive anniversaries may pass by without notice or may capture our attention only at marks such as five years, ten years, and so on. But the first one will be felt acutely, not only because a year has passed but because the hope that the pain is acute has vanished and the reality that it is chronic sets in.

Past days of pain are gone. We don't have to count every one, but on these anniversary dates, we remember that, even if the pain is long-standing, we need to live only this one day. We manage whatever pain we have and trust that, tomorrow, we will know how to live that day with a little more confidence. How we have grown!

FOR TODAY: I am proud on this day that I have not succumbed to pain. My anniversary date reminds me of how much progress toward better living I can achieve in a year's time.

April 29 ❧ Journey

*Courage is an inner resolution to go forward
in spite of obstacles and frightening
situations; cowardice is a submissive
surrender to circumstance.*
—*Martin Luther King, Jr.*

"It really gets old," my friend says, and I agree. It does get old, when the pain lingers on and on, and I'm finding that I have to expand my spiritual life and search for new and different ways to cope. It's a process that continues for me, rather than a destination that I reach. I don't expect to say, "I've made it now. The pain doesn't bother me a bit," but I'd like to say, "It's a daily process. The pain affects me less."

Like the main character in John Bunyan's *Pilgrim's Progress*, I have a burden on my back. I carry this bundle of pain up the Hill of Difficulty, past the Doubting Castle, through the Slough of Despond, and up the Mountain of Caution that he described.

I am helped by Patience and Passion and hindered by Doubtful on my way, while Hopeful encourages me to trek farther.

I may not have a clear view of significant landmarks, but I stay on the road. Reaching seemingly endless plateaus, I keep walking forward toward peace and contentment.

In my personal journey with pain, God guides and cheers me on when I want to retreat. He understands that having to cope with chronic pain "gets old," but He is with me, through all of it.

FOR TODAY: **God, the distance is long. Be my faithful companion on this uncomfortable journey.**

April 30 ❧ Caretaking

See simplicity in the complicated.
—Lao-tzu

Some of us are more familiar with pain, problems, and crises than we are with patience, peace, and joy. Ironically, many of us were drawn to crises even before our pain began, spending time rushing here and there, reacting to this crisis and that one. Much of our time may have been spent on fixing other people's problems, thereby overextending ourselves.

Chronic pain provides lessons in working out our problems and increasing our coping skills. We embark on a path of trial and error, to find what works best for us in meeting the challenges that life gives. Along the way we can ask, ''Is this the best thing to do? Is this what I really want?''

It is not selfish to ask, ''Is this good for me?'' We can expect fewer crises when we stop contributing to them. We can stop doing what we know is detrimental to our well-being. Finding the balance between taking care of ourselves and sharing time and resources with others is fundamental to our health.

FOR TODAY: **It is time to change patterns if I find myself falling into the trap of trauma and crisis again and again.**

MAY

May 1 ∾ Denial

Pride costs us more than hunger,
thirst and cold.
—Thomas Jefferson

Denying our pain is different from trying to distract our minds from it. With distraction, we still know and respect our boundaries, but we deflect some of the attention from our pain. With denial, we know we have pain, we divert our attention, but we do it to such an extent that we go beyond our boundaries. The reality of the pain might be too agonizing, so we subconsciously pretend that it's not there. We may be able to trick our minds for a while, but if we go too far, our bodies won't be able hide it from us any longer.

Denial of our pain can happen as a result of our pride saying "I can handle this" when we can't, or by overextending ourselves while assuming someone else's responsibilities.

We can face our pain and problems, change what we can, and then do our best. Pretending that the pain and problems don't exist will not help us.

For today: If I need to say "I can't," I will. It is not worth it to deny my pain to the extent of suffering severe consequences. I can face the reality of my situation today and not let others coax me to do more than I'm able.

May 2 ❧ Problem Solving

Back of tranquility lies conquered
unhappiness.
—David Grayson

Have you ever noticed how ingenious birds are? They find the most obscure places to build nests. This week I found one in a tiny space on the window ledge, in a space beside our upstairs air conditioner. Another one was atop a scoreboard on an athletic building. I even saw a bird taking apart the materials from last year's empty nest to rebuild another one across the yard. Yes, birds are quite ingenious. What creativity they exhibit in finding such out-of-the-way spots to house their young!

We who live with chronic pain are ingenious and creative, too. We constantly have to look for ways to live within our limitations, to problem-solve, and, like the birds, to make our homes comfortable ones, free from danger.

At home, insecurity can come in many forms. Maybe we are moody—too complacent or too depressed, too worried or too apathetic. Lack of emotional balance can upset everyone. We need to feel safe somewhere, and we want it to be in the home where love and security reside.

FOR TODAY: I will take great care to build my "nest," watching out for emotional pitfalls that can endanger my home.

May 3 ❧ Emotions

A tree as great as a man's embrace
  springs from a small shoot;
A terrace nine stories high begins with a
  pile of earth
A journey of a thousand miles starts under
  one's feet.

—*Lao-tzu*

Accepting and coming to terms with the emotional consequences is often more difficult than coming to terms with the ongoing presence of physical pain. Fear, depression, and anger are common when one is faced with chronic pain.

Fear often accompanies change. This emotion is related to the losses we have incurred, whether they are related to a job, family, or recreation. Trusting that we can cope and that either the recovery of or replacement of losses will occur can help overcome our fears. Another feeling that can affect all that we think, do, and say is depression. As immobilizing as it may seem, it can be made worse by separating ourselves from others.

Another common feeling is anger. The targets may be health professionals, insurance agents, employers, ourselves, friends, and family. Accepting life for what it is and not what we wish it would be is an important step. Guilt over the feeling of letting others down is an emotion that can undermine our self-respect and dignity. Learning to value a new sense of self can lessen guilt's self-defeating effects.

Most of us have been affected by fear, depression, and anger. This single admission is an important first step in our recovery from their power over us.

FOR TODAY: I will have days of feeling these emotions. I won't deny such thoughts but will bring them out into the open. Then I can work through and learn from them.

May 4 ❧ Living in the Present Moment

> *Oh, give us pleasure . . .*
> *All simply in the*
> *springing of the year.*
> —Robert Frost

I have beautiful red impatiens blooming outside the bay window of my house. I have been fascinated by their growth, seeing them creeping up, inch by inch, and spreading out to join with the other plants, making a wall of red. I am drawn to something I participated in but did not "make grow." I take pleasure in them as they are today, not looking back to the barren winter or envisioning their demise at the first frost of fall.

As usual, I have a degree of pain today. It can cast a shadow, separate me from my fellows, and make me blind to the beauty of the flowers. Pain wants all my attention, but I won't give all of it. I need the warmth like sunlight that I get from people I care about, things I enjoy, and places where I feel at ease.

The warmth is in this present moment. I may wither if I look farther to uncertain times, so I'll stay in this day and keep myself here, observing the flowers in the "springing of the year."

FOR TODAY: **I do my living today and will look for joy and beauty in each moment.**

May 5 ∿ Creativity

> *Most people lack imagination much more*
> *than they lack goodwill.*
> —Reinhold Niebuhr

Chronic pain tests our creativity. I once was upset that I could not go to the hairdresser for a permanent without suffering for days and sometimes weeks later. Getting up from the chair periodically was of no benefit.

Finally I worked out an arrangement whereby I could get a permanent at home while lying on my dining room table and letting someone else do the work. Because leaning over is difficult for me, I got in the shower at a particular rinse stage. I removed the rollers lying down in the tub. The perm turned out great. Another person who used a creative approach was the man who couldn't mow his lawn in one day because of the pain that it caused. What he did instead was to mow a section each day of the week.

Chronic pain forces us to come up with new solutions to problems. We find that with some planning and ingenuity, we can live with pain and do some things that we'd almost given up doing.

FOR TODAY: I may not be able to do an old activity in the old way. I will rethink my options and creatively design new ways.

May 6 ∾ Maturity

> . . . we could never learn to be brave and
> patient if there were only joy in the world.
> —Helen Keller

Each day is not a repeat of the one before, even though we may grumble, "The pain is the same, my life is the same, and I'm going nowhere." The statement is not true, because we are either maturing and gaining wisdom or we are simply growing older. We can sometimes play childish games, saying to our pain, "I'm angry at you, so I'm just going to sit here and sulk." Consider the game of hide-and-seek. We might say "I'm going to hide from you (perhaps in drugs, alcohol, or food), and you can try to find me." Maybe our game is a masquerade party, where we put on a mask that never stops smiling, and no one sees our struggles.

Chronic pain is a serious dilemma and not a game; it requires real coping tools and not just fantasies. One of the first steps toward maturity is to realize that we can't change our pain by running from it or denying its effect on us. Another step is to realize that we do not always need to be right. That awakening frees us to be open to new ideas.

Finally, maturity can help us to take action that we may have resisted taking, when we were too afraid to try.

FOR TODAY: **I am maturing through my experience with chronic pain by seeing my life with clarity, my pain realistically, and by admitting that my old ideas may need to be replaced with new ones. I will continue to question, to reexamine, and to try to make my life better.**

May 7 ❧ Explosive Anger

From disappointment, I gradually ascended
the emotional ladder to haughty indignation
and finally to that state of stubbornness
where the mind is locked like the jaws of an
enraged bulldog.
—Maya Angelou

I didn't know that I was capable of getting so angry at my pain, and sometimes my rage scares me. Pain forces its way in to steal away my time and energy, it strikes when I least expect it, and it lurks around every corner of my life. I'd like to scream at it and order it to never come back, ever, because I hate it so much.

There are times when positive words are repulsive to me —the very words that often help me change my attitude, accept the pain, and work with it. Sometimes I can't stomach such words as gratitude, patience, peace, joy, and contentment while I rage at the pain. I think of how easy it would be to feel good if I didn't have the pain! Of course I'm angry!

The anger fulminates inside until I feel as if I'm about to explode. I feel as if it will destroy me or provoke me to harm someone else and I get frightened. I can't hold it in any longer so I ask someone what to do. "Tell me what triggered your anger," "Work out," "Hammer nails into a block of wood," "Go ahead and cry," "Throw something that won't break at a pillow," I'm told.

Before I try anything, the hate toward my pain subsides. I've been liberated from my anger and from my potential to do harm. I'm done with it. I think to myself that I'm usually more in control of my emotions, but I remind myself that anyone would get exasperated by this pain. Anyone would, even me.

FOR TODAY: I admit I get angry. There is no shame in that. I can take care of it in a healthy way and not let it boil inside any longer.

May 8 ❧ Spring

Thaw with his gentle persuasion is more powerful than Thor with his hammer. The one melts, the other but breaks in pieces.
—Henry David Thoreau

The first signs of spring suddenly burst into existence. A bank of snow vanishes in a single warm day. The ice on the river, which cracked and boomed as it thawed, now flows swiftly, carried by shooting water. Fresh designs of green spread in all directions as the earth is warmed by lengthening rays. The silent air is broken by the chirping of returning robins. After months of waiting, the changes seem instantaneous. Suddenly there is a return to color, beauty, and new life.

My pain may make me feel that I am living in a dry, cold winter wasteland. The stark reality of pain contrasts with comfort, ease, luxury, cheer, and enjoyment.

Yet the change to color, beauty, and new life can be just as instantaneous for me as the resplendence of spring. The brightest and best day can follow the darkest day of pain. On days like these, spiritual comfort and new energy surround me. I open my heart to such nurturing, and I feel compelled to spread love to others.

FOR TODAY: **It is within my grasp to preserve the good in my life and let hope spring up. Perhaps spiritual nurturing and growing self-respect are what I need today.**

May 9 ❧ Insomnia

> *For some of them, pain is their life. It is the*
> *first sensation to greet them in the morning*
> *and the last they feel before drifting off to*
> *sleep, if they are lucky enough to fall asleep*
> *despite it.*
> —Philip Yancey

We with chronic pain also may be familiar with chronic insomnia. How to get to sleep and stay asleep haunts us as we toss and turn at night.

What is the answer? While sedatives are not usually recommended, a safe drug prescribed by our doctors, such as an antidepressant, may be part of the solution.

But what of the nonmedical, inexpensive ways to help us through our times of interrupted sleep?

Attempts to prevent sleeplessness might include having a consistent schedule of going to bed and rising, getting enough exercise to be tired at night, having a period of relaxation in the evening, and eliminating evening caffeine.

If we find ourselves awake at 3 A.M., unable to sleep, we might benefit from leaving the bedroom and finding something to read or doing some other distracting, quiet activity. If we still can't sleep in fifteen minutes, we may need to try something else, such as taking a hot bath. The fatigue from a restless night can make coping with pain more difficult on the following day. We do all we can to prevent and, if necessary, deal with this common problem.

FOR TODAY: If I can't prevent a fitful night, I'll do my best to cope. Sleep will come to me eventually.

May 10 ❧ Surrender, Choices

One thing I know: the only ones among you
who are really happy are those who will
have sought and found how to serve.
—Albert Schweitzer

"It's cold and rainy out, and there's nothing to do" is what disappointed children say who cannot play outdoors. They expect the parent to provide suggestions, but often reject the ideas offered because they would rather have a sunny, warm day outside.

We may make the same complaint when our pain either prevents or makes more difficult the things we used to do. A friend described her depression after being unable to return to the "helping profession" she loved. "I know that if I can't change something, I have to change my response to it," she said, but her words sounded hollow. I knew that if I offered other options they would be rejected, because she was not yet ready to consider other alternatives.

Another friend lost the ability to use her hands for sewing. She struggled with having to surrender her talent. Now she says that she would never have taught her boys to sew and seen their proud faces when a project was finished had this not happened. She saw her talent demonstrated by her children.

Is there a skill we can teach, a tradition to pass along, or a way to modify a favorite activity? We ask such questions to give ourselves the most satisfying choices.

FOR TODAY: **I have a patient and steady need to make my contribution to humanity. Surrendering the old ways brings me closer to realizing occasions of joy and opportunities for service that diminish my losses.**

May 11 ∾ Isolation, Worry Over What Others Think

> *(Of Vincent van Gogh) He also learned that*
> *isolation is a sort of prison.*
> —Irving Stone

We sometimes care too much about what others think. In moments of weakness, we are ashamed that we're different and may be self-conscious about being unable to do certain things. I have moved beyond thinking that I should have been able to find something to cure my pain, but I still cringe when someone says, "You still have a problem with that?"

It tells me that maybe I'm not yet totally accepting of my pain. I'm not where I once was, though. I'll go to places that I used to shun and not feel guilty for being unable to stay there an entire day. I won't let someone else's reaction to my pain drive me into isolation, either.

Solitude can give me time to develop my thoughts and enlarge my spiritual life, but I can't live in seclusion for long. I want to surrender my self-absorption, reenter the world, and answer the question about the presence of my pain with a matter-of-fact statement: "Yes, I still have a problem with pain, but I'm doing all right." Without apology and self-reproach, we can be comfortable among others again.

FOR TODAY: **Only I know the nature and effects of my pain. I won't let someone else's comments dishearten me.**

Never, "for the sake of peace and quiet,"
deny your own experience or convictions.
—Dag Hammarskjöld

"Sometimes when I feel pressured, I take shortcuts and forget good body mechanics. Sometimes I don't want to slow someone else down, and I cut corners. In the end, I only cause myself more pain," my friend said.

At one time, she had a hard time sitting on the floor because she needed the support of a chair. But when she played with her two-year-old son or when she read to a circle of preschoolers on the carpet, she minimized how important it was for her to sit in a chair. The consequence was great pain on the following day. Now she makes sure a chair is available to sit on.

Sometimes the time we take to accommodate our needs is very short, compared to the time we're in pain due to poor or insufficient planning. Without thinking, we may operate on "automatic pilot," as if we have no pain, but always there is an accounting.

Only we know what we need, and it is a relief to know that, with planning, we don't have to deny those needs.

FOR TODAY: **I don't want to cut corners, if it puts me at risk for more pain. The time I invest in planning will pay dividends in pain prevention.**

May 13   Fear

*No passion so effectively robs the mind of
all its power of acting and reasoning as
fear.*
—Edmund Burke

Fear can cause tension, which can intensify our pain. We may feel terrified, but we need to ask if there is a present danger. If the fear concerns the future, we realize that there is not an immediate hazard to our well-being.

We need to confront our fears, instead of avoiding situations of which we are afraid. I might think, ''I can't leave town because I feel safer at home. What if my pain gets worse 'out there'?'' Because of an irrational fear, I may miss an opportunity to enjoy myself. In fact, the pain may become worse by staying home.

Facing our fears by saying them out loud or writing them down may help defuse them. We can try assigning a number from one to ten as to how anxious and fearful we feel, recording it every fifteen minutes. We will see that our fear does not go on forever and the level of our anxiety eventually will decrease with time. We can call a friend, no matter how foolish we think our fears are.

With regard to the future, most often ''What will happen if . . . ?'' never materializes. Worry has not protected us; it has only wasted our time. We have to let it go.

FOR TODAY: I will face my fears rather than nurturing them and becoming more anxious. I will let go of tomorrow's fears and take care of today.

In the midst of staggering disillusionment,
many cry for the bread of faith.
—*Martin Luther King, Jr.*

I know about disillusionment. I have known the feeling of devastation when no cure and no definite cause could be found for my pain. I've asked if there is anything to hope for and anyone to trust. I have cried ''for the bread of faith'' when the life I once knew was dismantled.

My arguments with God as to why I have the pain have forced me to decide whether to alienate myself from God or bring myself closer to Him. I feel the most alienated when I expect the pain to be removed as a reward for a faithful life, or when I see pain as a punishment for an unfaithful one. I trust God most when I accept that He did not cause the pain and when I am accepting of the fact that He may not intervene. I trust by believing that He can be relied on to stay by my side and give me the tools for building a quality life.

While the definition of quality may differ for each individual, the tools I need include patience, courage and gratitude. Using these, faith, hope, and love are kept alive.

For me, love of life pours out of the reconciliation I make with God and the subsequent revitalization of faith and hope.

For today: **God, please replenish my spiritual resources and give me an ample supply of the tools for living.**

May 15 ❧ Guilt

Courage is the price that life exacts for granting peace.
—Amelia Earhart

"I told my friends that they would need to take a taxi from the airport to my house," the lady said. "I knew that it was the only way that I could enjoy their company. Picking them up from the airport would have been too much for me."

There was no talk of feeling guilty for being unable to greet them at the airport, but rather an honest estimate of her limitations, an example of setting priorities, and the ability to communicate her needs to her out-of-town visitors. It sounded so simple that day, but it had not always been so easy for her to do.

After much experience of living with chronic pain, she had learned how to act in her own best interest, to express honest feelings comfortably, to exercise her own personal rights, and to gain confidence in her ability to work around the limitations that existed and thereby be much more receptive to and considerate of others.

She had learned the lessons well, and her visitors were welcomed without guilt.

FOR TODAY: **I will replace guilt with a pride in being able to take care of myself.**

May 16 ❧ Anger

When angry, count ten before you speak; if
very angry, a hundred.
—Thomas Jefferson

We can be angry about a lot of things: our pain, the misunderstanding of others, our limitations, and our fatigue as well as all the everyday irritations that most people experience.

We must not deny the emotion of anger because that only makes the situation worse. It causes our whole being to be tense. We first look at ourselves. Acknowledging what we are angry about, we ask ourselves if there's anything that we, at this moment, can change. For example, if we are angry at feeling tired, we can plan time to rest.

If we are angry at another person, we can uncover if we feel threatened (for example, "I'm angry because I feel that the other person doesn't respect my opinion and my self-esteem is threatened"), rationally explain our dissatisfaction to that person, and be open to discussion, calming our minds before we speak.

As for our pain, we realize that all our raging at it will not make it go away. When we come to terms with it, our lives can move forward. Anger will return from time to time, as it does to most people, but we need not live under its control.

FOR TODAY: I will examine what I'm angry about and decide if there is anything I can do to change the situation. If I cannot, I need to loosen my grip on what I can't change, thereby letting my anger dissipate. Then I can turn my attention to things that I am capable of changing.

May 17 ❧ Choices

A life spent in making mistakes is not only
more honorable, but more useful than a life
spent in doing nothing.
—George Bernard Shaw

What choices are open to us who are hampered by pain?
There are more than we may, at any one moment, imagine.
One day a person with chronic pain realizes that everything has changed and yet nothing has changed. The sun
still rises and sets, the seasons move on, and the birds
migrate.

Pain affects every aspect of our lives, but nothing has
changed with regard to our wants and needs. I can think of
examples of people who have made choices. Some may
want to return to work but can't perform the old job, so
they may retrain or start their own business. Another ac-
cepts household help when needed. One person gives up
chasing after a cure and, without all the time spent at doctors' offices, has more time to spend with family and
friends. Another can't attend some of the children's func-
tions but thoroughly enjoys those that he can. A man and
woman have changes in their sex lives, but adjust by talking with and trusting their partner in order to achieve satisfaction and a level of comfort. Some are retired and can't
leave home as much, but still meet at the coffee shop occasionally with friends.

Nothing has changed in what we want out of life in the
way of work, hobby, social involvement, and sexual satisfaction. Everything has changed because of pain, but solu-

tions exist, different for each of us. We will open our minds to find them.

FOR TODAY: I see options and perhaps tomorrow I will see more of them.

May 18 ∾ Exercise

You never know what is enough until you
know what is more than enough.
—*William Blake*

Exercise is an integral part of my life. I need to do it every day or my pain level increases.

Sometimes I am able to follow my prescribed routine. At other times, if I have exceeded my limitations, I can only stretch and walk.

I have to be ever aware of what my body is telling me and to not increase my exercises too fast. A setback spells both physical and emotional pain. It is then that I need to be more mindful of pacing myself the next time.

Each of us is unique in our abilities, but a basic activity for me is walking every day. As I walk, putting one foot in front of the other means more than mobility. It symbolizes taking care of myself and going forward.

If I stop exercising, I've given up. I must keep moving.

FOR TODAY: **My goal is to be as functional as I can be. I'll be proud of any progress I make but not berate myself if I exceed my limitations while trying.**

May 19 ❧ Change

*Since we can't search our motives (the eye
sees, but it can't see itself) the only
alternative to shuddering paralysis is to leap
into action, regardless of consequences.*
—Alan Watts

Change can be difficult because of the risk of failure and
the discomfort of venturing into the unknown. We do need
to consider consequences, but not be so afraid of the attempt that we become paralyzed into inaction.

We have already become all too familiar with the
changes in our lives because of pain. We have had to learn
what is within reach of our abilities, whom we can turn to
when we need support, and how to find distractions from
pain.

Maybe we have reached a point where we need to make
more changes. Possibly we have been only surviving from
day to day, and now we are eager to live. Maybe we see
that we have wanted other people's approval through
achievements, and now we just want to be loved. Maybe
guilt has haunted our days, and we want to be free of it.
Maybe we have neglected our health in some way, such as
not exercising consistently, and we want to set up a regular
program.

Change involves doing things in a different way. We can
overcome our own resistance, take on the challenge, and
be patient with ourselves along the way.

FOR TODAY: **I can assess what adjustments I need to
make today and take the first step toward change.**

May 20 ∿ Trust

> *It is not for us to arrive at knowledge. We
> know, as we love, by instinct, faith, emotion.*
> —Isadora Duncan

My spiritual advisor once told me that there are three
things that God won't do: He won't let me down, He
won't let me off, and He won't let me go. I vaguely under-
stood the first one, but I needed to have all of them explained.

He won't let me down: He's always there walking beside me, caring, hurting with me. He hasn't removed my
pain but has loved me through it.

He won't let me off: He uses me according to my talents, abilities, and personality, in spite of the pain.

He won't let me go: He lets me remember how much I
need Him when I get complacent, and He carries me when
I stumble.

I needed to hear what God won't do to better understand
what He will do. Now I understand that there is One who
loves me. He's not "out to get me" but to sustain me in a
world of calamity that has invaded mine.

FOR TODAY: **God walks beside me, uses me, and reminds
me of the need I have for Him. Whatever my past conception of God, I can trust that He loves me now. This
love calms me today.**

> *If you look healthy, people expect you*
> *to behave in a healthy fashion,*
> *free of limitations.*
> —*Cheri Register*

The other day I saw someone I hadn't seen for several years. She said, ''I hear you're doing fine these days—a new part-time job and everything.'' I nodded and said that I was doing better and I liked my job. The inside of me wanted to shout, ''But I still have constant pain every minute of every day! I'm *not* fine, and you don't know how much it takes to handle my three-hour-a-day job. I'm *not* that much better and I'm not fine!''

But I didn't say what my insides were dying to say. That would be too much like the old days, when a simple ''How are you doing?'' that was meant as a polite gesture in order to start a conversation would bring a five-minute (it was probably longer) lecture on ''My Life Stinks and I'll Tell You Why.''

I don't have to let the whole world know how I'm doing. If I'm asked, my answers are short, and my honesty depends on the seriousness of the person who asks and how much I want to share. It may be ''Fine,'' ''I've had better days,'' ''About the same,'' or just ''Okay.''

A one-on-one conversation with a friend, especially one with chronic pain, is another thing. I can be brutally honest and get the encouragement I need. I can let out the words ''I'm not fine!''

FOR TODAY: I have options for my response to ''How are you?'' It depends on the person asking and how much detail I want to go into. I reserve my detailed honesty for those who truly understand.

May 22 ∾ Talents

*I am only one, but still I am one. I cannot
do everything, but still I can do something. I
will not refuse to do the something I can do.*
—Helen Keller

One afternoon I went outside to see what my daughter was
doing. She had a heap of newly mown grass, a glass of
water, and a pile of mud beside her. "What are you doing?" I asked, looking at her dirty hands. "I'm making a
bird's nest," she said, beaming. "Ain't I good at it?" After snickering at her poor grammar, I had to agree. Beside
the heap of grass was a perfectly good bird's nest. She had
truly made something fine with her hands.

As Helen Keller says, there is something for all of us to
do. For some of us, our chronic pain is an annoyance in
the midst of maintaining a full occupational and social
life. For others, the pain is severe and disabling. Some
have constant pain and others have it intermittently. Some
live with others and some live alone. As different as we
are, we all have something to contribute to the world. Each
of us is unique, which means that we are free to discover
what talents and skills we have to offer, regardless of
whether someone else can do those things better or not.

In Keller's quote, she tells us not to so belittle our talents or wish we had different ones that we refuse to use
the ones we have. Let's ask, "What am I good at?" and
do "the something" we can.

FOR TODAY: **I accept with gratitude the talents that are
mine. I'll share these priceless gifts with the world today.**

May 23 ∾ Creativity

Adversity has the effect of eliciting talents,
which in prosperous circumstances would
have lain dormant.
—Horace

I love to read biographies of famous people who have overcome disabilities by modifying activities in order to continue to do what they most enjoy. I ask myself if I am settling for less than is possible due to my limitations.

What I have learned to appreciate in these stories is that others, too, once struggled with the common emotional reactions to chronic pain that I have. Being talented and famous did not make them immune to the struggles, but love of their talents and the use of creative responses enabled these people to continue using them in unexpected ways.

I think of Renoir, the famous artist whose hands and legs were afflicted with rheumatoid arthritis. He found that it took too much energy to try to walk and paint, so he chose to paint while in a wheelchair. In order to work, he had to fold a cloth on the brush handle and strap his hand to it. What he considered his best work, ''Women Bathers,'' was done during this time when the freedom to use his hands was limited.

FOR TODAY: **I won't give up my favorite activities without seeing how I can make modifications or without trying satisfactory alternatives to continue doing what I love to do.**

*No one would ever have crossed the
ocean if he could have gotten
off the ship in a storm.*
—*Charles F. Kettering*

We want to look back and say, "My chronic pain hasn't
been meaningless. Some good has come from it." It
seems that if we only had an answer to the purposelessness, we could make order out of the chaos in our minds.
The trouble is, the answers don't readily come.

It seems like I'm a traveler without a map and no clear
idea of where I'm going. I know that I've covered new
territory, but I don't know why. I ask for directions, but no
one has any. One would conclude that I really am lost.

Ironically, I don't feel lost. I still don't know why pain
entered my life or where exactly I'm being led, but one
thing is sure—I do not have the hopeless resignation to an
unhappy fate that I once did. God helps me to come to
terms with chronic pain and to achieve a deeper level of
acceptance. There is an ebb and flow to my acceptance
level, to be sure. It is not static but changing.

My faith falters sometimes but I still believe that God
will show me what to do and where to go next. Because
He's helped me already, I need not panic while He is there
to help me cope with storms.

For today: **God, show me where You want me to go and
what You want me to do on this journey. Help me continue to take steps forward.**

> *Drag your thought away from your troubles*
> *. . . by the ears, by the heels or any other*
> *way you can manage it. It's the healthiest*
> *thing a body can do.*
> —Mark Twain

We read this and say, "But it's not only my thoughts that are troubling me—it's my body, too. And I can't drag *it* away." The pain is a real part of what has happened in our bodies, but our thoughts can be part of the problem, too.

A little indulgence in feeling sorry for ourselves may lead us to recognizing what issues are bothering us, but if excessive self-pity fills our thoughts, we may avoid problem solving. We may choose to resign ourselves to feeling bad, seeing that as our only option. It then becomes easier to look at someone else and say, "I have been denied all that he or she has," which deepens our self-pity.

We have talents and abilities. Perhaps it will take a little longer than we thought to discover and develop them. There is always something that we can excel at and be proud of. We have our own prized possessions, not the least of which is being ourselves—which no one else has the ability to be.

FOR TODAY: I can reflect on my personal growth, rather than analyzing my failings today. I take pride in the emerging person that is me.

> *The deepest principle of human nature is the*
> *craving to be appreciated.*
> —*William James*

In our society it's easier for us to say, "The deck looks nice," rather than, "You really do a fine job with lumber," or "The pie tastes good," rather than, "You're a good cook." The implication is that we did good work and our product shows it. If our product pleases someone and we are thanked, we feel appreciated.

What happens when we are unable to do the things that, in the past, brought us recognition? A friend describes to me how her self-confidence was shaken when nerve damage took away some of her abilities, such as her beautiful piano playing. Others appreciated her ability, as well, and now she feels the loss of both her talent and the compliments. Now she is trying to discover different aptitudes.

This loss of abilities can't take one thing away—the ability to show affection to others even if in doing so there is no tangible reward. Speaking kindly to someone, listening attentively, or using whatever other abilities we have gives us a feeling of pride. We should never stop trying to realize our full potential. Even without feedback from others, we can still honor our own willingness to keep venturing on.

We all like to be appreciated. Finding even small ways to be useful enhances those good feelings.

FOR TODAY: **God, smile on me, even if no one else shows appreciation.**

May 27 ❧ Friends, Asking for Help

The only gift is a portion of thyself.
—Ralph Waldo Emerson

I want to ask for help when I am in pain, but sometimes I find it hard to bring myself to do so. To admit that in some areas I am helpless is hard on my ego. It's hard to swallow my pride. Another reason that it is hard to ask is that I am afraid that I will burden people who already are busy or have enough problems of their own. At the same time, I am afraid that friends will not come to me for support because they think I have enough problems. What a vicious cycle!

The problem with being more on the receiving end of help is that we feel guilty for being unable to return to the giver what has so generously been given to us. The best way we can deal with this dilemma is to do what we can within our ability for the other person. Simple gestures like sending a card or making a phone call can mean a lot.

What I want most is a mutual friendship, one of give and take. I won't keep score of how much I have received and how much I have given. If I cannot repay someone for help right away, I trust that eventually I'll be the one to be the helper, even if it is to assist someone whom I hardly know instead of a friend.

FOR TODAY: **I will do what I can to befriend someone today.**

May 28 ❧ Medication

*We should not let our fears hold us back
from pursuing our hope.*
—John F. Kennedy

We've had a lot of hope that a drug would take away our pain. Medications are never the sole answer to chronic pain, because the narcotics that help the most are most effective for acute pain, and chronic pain is more complex.

To avoid some of our painful situations, we can learn to prevent extreme pain by living within our limitations. Dulling the mind and creating a tolerance or addiction are side effects we don't need. We want to use as little medication as possible, but what and how much is a topic of controversy.

Another drawback to medication use is its cost. Most of the time we want to take only the safest drugs and those that will help us, at the lowest cost. At the same time, if a drug such as a prescribed antidepressant medication is expensive but helps us sleep or gives us a sense of well-being, we can be grateful that it works, knowing that it is all right to have help in staying as functional as possible.

Medications are not the sole answer, but neither should we close our minds to their possible good effects.

FOR TODAY: I will try to prevent severe pain by operating within the boundaries of my limitations and by not being overly dependent on medication to help me through my day.

> *We can all do good deeds, but very few of*
> *us can think good thoughts.*
> —Cesare Pavese

Stress gives us a chance to discover much about ourselves, including the thoughts we think. Stress involves demands on our time and changes that we have to adjust to. Chronic pain brings changes with it that constitute a major adjustment. We must meet and deal with an accumulation of everyday problems.

One way to combat stress is to alter irrational ideas. We may have misconceptions, such as "I should be better at deciding this," when more supportive self-talk might be "I need more information in order to know what I should do next."

We may have irrational ideas about our pain. I have been guilty of "awfulizing" it when feeling sorry for myself. My attitude is much different when I consider it as being a part of my life that I can live and work with. Of course, sometimes it *is* awful, and by admitting to myself the way I feel I acknowledge the fact that some days are worse than others.

Sometimes changing how we verbalize our feelings can make the emotion less stressful. For example, by saying "disappointed" rather than "depressed," we can tone down the emotional intensity.

Thoughts and self-talk can color our response to stress. To help reduce stress, we can work to change those thoughts.

FOR TODAY: **How stress affects me depends partially on the meaning I attach to it. Which of my thoughts need altering today?**

May 30 ❧ Compassion, Reaching Out

People only see what they are prepared
to see.
—*Ralph Waldo Emerson*

We think we have cornered the market on suffering. In our obsession with pain, we have so little room for others. We have been so busy going to doctors and a whole array of health professionals; we have been trying this treatment and that—sometimes traveling from one side of the country to the other; we have asked numerous people what they would do in our situation and clung to every new book and newspaper clipping that offered a cure. It has taken so much time and energy, and we feel so different, even from other people who suffer, too.

I thought I'd have time for other people's problems once my pain problem was alleviated, but I found myself getting lonely because time passed and still the pain persisted.

One day I called a former coworker, wanting to make contact again but not expecting much to have changed in her life. I was surprised and disturbed when she told me that she was very ill with diabetes and waited by the phone every day to hear news that a kidney-pancreas donor had been found for her. How wrapped up in my own problems I had been!

There are times when I have so much pain or am so overwhelmed with coping with it that I can't reach out. But I am making a greater effort to be less self-absorbed and more aware of how I can at least listen, and perhaps help relieve the sufferings of others.

For today: **I will be available to someone who needs what I can give.**

May 31 ❧ Attitude

If you are sitting on a hot stove, a minute
can seem like an hour, but if you are doing
something pleasurable, an hour can seem
like a minute.
—*Albert Einstein*

A doctor once told me, "You'll have good days and bad days." If we only see our pain as physical, we may have too few good days. It's a narrow definition of our pain.

The other parts of us—mental, emotional, and spiritual —can be having a great day, even while our bodies are having a difficult one.

For instance, I once took a vacation to an island, and many things delighted my senses. There was the sight of the cloudless sky, the feel of the softly blowing wind, the sound of the collapsing waves onto the shore, and the smell of the salty ocean. Other living things presented themselves, such as the band of sandpipers moving along the beach, the crab burrowing under the sand as I came closer for a look, and the porpoises, whose dives appeared playful rather than searching.

It was a wonderful day, in spite of physical pain.

FOR TODAY: **I will appreciate a good day by using all my senses. What can I see, touch, smell, and hear today that will bring a smile to my face and joy to my heart?**

JUNE

*The Infinite Goodness has such wide arms
that it takes whatever turns to it.*
—*Dante Alighieri*

An engaged couple was asked in premarital counseling,
"What makes you think that your marriage will survive
while there are so many divorces today?" One of them
answered, "We'll work together, and, with prayer, we can
handle all that comes our way." On first glance the words
sound trite, but this can be seen as a more realistic and
thoughtful response than, "We won't have any problems
and we'll live in perfect bliss."

Does prayer help when it comes to pain? I believe it
does. I pray, even though I see that my pain is with me the
next day. Pain is one of the areas of my life that is difficult
for me to handle alone, so I reach out for spiritual
strength.

Prayer is a call to the Great Spirit who cares about me. I
ask for the energy and strength to cope with not only pain
but other things that I have no control over, such as family
illness, various losses, or the future.

Prayer is my offering of my problems to God. At some
point, alleviation of my troubles or the strength to cope
with them is what I get in return.

FOR TODAY: **Like the engaged couple, I will depend on
God to work with me to handle all that comes my way.**

June 2 ❧ Morning, Uncertainty

But where shall we set our limits, how much do we dare to occupy ourselves with the future?
—Sören Kierkegaard

"I wake up so stiff in the morning that I can hardly move," a friend tells me. "I almost hate to go to sleep, because I don't know what shape I'll be in when I wake up."

The uncertainty over the daily status of pain can be frustrating, and it can lead to a sense of dread about the future. Many physical conditions have this uncertainty as their hallmark. For those who are bothered by barometric changes in the atmosphere, a weather forecast of dreary, wet days ahead can spell an anticipation of greater pain.

My friend says, "I try to ignore the pain when I wake up. I'm helped by limbering up and taking a hot bath or shower. After that, my attitude improves."

We can't totally ignore pain and stiffness, but we can learn to place such mornings into the perspective of the day. While we still may have pain and limited freedom and mobility, we can find at least one thing at the close of each day to be grateful for. By feeling grateful for something in the present, we'll have less time to worry about how we'll feel tomorrow.

FOR TODAY: Gratitude has healing effects, so I'll appreciate at least one thing today. Is there a problem I'm dwelling on? I'll pray for the best outcome.

June 3 ∾ Guilt

> *Whether justified by objective facts or not,*
> *guilt is a useless response to pain, because*
> *it obviously fails to make the pain go away*
> *or even diminish.*
> —Dr. Patrick Wall and Mervyn Jones

Guilt doesn't work to make the pain go away. We may have justifiable reasons for feeling guilty; for example, we may blame ourselves for causing an accident. But many kinds of chronic pain appear for no reason. So why do we spend so much time feeling guilty? Perhaps we think that our pain is a punishment for something we have done or have failed to do. Let's start to look at pain and suffering differently. Pain happens, period. Of course, if we are at fault, it is time to make apologies, ask for forgiveness, and change our behavior, but in many cases we feel guilty over things that we would change if we could. How can we justify feeling guilty over what we can't change? We do the best we can with whatever resources are available.

Extended guilt only makes our problems worse. If we have taken needed actions, we can quit punishing ourselves. We can get out from under guilt's oppression and be freed from it.

For today: Guilt keeps me stuck in the past. If I have harmed someone, I can make amends. If not, I will concentrate on this day's actions and plan those of tomorrow.

June 4 ❧ Habits

*To promise not to do a thing is the surest
way in the world to make a body want to go
and do that very thing.*
—Mark Twain

"Eat your peas; they're good for you." Most of us have
heard this as children. There always seemed to be some
green vegetable that we turned up our noses at. Yet we
were ordered to eat it because it was good for us.

With chronic pain, we are called upon to make changes
in our lives in order to live well and as normally as possible. Some of these changes include learning good habits.
Sometimes we resist these changes, just as children refuse
to eat peas or as an amateur golfer unconsciously resists
unlearning habits of a poor swing.

Good habits involve doing what we need to do and not
doing what is harmful. Superficially, these seem like simple concepts, but neither is. When we complicate what we
need to do with excuses such as, "But I can't do this for
myself, because other people take all my time," we hurt
ourselves. When we don't refrain from what is harmful,
with excuses such as, "I have to work at this all day and
night," we are not doing what is good for us, either.

Old habits, like a golf swing, are hard to break and, like
peas, not everything that is good for us tastes sweet, but
living well is our aim.

FOR TODAY: **I am willing to consider doing what is
healthy and changing the habits that are harmful to
me. I don't have to make promises about it today, but
only endeavor to take care of myself as well as I can.**

When spring comes, the grass
grows by itself.
—Lao-tzu

Life can be so complicated with its deadlines, time constraints, and pressures. We wonder why our adult lives can't resemble the stories we read to children. In many children's books there is sharing, love, and cooperation. Friendly animals show courtesy and concern for one another.

Would we be more childlike if only we had more time, or is something else holding us back?

We can relax while watching a happy child do such things as take time to play with kittens, sit and rock on a willing grandmother's lap, find empty bird nests, skip rope, or play until the sun goes down.

Some adults have had childhoods with greater problems than a splinter in the hand or a scraped knee, however. Those with chronic pain may have these histories, too. Past abuse and neglect may add self-loathing and shame to their hurdles in coping with pain.

Recovery from a painful past is possible, though. There is still time to let the childlike part of our beings teach us to create lives that are more spontaneous, carefree, and simple. We can learn to have more dreams and fewer plans when we decide that it is necessary for us to settle our pasts and learn how to play.

Many things, like the grass, grow naturally. If we allow it, we can let childlike peace and serenity happen, too.

For today: **I want my eyes to be like those of a child to see and love my world.**

June 6 ∾ Healing

Will it come or will it not, the day when the
joy becomes great, the day when the grief
becomes small?
—*Gunnar Ekeloff*

In a letter to my editor, I told her that every time I wrote
about chronic pain, a part of me healed. A calmness came
over me even as I wrote those words. I wondered myself
what I had meant by the word "healed."

I realize now that to be healed is not to be cured, but
somehow to be converted to a new way of thinking and
feeling. To me, it means that I realize that there is more to
me than the pain, that there is a wholeness to me that
stays, no matter what. By having an attitude of being
mostly well and able, I can cope with pain better. In experiencing healing, I feel a closeness with others and a
peacefulness within myself.

We must find our own avenues to healing. For me, healing happens when I face the truth about my pain, instead
of reacting to it in a fearful or self-pitying way. I try to
deal with it more positively by being grateful for what I
can do and modifying or letting go of what I can't. Stillness, prayer, meditation, self-nurturing, and reaching out
to others are all ways that assist me. These help me iden-
tify who I am and what my needs are, so that I can be
transformed from an "uncured pain patient" to a person
like anyone else, with values, beliefs, and dreams. If we
can't be cured, we work to adapt and be healed, as fully as
we can.

For today: **My healing journey goes on. I'll keep the
vision of wholeness before me.**

June 7 ❧ Life's Injustice

> *I have always depended upon the kindness*
> *of strangers.*
> —Tennessee Williams

We bring our histories to our experience of chronic pain. One person says, "I had an abusive, alcoholic father, and when I can bear to think of God, it is in terms of 'her,' instead of 'Father.'" Another says, "My mother and I have always had a battle of wills. Not only do I not have her support, but I have trouble with female friendships. All my close friends are gone, so it must be due to my unconscious need to get rid of them." A divorced person says, "I live alone, with few friends and no family. People treat me differently now that I have this pain. I isolate myself and I know that I'm alone more than I should be."

One who has suffered abuse, rejection, childhood neglect, or an inadequate support system may ask, "All of my life has been hard. Why is it still?"

Locked in a cycle of emotional pain and driven by loneliness, we may need to accept a new identity for the God of our understanding—a personal God who helps us to work through our pasts, helps us forgive others for harm done, and enables us to risk rejection.

We can gain profound healing if we refuse to stand still, but instead use spiritual courage to deal with our pasts, to forgive others, to face our pain, and to let peace be ours.

FOR TODAY: **Pain has inspired me to relate to the new God of my understanding, and I am willing to reach out to someone whom He has sent to help.**

June 8 ❧ Pacing, Limitations, Social Life

> *Life is not meant to be easy, my child, but*
> *take courage; it can be delightful.*
> —George Bernard Shaw

How can we enjoy social events when in pain? We have to think differently. I once was looking forward to two weekend activities of seeing friends and relatives that I had not seen for years. On Friday night, the Pain Monster woke me up at 3 A.M. for reasons that were obscure. Resting little until daybreak, I could not imagine being able to socialize, but I trusted that there would be a way if I lowered my expectations.

At the outdoor party, I limited my contacts to fewer people, rested inside a few times when the pain became severe, concentrated on the music being played, and left at a reasonable time. Thinking about the evening later, I focused on whom I could visit with rather than all those with whom I could not.

I woke up the next morning minus a pain flare-up from the night before. Pacing had worked, giving me hope that it could work again.

FOR TODAY: **There is a way to make social life possible for me. I will use moderation in this area, too.**

June 9 ❧ Advice

*Those who cannot remember the past are
condemned to repeat it.*
—George Santayana

We have to be careful about taking advice. Newspaper clippings about people whose pain has been completely alleviated can make us feel guilty and jealous instead of hopeful, especially if we have already tried the treatment that worked for the person in the article.

Advice has its pitfalls. We may take someone else's advice without holding it up to the light of our present reality, or we may take simplistic sentences out of books that sound helpful and think, "That's it! Doing that one thing will turn my pain around."

The most dangerous thing is to follow advice without comparing it to our past experience. When deciding whether to go somewhere, a friend advised, "You're going to hurt anyway, so just go." What she was saying was, "Don't bow out of activities because you have pain, because even at home the pain will be there." Reverting to past behavior, I took a careless attitude, went, and created a pain flare-up by recklessly exceeding my limitations, telling myself, "I'm going to hurt anyway."

If we get advice, we can say "Thank you. I'll think about it." There is much advice that will not apply to us. It is important to look at the advice rationally and judge it for ourselves.

FOR TODAY: If I get advice from someone today, I will look at it carefully and in the light of my past experiences.

June 10 ❧ Tears

*Tears are the safety-valve of the heart, when
too much pressure is laid on.*
—Albert Smith

I don't like to cry. It makes me feel weak and out of control, but after it is over, I am relieved of the pressures in my heart.

"Why are you so irritable?" someone asks on a difficult day when I am trying, with limited success, to contain my frustration.

Tears start to flow. This time, I am helpless to stop them. Each tear brings another, and they send more, until I cry hard and long over circumstances, emotions, and responsibilities. All of it comes out—all the anger, frustration, disappointment, and pain. A torrent of tears falls over the things that oppress my heart. Tissues are torn from the box, while my face becomes contorted and my eyes red and swollen. Finally I regain composure, drying my eyes and blowing my nose. It may not be a pretty sight, but it is a necessary one.

If we need to cry, we can allow ourselves to do so. This safety valve releases pressures, and it can result in profound relief.

FOR TODAY: **I won't be ashamed if I feel a need to cry. Sometimes it is the best thing I can do.**

June 11 ❧ Hope

*Everything has its wonders, even darkness
and silence, and I learn, whatever state I
may be in, therein to be content.*
—Helen Keller

"I have chronic pain, but it doesn't have me," said an older person. Can I say the same, or does it "have me"?

I can now tell when it does and when it doesn't. It "has me" when I slide into the habit of wanting to be alone too frequently, when I don't care about doing my favorite activities, and when I get irritated at people and things that usually don't annoy me. It "has me" when pain is all I can think about.

It doesn't "have me" when I think of someone or something besides myself and the pain, when I appreciate the small things, such as the first rose blooming, and when I can say "I'll try" rather than "I can't."

I choose freedom from the emotional enslavement of chronic pain, but to do so, I enlist help. A spiritual power, whom I call God gives me courage and perseverance and helps me see over the wall that chronic pain has erected between me and the world. The pain may stay, I may be exhausted, but it doesn't have to "have me." I have hope, and hope is restorative and healing to my spirit.

FOR TODAY: **I proceed in the hope that chronic pain will not rule my life. I will live today with health and wholeness in mind.**

June 12 ∾ Isolation

*Talent develops itself in solitude—the talent
of prayer, of faith, of meditation, of seeing
the unseen. But character grows in the
stream of the world's life.*
—Henry Drummond

If we have found comfort in things that are spiritual in
nature, such as prayer, faith, and meditation, it is tempting
to remove ourselves from other people and not deal with
the petty, mundane, irritating, and multitudinous demands
of everyday life. We see spiritual retreat as a desirable
alternative to tension and pain, but it also has the potential
for being an unhealthy form of escape, if we fail to reenter
the physical world.

If "character grows in the stream of the world's life,"
we have to find a balance between the physical and spiritual worlds we live in.

The physical world can indeed cause us added tension,
but it is here that we function and do business, pain and
all. It is in this physical world where our temperament is
revealed, our attitudes are tested, and our moods are
brought to light. Isolation, where we can control our environment if not our pain, seems easier and more appealing,
especially under the auspices of spirituality.

Prayer, faith, and meditation can deepen our spiritual
lives, but those means were never meant to separate us
from others or to give us a place to hide. With spiritual
help, our characters are meant to grow.

FOR TODAY: **I want to be able to function in the here and
now, so I will give attention to my responsibilities in my
physical world.**

June 13 ～ Special Moments

Even the most starless midnight may herald
the dawn of fulfillment.
—Martin Luther King, Jr.

For many of us, individual days at one time were not special. They were simply a unit in a growing line of digits that marked our days with pain. Few things seemed important, compared to finding complete and total relief from suffering. We refused to participate in life if this was all it offered. We limited our social lives and found it hard to smile.

In our own way and in our own time, we became tired of our misery and became open to the possibility of living a more fulfilling life, in spite of the pain. From there we grew to wanting to live meaningfully, and found that it was necessary that we allowed ourselves time to relax. We worked toward improving our attitudes and physical function, and we quit fighting for what we thought was our right.

Now we appreciate the special moments: a holiday get-together, a good meal, the laughter of a child, and the beauty of a sunset as it changes from red and blue, to pink and lavender. We cherish these simple but bright spots in our lives.

Each day holds the promise of special moments, and these moments soften us and lighten our burdens.

FOR TODAY: **I know a new freedom when I look for and sometimes help to create these special moments.**

> *Be not angry that you cannot make others*
> *as you wish them to be, since you cannot*
> *make yourself as you wish to be.*
> *—Thomas à Kempis*

At times, I receive unsolicited advice that irritates me. I want to stop the person from offering advice, but I realize that I have no control over anyone else, since it is just as difficult to change myself.

Many of us have difficulty in enlisting the help of others, and other people may advise us simply to ask someone we live with for help in getting our work done.

Yet other issues go along with expecting others to aid us. They include our struggle with dependence vs. independence, balance vs. perfectionism, and changing our attitudes vs. changing someone else's behavior. If help is not forthcoming for whatever reason, we do what time, energy, and pain levels allow us.

Sometimes we are grateful to a relative, friend, or outsider who offers us constructive, effective solutions that we had not considered.

Sometimes we have tried a particular bit of advice without success. We thank people for their suggestions and concern and do what works for us. If some method is not an option, we can be honest and say so in a kind way.

For today: I'm grateful for concerned advice but I must decide which I want to follow.

June 15 ❧ Faith

*Then when you failed in everything, when
what you had slowly built up was blown
away in a moment, and you must toilsomely
begin again from the beginning . . . then
you still held fast to your expectation of
faith, which is victory.*
—*Sören Kierkegaard*

I have faith enough to get me through today. I cannot speak assuredly for tomorrow, with its unknown cares. The work of coping with pain sometimes seems endless and the very thought, depressing. Pining away inside my house increases my distress. When I do so, I become weary too soon and I lose the sufficiency of faith.

The confidence of faith provides the constancy necessary for me to meet challenges. With faith, I can be led to active participation in the management of my life rather than being submissive and morose over it. Faith allows me sight to see the beauty of today rather than envisioning the dangers of tomorrow. Faith leads me into service for another life and away from performing only the duties of my own.

The confidence of faith gives therapy to my soul. Self-respect is rooted, the mists of tomorrow disappear, and I am in a place to gratefully receive these hours with which I am entrusted. Even trifling responsibilities may be of utmost importance to the God I trust with my day.

FOR TODAY: **Even one day with pain can seem endless, and I can't predict the future. The constancy of faith in my personal God will guide me through these twenty-four hours and help me look beyond the pain.**

June 16 ❧ Social Life, Moderation, Balance

One cannot have wisdom without living life.
—Dorothy McCall

Sometimes I feel stuck. If I protect myself from increased pain and isolate myself, I am more inclined to focus on my pain. If I stay involved, I risk flare-ups. An active social life can increase my pain.

Seeking a balance is the answer. Once I was invited to attend a wedding, reception, and a birthday party for an old friend on the same night. I didn't know if I would be able to handle the sitting and standing at each event. Missing one was an option, but I decided to test my ability by pacing myself and spending less time at each one. It worked. I wasn't able to talk to all the people I wanted to. I had to leave early, and I did have a minor flare-up of pain, but I reminded myself that attending the activities was the choice I had made. Recognition of this didn't remove all my sadness and frustration at not being able to stay as long as I wanted, but in the end I felt very good about not exceeding my limitations and enjoying myself in the process.

Although I felt like Cinderella at the ball, having to leave before I was ready, I was grateful to be invited, to be able to attend, and to have delightful though short conversations at each event.

FOR TODAY: **I can focus on the people I am with and not on all the people I can't be with. It is part of focusing on what I can do instead of emphasizing what I can't do.**

> *"Emotional"* is perhaps the last word we
> can apply to some of the most
> important events.
> —C. S. Lewis

From A to Z, from annoyed to zealous, we can list a feeling for almost every letter in the alphabet. We can go back to such a list and decide which ones we call "good" and which ones we call "bad."

We can look at which words describe joy, which describe sorrow, and which describe shame.

Do we feel good when, in spite of our pain, we have times of security and content? Do we feel bad when we are trapped and deprived? Are we ashamed when negative emotions turn into underlying attitudes, such as believing that a disability has made us inferior to others?

Feelings will come, and we must remember that it is how we act on our feelings that matters. We work toward acknowledging them and choosing to respond in a healthy way, not in a way that will hurt others or ourselves. Repressing negative emotions only causes us more stress and tension; admitting our feelings, first to ourselves and then to another person, will go a long way toward lessening the negative emotions' hold on us.

FOR TODAY: **If I am troubled, I can admit it, talk to someone, or write about it. I don't have to hold my feelings in.**

June 18 ❧ Growth

We can never have enough of nature.
—Henry David Thoreau

Last year my husband and I looked at the pine tree in the backyard, discussing possible reasons for its change in appearance. Most of the needles were dry and brown. He said that he had watered it, but I wondered if the tree had been transplanted too soon or if it had been watered too late. It had grown rapidly from a tiny seedling to a tree that was six feet tall. It was the nicest of evergreen trees, with feathery soft needles and upstretched branches. Although the neighbor's blue spruce was taller, our white pine tree was much more spacious, with places to look through at various levels. The blue spruce barely moved with the wind, while the pine tree's light branches and needles seemed to dance with the slightest breeze. The blue spruce seemed solid, while our tree seemed more carefree. I hated the thought of it dying.

Later we found the brown needles underneath the tree and each branch holding new, green needles. The needles had died, but not the tree. I had almost given up on it, but it was simply preparing for new growth. Today it stands twelve or fifteen feet high.

The neighbor's tree met the neighbor's needs and expectations, as ours did mine. If it could think, would it feel inferior to the taller one? As the tree might, there are times when I compare myself with those who are not hindered by pain and I feel less of a person, though I tell myself I am not. My tree has reached its full height but continues to show new growth. I never stop growing, either.

Doubts about my place and purpose come and go but I

never give up, believing that I am a person who is growing in dignity each day.

FOR TODAY: I will let go of the old and prepare for the new. I can hold tight to my values and grow in strength and love.

June 19 ❧ Exercise

> *Deal with it before it happens. Set things in*
> *order before there is confusion.*
> —Lao-tzu

Exercise is necessary for all of us. Its benefit isn't limited to people with musculoskeletal pain. Individuals with other pain problems benefit, too. Vascular systems need to be toned up for people with migraines, and a host of other problems require more than average amounts of exercise, not only to prevent inactivity and to gain or maintain strength but to help encourage physical and mental relaxation at the end of the day.

Most of us know that it is a wise precaution to get a doctor's approval before beginning an exercise program and then to start gradually. We have to allow our bodies time for conditioning.

Unrealistic goals for exercise can cause us guilt and make us feel as if we'll never progress. Depression can follow if our goals go unfulfilled. The whole problem is that our expectations for progress are too high.

We can incorporate some fun into our exercise. A man who bicycles with other members of a bicycle club says, "It's nice to see the progress I make and that I can reach my target heart rate, but mostly I do it for fun. It makes me feel good."

Exercise is important to give us that sense of wholeness that brings our bodies, minds, and spirits together. We move and then we rest, satisfied that we are toning our bodies and refreshing our minds and hearts.

FOR TODAY: **Even a short walk will enhance my sense of well-being today.**

June 20 ❧ Distraction

> *Why, what is to live? Not to eat and drink*
> *and breathe—but to feel the life in*
> *you down all the fibers of being,*
> *passionately and joyfully.*
> —Elizabeth Barrett Browning

I read once that our pain plus the perception of it equals our pain experience. I wanted to know how to change my pain experience.

First, I spent a lot of time reading about my condition, thinking that if I knew more about its nature, I could control it better. I believed that knowledge of my diagnosis was an essential prerequisite. I didn't get far because the doctors weren't sure where the true origin of my pain was in the first place. I didn't think this was logical because I believed that every pain should have a cause and then a simple progression of healing from beginning to end. What I finally learned is that not all pain can be explained, and even if it can be, sometimes it just can't be fixed.

That took care of the pain part of the formula. More of my attention had to be focused on how to change my perception of the pain. I learned ways to distract my mind from the pain and thereby become less depressed. If I couldn't change the pain, maybe I could change my perception of it.

Looking for the good in situations, planning activities, and if necessary putting a time limit on those activities helps improve my experience of life and my experience of pain. For example, going to the zoo for a few hours rather than a full day gives me happiness and an optimistic attitude about all living things. Since I can't change my pain, I search for ways to divert my attention from it.

FOR TODAY: The best way to alter my pain experience is by doing something I like to do. I'll take time to do one of those things today and notice my pain being pushed into the background.

June 21 ∾ Financial Worries

Dear God, be good to me;
The sea is so wide,
And my boat is so small.
—Breton fisherman's prayer

Many of us are struggling financially. For many who cannot return to former jobs, income often decreases. At the same time, the bills may increase. Medical costs can skyrocket, and we may have many debts from all the procedures, medications, and health professionals we have turned to in hopes of a cure.

We can become fixated on our debts and fall prey to the fear of *"What if?"* "What if my pain gets worse and I really do need an expensive procedure done?" "What if I get turned down for health insurance?" "What if my spouse leaves me?"

As a result of our financial insecurity, we may even make matters worse. We may buy material goods, grabbing for possessions before the day that our "what ifs" come true.

We need to take a deep breath. We need to tell ourselves that we have what we need. We can contact our creditors. We can seek financial advice. We can have confidence that we will be financially responsible for this month and be able to plan for the near future.

Most important, we can let go of the minute details of tomorrow's financial future. This frees us to do what we need to do today and live with what we have. If we do not have enough to live on, we can use appropriate governmental resources. There is no shame in doing what we need to do in order to survive.

FOR TODAY: I can easily be overwhelmed by financial insecurity, but I know there is a way out. I'll try to concentrate on my current needs, keep a good perspective, and ask the appropriate people to show me the way.

> *He who thinks he can find in himself the*
> *means of doing without others is much*
> *mistaken; but he who thinks that*
> *others cannot do without him*
> *is still more mistaken.*
> —*François, duc de la Rochefoucauld*

We need one another for our lives to be whole and satisfying, but do we too readily think that others cannot manage without us? Because of this belief, have we unknowingly usurped others' ability to take responsibility for themselves? Have we forfeited time from the things we need to do?

Delegating tasks to others is hard, if we have assumed a supervisory role at home or work. Perhaps the other person doesn't do things in the same way as we would like or, in our opinion, does not do them as well as we can. Perhaps someone tells us, "That's your job, not mine." Perhaps others convince us that we expect too much from them.

We with chronic pain want to make our time count and our energy last. Because we want to be as independent as possible, because we want to foster self-reliance in others, and because we want to come together in mutual, healthy dependence, delegating and sharing tasks with others may be the answer, no matter how imperfectly done.

We can look to delegating and sharing responsibilities when we find ourselves resentful over having to "do it all."

FOR TODAY: **My time, energy, and peace of mind are important enough for me to communicate my needs for help today.**

> *I'm happy because the world is round.*
> —*Pierre Teilhard de Chardin*

Robert S. Eliot, M.D., author of *Is It Worth Dying For?*, had a heart attack and vowed thereafter to reduce his level of stress. He learned to increase the awareness of the overload signals his body was giving him and to work out a self-management program to change his lifestyle and his reactions to stress. He now refers to stress as a friend that can help him live a healthy and creative life.

We often feel pressured by an accumulation of small issues and irritations. Pain is no small problem, but what place does it take in the context of our lives? How much do we worry about how others judge us? In reality, probably few people are really watching how we live. Around others, we don't always have to wear a mask of contentment, but neither do we need to remind them daily about how we feel.

We can flow with the stress that comes from chronic pain and be ourselves rather than be who we're not. Unable to change things or people, we may find that even minor irritations may be smoothed through acceptance.

For today: I can change and adapt in order to go with the flow and have my body work for me. If excess stress sends signals of more pain, I'll try reducing what I can and do my best to manage the rest.

June 24 ❧ Loneliness

> . . . I think the greatest suffering is being
> lonely, feeling unloved, having no one. I
> have come more and more to realize that it
> is being unwanted that is the worst disease
> that any human can ever experience.
> —Mother Teresa

When we have to miss an activity because it would not be worth the increased pain, we need to first ask ourselves whether there is a way that we can modify the activity so we can participate.

For example, if eating out bothers us because of the hustle and noise, can we find a quiet restaurant? If it bothers us because we cannot sit long, can we find a place that has booths so we can semirecline or find a table that we can stand beside periodically, out of the way of restaurant workers? If we are uncomfortable at a movie theater, can we rent a movie instead?

When we cannot get out, we worry that people will quit asking us to join them and that we will be forgotten. We fear losing our friends, and we even fear that our families will be content to exclude us.

When it is impossible for us to join others, we feel unwanted. We can try to combat the loneliness by thinking of the things we always wished we could do if we had uninterrupted time by ourselves. We can do these things or we can call someone else who is home, too. We can tell God about our sorrow or we can cry. Any of these options is okay.

FOR TODAY: **If I feel lonely, I can try to make accommodations in order to participate. If that cannot be done, I can try to fill the void until I can be involved again.**

June 25 ❧ Play

To be released from the "You must *survive"*
double bind is to see that life is at root
playing.
—Alan Watts

A child transforms a bunk bed into a battleship, a room
into a schoolhouse, and a closet into a secret hiding place.
Real things become imaginary and the imaginary becomes
real. Life is play, not work, even though play often imi-
tates the work of an adult. Play is both a release and a
preparation.

Perhaps we have let chronic pain rob us of our desire to
play. We may see life as somber and serious, not fun and
playful. Play can be a release for us, and the methods of
play are numerous.

Play can take place on a playground or park; it can happen on a playing field or gymnasium. It can happen by
oneself while engaged in a hobby or with others, while
playing a game, singing a song, or in sharing the amusement of a good joke.

Play can release us from the solemnity of chronic pain,
and release is what we badly need. It can give us a chance
to enter into a child's world and participate in the wonder
and joy that life can offer.

FOR TODAY: **When was the last time I set aside time to
play? I'll take the time I need for this release and try to
see more fun and joy in the world.**

June 26 ∾ Pain Flare-up

Limitations are sometimes the lens
which can bring our life into
deeper and finer focus.
—Tim Hansel

I didn't know this would happen. I didn't see it coming. There was a little bell in my head that rang "Caution," but I was only vaguely aware of it. What seemed to be an innocent activity turned into disaster because I didn't watch the signals. What happened? Like a powerful train engine hitting me, my pain flared. I should have seen it coming but I hadn't taken the time to look and listen.

One example is the time that I decided to go to a long movie. I was uncomfortable sitting but I stayed anyway. The thought occurred to me that I should leave, as if a faint "caution" bell were ringing, but I ignored it. Later I experienced severe pain and incapacitation.

I now try to keep my ears open to the voice that says "Watch out" and stay far from the cross arm that says "Don't cross, delay—pain is coming."

FOR TODAY: **I will watch for signs of impending pain and learn to listen to my body.**

> *Anger as soon as fed is dead;*
> *'Tis starving that makes it fat.*
> —Emily Dickinson

I can express my anger rather than fuel it further by holding it inside as a deep, gnawing resentment. When I give voice to anger as it occurs, I not only let it defuse faster, but expressing it quickly places the incident in a better perspective.

The best example of how I express my anger was dealing with a flight attendant on the day I made a plane stop on the runway. I had been operated on two months earlier, and my back was weak. Riding in a car for a long distance was impossible. As we hadn't taken a family vacation for several years, we decided that we all needed a reprieve. I thought I'd be able to find two seats to lie across. Unfortunately, not only was the plane full, but, because of turbulence, I needed to sit with my seat belt on for an extended period. I had expected to be able to move around at our layover airport, but we arrived late and our next plane left almost immediately.

After the plane began to taxi down the runway, I lowered my painful body to the floor—I was unable to sit any longer. In about thirty seconds I felt the plane come to a grinding halt. A flight attendant grabbed me up by the arm, put me into my seat, and said, ''You have to wear your seat belt. It's for your safety as well as that of the rest of the passengers.''

''I know,'' I said angrily, ''but I'm having severe pain.''

''We know you are,'' she said—how did she know this? —''but you have to take your seat.'' I sat and cried tears of anger and pain. As soon as the seat belt light went off, I went back to the floor to relieve my pain.

I could let the anger dissipate. The flight attendant was doing her job. She didn't understand my pain, but I didn't have to make it worse by resenting her attitude and actions. I might have done the same thing, if I'd never known pain as I do.

FOR TODAY: **When I travel, I must carefully consider my options. Others may be insensitive to my needs. Holding resentment only harms my peace of mind.**

June 28 ❧ Fear

*It is almost incredible. I again saw the
world bright and joyful before me and no
longer succumbed to fits of suffocating fear.*
—Herman Hesse

Sometimes the unknown summons me, but I hesitate to answer its call. The spot I am in may be uncomfortable, but I am acquainted with it. I fear breaking away from its familiarity. I stay in the same place because I'm afraid to move. The unknown may include a decision about a new activity, work, relationship, or lifestyle.

I can look back on other times in my life when change threatened me. I was afraid of taking the first step but, in time, took it. I was afraid of following a different course, but hesitantly I followed it. I was afraid of plunging in, but finally I jumped. Many times good things happened by taking action in spite of fear.

These experiences enriched me, although the risks intimidated me and fear seemed to jeopardize my journey. I continue this journey of life made easier through past experiences and support from other people.

I trust that I am moving along at the right pace and that the uncertainty is not a roadblock but a bend in the road that I may need to follow.

FOR TODAY: **I will summon all my courage and strength to follow new paths when I need to.**

June 29 ∾ Suicidal Depression

When I can get people to accept themselves
as whole individuals, lovable as they are,
they become able to give from an inner
strength.
—Bernie Siegel, M.D.

A commercial for using seat belts says, "Do it for those who love you," as if to say, "We know you don't value your life much, but do it for the ones who care about you."

Most of us have at least one person who cares if we live or die, even if we do not value ourselves very much. Even if we can't see a purpose to our lives, we can think about this person or those people whom we would not want to hurt.

It's hard to admit to suicidal thoughts, but whether they are fleeting, persistent, or used actually to plan suicide, many of us have had the thought of wanting to end the pain by ending our lives. We feel we can't go on a day longer with it. Suppose we ask, "How would _____ do without me?" only to answer to ourselves, "They would feel bad, but they'd get over it and be better off without me. I've already figured out how I'd do it." At times like these, we should seek help. That is depression at its deepest. For the sake of those who love us, we must seek help.

FOR TODAY: If I have serious thoughts about suicide, I know where to get help. If I am depressed, I will find someone to talk to, knowing that wisdom and guidance speak through the voices of others.

> *This would be an unbearable world were*
> *God to have only a single light, but we may*
> *be consoled that God has two lights: a light*
> *to guide us in the brightness of day . . .*
> *and a light to guide us in the dark of*
> *midnight when we are thwarted and the*
> *slumbering giants of gloom and despair rise*
> *in our sails.*
> —Martin Luther King, Jr.

How can we accept the unacceptable? Chronic pain is fierce, powerful, and sometimes crippling. It does damage to us and the people we are in contact with. It causes us to lose time that otherwise we would have used for worthy endeavors and ambitious pursuits. It changes us in ways that we are not always proud of. How, then, can we accept chronic pain?

Facing its impact on our lives is the first step toward moving out of its grip. It is not easy to surrender to the fact of having pain, but it can be the stepping-stone that leads us to a life of promise and reassurance. We can go on to working toward quality in our lives again.

We may feel, at times, as if a bird of ill omen were flying above us, leading us to a cave of despair, but we do not have to follow it. Through gloomy clouds there is also a ray of hope, and it is this that I gaze upon.

For today: **Within me is a source of hope, available to me for comfort, guidance, and peace. I know too well about pain's impact, and trust that I will have the fortitude to realize my dreams.**

JULY

*They do not love who do not show their
love.*
—*William Shakespeare*

As we may have already discovered, chronic pain affects
our families, also. When we have felt helpless and hopeless, our families have, too. Both we and they long for the
time when pain is not an issue and family life can return to
"normal." We all want to laugh and love again, without
pain at the center of family life.

When the pain stays, it affects everyone. We may want
to withdraw rather than have the family make concessions
for us. Family members can feel alienated from each other
instead of coming together to work around the pain problem. Plans can get upset because of sudden flare-ups.

Pain doesn't have to be a wedge between us and our
families. We can listen to what our families want to do and
tell them what is realistic for us to participate in. Pain is
not static, and its unpredictable nature can confuse our
families. But communication helps, even when we feel
that they don't understand what it is like for us to have the
pain.

Within our limitations, we can stay involved and push
pain out of center stage. We can be the initiators of harmony, sharing, and togetherness. With our families, we
can pull together rather than be pulled apart by pain.

FOR TODAY: **I don't want pain to destroy my family life.
With honest communication and the willingness to
work together, we can enjoy one another again.**

July 2 ∾ Fun, Structure, Social Life

Let us live while we live.
—Philip Doddridge

I need to be more spontaneous. When it comes to my social life, planning events doesn't mean that they have to be big productions. If I want to see people, I don't have to plan an elaborate dinner. I can ask my guests if they want to grill and bring a potluck supper to a picnic. Next time we can order carry-out pizza or Chinese food. I have options to consider. Spontaneity can simplify things and save energy for the more important activity of talking with my friends.

But in my day I need structure, too. I need a consistent schedule to avoid feeling purposeless and useless. Accomplishing even tiny tasks makes me feel better about myself.

In our pain experience, fun is almost foreign to us sometimes, because pain has made us overly serious. The enormity of the problem makes us very somber until we see that having fun and laughing relieve us momentarily of the consciousness of pain. We can put fun back into our lives, sometimes spontaneously and sometimes on schedule, with friends we welcome into our homes.

FOR TODAY: I need to "lighten up" and do some things just because I enjoy doing them. Pain doesn't need to rob me of a social life. I don't need to put off calling friends until I feel better. Today is the day to feel fully alive by putting my energy into enjoyment.

July 3 ❧ Life's Injustice

Fear not . . . I am your shield.
—Genesis 15:1
The Bible, Revised Standard Version

"Where is God in all of this?" we ask. Maybe we had once given the question a passing thought while we listened to the report of some tragedy on the news. Now we are agonizing over where God is in the midst of our pain.

Harold Kushner, in *Who Needs God,* says that God is something abstract when things are going well but becomes real when we talk to God as a real presence in our lives. He says that God is not found in happy endings but in the human being's capacity to cherish a value or cause as something greater than life itself, and that such a recognition makes human life precious. Kushner relates a story of a Soviet Jew who, though imprisoned, reminded himself that he was freer than his captors because his mind, unlike theirs, was not enslaved.

We can feel imprisoned by our pain and ask, "Where is God in all of this?" The shackles on our physical selves may not be removed but our spirits are free—free to affirm the preciousness of life. Our free spirits are made strong against the tempestuous powers of our pain, helping us to resist the pull toward a sea of agony and despair.

My faith is with me through the valleys and in the depths. Even there my life is precious.

FOR TODAY: **I will relax and accept spiritual strength and presence for this day.**

July 4 ❧ Freedom

I felt a deep joy. This is how great visionary
poets see everything—as if for the first time.
  —Nikos Kazantzakis

I've seen bald eagles sitting in the trees of a nearby wildlife refuge. Imagine the exhilaration I felt one March as I
counted ninety of the rare birds on the ice of the lake!
Using binoculars, I observed one and felt that I could almost touch it. Suddenly it flew into the air. I watched with
awe as its wide wings soared and dipped and it glided to a
distant tree.

I envy its freedom in this place of refuge. I wonder if I
would have pain if I could fly. I wish I could soar, dip, and
glide away from my pain. Sometimes I can mentally fly
away, but then it eventually makes itself known. Physical
freedom is something I once took for granted.

With the realization that life holds no guarantees, I realize that I am at liberty to appreciate the freedoms that I do
have. I am grateful for the most fundamental freedom—
the ability to breathe unassisted. I think of this as I walk
behind a person connected to an oxygen tank in a busy
shopping mall. I take my own respiratory ease for granted.

I take spiritual freedom for granted. I am free to ask
God for help and to gain the freedom that my spirit needs
to rise above the pain that can weigh me down, or to ask to
be pulled ahead when I fall and tarry behind.

My mental and spiritual freedoms may not be apparent
to others, but I know how valuable they are in letting my
whole self be more free.

FOR TODAY: **God, You help me find freedom from despair. Help me see that in You my spirit finds refuge.**

July 5 ❧ Helping Others

> *The sage never tries to store things up. The*
> *more he does for others, the more he has.*
> *The more he gives to others, the greater his*
> *abundance.*
> —Lao-tzu

Everyone has probably heard that by helping others, we help ourselves. This can be particularly true for people who suffer from chronic pain. We can think about our needs so much and how others can help us meet them that we lose sight of how we might help someone else.

Is there volunteer work we are capable of? Are others aware of our willingness to assist as much as we can? Do we know of others who have problems and just need someone like us to listen to them?

We may also show our graciousness toward those we don't know. It could take the form of smiling at a passerby on the sidewalk, helping a lost visitor with directions, or reminding someone to shut off car lights. Helpfulness can be shown in even the smallest ways.

The help we give almost always comes back as a gift to us.

FOR TODAY: **I will do a stranger a service or come to the aid of a friend. It is satisfying to think that I can help.**

July 6 ∾ Pain Management

A man doesn't learn to understand anything
unless he loves it.
—*Johann W. von Goethe*

At one time I wondered how I could fathom a new way of life, restructured by pain. I couldn't, because I didn't love my life any longer. It's not easy to get such love back once it's gone.

I've had to tell myself to go through the motions of my responsibilities, even if I didn't care; to exercise, even if I didn't think it would help; and to set aside time for relaxation, even if I thought I had none to spare. By taking action, I feel more in charge of my pain and thus of my life. As a result, I find it easier to say no to someone when I need to and to say yes to life, even when it hurts.

We can always make progress in restoring quality to our lives. We can love life again when we realize that our innermost selves are not at pain's mercy.

FOR TODAY: **I love my life. I'm willing to learn how to take charge of my pain, which will help me love life even more.**

July 7 ❧ Time

It is now, in this very moment, that I can
and must pay for all that I have received.
The past and its load of debt are balanced
against the present. And on the future I have
no claim.
—Dag Hammarskjöld

Time can be either our master or our servant. It can rule us or we can dictate, to some extent, what we want it to do for us. Our circumstances have much to do with our relationship with time. Raising a young family, maintaining a hectic work schedule, and/or keeping up with a busy social life can make us feel pressured. If we are disabled and inactive, however, time can feel like a different sort of oppressor. We either have too little time to accomplish what we want or time weighs heavily on us.

To some extent, time is relative to how we think about it. Albert Einstein once said, "If you are sitting on a hot stove, a minute can seem like an hour, but if you are doing something pleasurable, an hour can seem like a minute." We can compare a painful twenty-four-hour day that drags on with an enjoyable day spent during a two-week vacation to see the contrast.

Perhaps we need to change our thoughts about time and not time itself. Giving time our fullest attention will bring more meaning to it. Even when we are in a hurry, if we make time our possession we will feel that we have some power over it. We will also see that some things can wait and that other things will need to be given up.

Best of all, we can preserve some time for silence and emptiness. Thus, with renewal, we can conquer time.

FOR TODAY: **There are ways to slow down time. It may mean having to say no to someone or something today, but it will be worth it. I will protect my time, so that it does not oppress me.**

July 8 ❧ Fear of Failure

> *Do not be too timid and squeamish about*
> *your actions. All life is an experiment. The*
> *more experiments you make, the better.*
> *What if they are a little coarse, and you*
> *may get your coat soiled or torn? What if*
> *you do fail, and get fairly rolled in the*
> *dirt once or twice? Up again; you shall*
> *never be so afraid of a tumble.*
> —Ralph Waldo Emerson

Fear of added pain and fear of failure can keep us stuck. We can allow ourselves to dwell so much on past medical treatment failures that we are immobilized. We may fear that a new exercise will cause a setback. Or we may simply be afraid to gamble on any unnecessary activity. Sometimes what we call fear is actually shame. We may be ashamed that a certain treatment has helped a number of people, but it did not help us. Or ashamed that we may begin an activity and be unable to finish it.

It's time to ease up on ourselves. There are plenty of reasons to do so: (1) Just because something has failed to help us does not brand us as failures; (2) Living life the best we can is good enough; (3) Every day we start from where we are and do what we can; and (4) Even failures can be important experiences that may lead to personal success.

For today: **I can put shame behind me and believe that I am not a failure. At least I have tried, and experimenting takes courage. I can take risks toward living a fuller life.**

July 9 ⚬ Fun

The shell must break before the bird can fly.
—Alfred, Lord Tennyson

With whatever abilities I have and with whatever power is mine, I will say yes to life today.

My chronic pain tempts me to say no, to not venture out, reach out to someone else, or have fun. Recovery from the negative effects of chronic pain is about more than merely surviving, it is about making a good life for ourselves.

If I search, I can find activities that make me feel good, even though I have pain. Basking in the sun, swimming, picking out a funny card, spending time with family and friends, getting a massage, buying someone flowers, taking a walk, reading a good book, petting my dog, and listening to music are some of my favorite options.

It is easier to say no and to keep myself hidden behind a wall of pain, but if I venture out slowly, believing that my efforts will be worth it, I can say yes again. A good day awaits me today.

FOR TODAY: **Today I will do something enjoyable or fun. It is time.**

> *Courage is not fighting back; it is the power*
> *to endure.*
> —Robert Frost

It's a remarkable sight. Outside my upstairs window, a plant grows out of the drain spout on the roof. The narrow metal spout is clogged with twigs and dirt, and there, amid seemingly impossible conditions, it grows—not a small plant but a sunflower that is now a yard tall.

I look at it and smile. Where did the seed come from? How can it place roots in those scanty materials? How big will it get? Yesterday it flowered, as if to smile on the yard far below it.

To me, the sunflower represents survival against great odds. It represents natural growth in an unnatural setting. It represents believing it belongs there because that is where the seed landed.

It represents an unquestioning response of growth to "Why am I up here instead of down there?" It represents acceptance and patience.

The remarkable thing about chronic pain is that we, too, are surviving against great odds. It takes acceptance and patience to keep growing as a person, but in spite of an unnatural condition, we will flower, too.

FOR TODAY: **I have great potential in spite of the odds I face. Today I'll work toward fulfilling that potential.**

July 11 ∾ Music

Life is extremely simple but it suits me.
—Alice B. Toklas

Children dancing, adults tapping their feet, and people clapping describe the outdoor concert scene as smiling faces listen to the horns, saxophone, and drums of a Caribbean jazz band.

In other places in the city, people are humming old favorite tunes and remembering their youth; others are changing the radio station in search of a romantic melody; and still others have turned up their music so loud that even sirens can't be heard. Everywhere, music is alive.

Music is part of our heritage, our culture, and ourselves. Each of us has individual likes and dislikes in music. Besides listening, some of us have learned to play an instrument and experience firsthand the pleasure that it brings.

For us with chronic pain, we can listen and "lose ourselves" in music, whether it is a soothing classical piece that relaxes or an upbeat song that invigorates. Whether for comfort or for energy, music can be the therapy that leaves us happy.

FOR TODAY: **My ear is not the only part of me that receives and responds to music. Music has benefits for my heart. What kind shall I listen to today?**

July 12 ❧ Decisions

What is strength without a double share of
wisdom? Vast, unwieldy, burdensome,
proudly secure, yet liable to fall.
—John Milton

"Some of the things that are good for my head aren't good
for my body," I told a friend with chronic pain. At the time,
working, learning new things, and occupying myself with
activities helped my mental state, which affected my attitude toward pain. I liked to be busy, but during this conversation, I was anticipating a pain flare-up because I had to
travel many miles to attend a workshop.

My friend responded to my complaint with, "Then you
have to choose." I couldn't count on her for a "poor us" or
an "Isn't it awful?" She put the responsibility for the decision in my lap.

We can be pulled in many directions by what we want to
do or what others want us to do. Sometimes we are willing
to risk the consequence of more discomfort in order to join
in, to be a part of, or to be different from another person or
group. Sometimes it is worth the risk, and sometimes it is
not.

We might want to throw caution to the wind and do all
the things we'd like, but there are times of choice and compromise. It is our responsibility to decide. We may need the
counsel of another, but personal choice is ours alone.

**FOR TODAY: What alternatives do I face? How important
are they? What are the consequences of saying yes or no
to each one? I'll trust what my heart and mind tell me to
do, and try again if I fail to make a good judgment.**

> *I was gratified to be able to answer*
> *promptly and I did. I said I didn't know.*
> —Mark Twain

We cannot blame doctors entirely for not being able to help us. They feel that their job is done if they have performed the appropriate tests and procedures, prescribed medication, and sought to find a cure for the pain. They're trained to think about medical problems, but they sometimes ignore the holistic ones that include issues at work or at home. Some doctors refrain from asking personal questions and may hesitate to suggest psychological help because some patients may be offended. Both doctor and patient may feel uncomfortable.

We may need to consult our doctors about new medical problems or rehabilitation plans, but after a time we will rely on much less medical help to cope with chronic pain.

Without blame or remorse, we can transfer the burden of dealing with our problem from our doctor to ourselves, shouldering it with assistance from spiritual help, from others with chronic pain, and from our own inner resources.

FOR TODAY: **I have the courage to deal with chronic pain in my own way. My doctor will no longer be my sole source of help.**

July 14 ❧ Empathy

Achieve greatness in little things.
—Lao-tzu

Although we may come together to share our strengths, it is in our weakness that we relate to one another. This is particularly true for those of us who know others with chronic pain. The person who seems to have all the answers may seem too distant for us to relate to.

A woman with chronic pain confided, "When she told me that she was always a happy person, it made me feel like I shouldn't have been feeling bad."

Even if we have found something to be enthusiastic about, we should feel empathy for those who are struggling. We may be the ones who need an understanding ear at our next encounter.

We can apply this to our everyday relations, also. Chronic pain has given us the opportunity to have empathy for others undergoing physical, emotional, and spiritual suffering.

We may not be able to effect an instantaneous change for another person, but relating our weakness can lead to binding together our strengths.

FOR TODAY: I can lift someone up by sharing what we have in common. I'll include my experiences with the low times, too.

July 15 ∾ Fun

> *But all memories return, especially the*
> *sharp-set memories of our youth.*
> *—Ellen Anderson Gholson Glasgow*

Remember how carefree summer was as a child? Maybe there was the splashing at the pool, running through the water sprinkler, screaming on the roller coaster at the amusement park, going on a long family vacation, or staying up late and sleeping in the next morning. Perhaps when we got older, there were hours of water-skiing, doing a backward flip off the diving board, or fishing until it got dark.

Adulthood has spoiled some of our fun due to its time-consuming responsibilities. As people in pain, we envy both the relaxation and the excitement of a child's summer. Because we may have limitations due to pain, our thinking may get distorted; we may feel we can no longer enjoy summer.

Perhaps we haven't thought through our options. How about having a picnic with friends? Or swimming, not for the thrill of doing acrobatics off the diving board, but for the good feeling of staying fit? Or letting someone else pack for the family vacation to conserve our energy for the trip? Or sunbathing, more for the relaxation than the tan?

One year I knew three people who took vacations, and their conclusions about traveling while in pain were the same. "It took nine days to travel 1,500 miles because I had to get out of the car so often and walk around, but it was worth it," one said. Another said, "The trip really aggravated my pain, but the scenery was worth it." The last one said, "I was able to do more on this vacation than I thought I could. Just discovering that was worth it."

They wanted to have fun, even if it meant taking the risk of having more pain. All in all, it was worth it.

FOR TODAY: **Like a child taking back a favorite toy, I'll take fun back for thirty minutes during this day. Tomorrow I might allow myself an hour's worth. After that, there may be no stopping me!**

July 16 ❧ Enthusiasm

> *Nothing was ever achieved without*
> *enthusiasm.*
> —*Ralph Waldo Emerson*

She spoke with such passion about her garden. ''I go out, pull some weeds, and sit on my bucket, looking at how all the tomatoes, beans, peppers, and squash have grown. Every day it's what I look forward to, and it's something I can still do.'' Her eyes sparkled as she described something she truly loved.

My friend with constant pain feels that this summer she is able to do less than she was able to do last year. She says that she gets angry about it sometimes, but she can't afford to focus on the losses. Instead, she is grateful for what she can do now.

I see in her a concentration on the ''living'' part of living with pain, where I've sometimes had more of my focus on the ''pain'' part of the phrase.

There was excitement, there was enthusiasm, and there was fervor in her voice. I wanted desperately to find my own passion for living and to not let pain stand in my way. By her gentle example, she helped lead me to the understanding that, indeed, life is worth living.

FOR TODAY: **I can find something to be enthusiastic about and find people to share my enthusiasm with.**

July 17 ❧ Pacing

Life was meant to be lived and curiosity
must be kept alive. One must never, for any
reason, turn his back on life.
—Eleanor Roosevelt

I know someone who is excited about her new outlook on life. She knew that "life was meant to be lived," but it was getting increasingly hard to believe that she could do anything to affect her pain. Once, feeling hopeless, she said, "I have dreams about being in the coffin and people standing above me, laughing."

Today she has learned how to pace herself, and for her this has made all the difference in being able to do more with less pain. She no longer has nightmares, and she feels good about living again.

In order for us to live within our limitations, pacing ourselves by doing activities in stages is important. Our pain levels may decrease if we plan ahead to estimate how much we can do, how long it will take, and how much rest we'll need to accomplish tasks. We may wish we could do things the old way and get them done quickly. We may be impatient with our new pace, but we must learn to accept and adjust.

Pacing ourselves involves setting priorities and working toward goals. It is exhilarating finally to be successful at accomplishing goals that we believed were out of reach.

As Eleanor Roosevelt said, we must keep curiosity alive as to who we are and what we can do, and we must never, for any reason—not even for chronic pain—turn our back on life.

FOR TODAY: **In learning to pace myself, I will carefully plan today's activities by first taking stock of my pain and energy levels. Putting thought into planning will simplify my day.**

July 18 ❧ Accidents, Birthday

*I am not afraid of storms for I am learning
how to sail my ships.*
—Louisa May Alcott

Accidents happen to everyone, but they seem to have more severe consequences for us who are already in pain than they do for others.

One hot summer day I went to recline on a lawn chair and, because I hadn't set it up properly, it collapsed under me. There was instant, intense pain. I could count on the pain persisting for many days. I felt crushed, defeated, and angry at the accident that caused me such additional pain.

The day of the lounge chair accident was my birthday. It was a day that people commonly think of as "their day" —a day of taking one's ease, a day of reprieve from demands, and a day to celebrate being alive. Instead, there was the threat of it being Pain's Day.

I determined not to let the pain take my day away from me. I prayed to recover quickly and not to be plunged into despair.

I returned to the lounge chair, secured its legs, and eased into it. The pain eased minimally. I began to write about my feelings. Gradually I calmed down and regained my composure. I had fallen, but not so far that I couldn't lift myself up.

FOR TODAY: **Today is too precious to give over to pain. An accident may happen whereby my pain increases, but my emotional distress can be calmed, so that I experience a new level of healing and wholeness.**

July 19 ❧ Choices

*What man actually needs is not a tensionless
state but rather the striving and struggling
for some goal worthy of him.*
—*Viktor Frankl*

Accommodating and compromising—it sometimes seems that that is all we do. We would rather say no to activities if we can't do them the "old way." Still, accommodation is often the way that we get things done. Choices become less "I choose to do this" or "I choose not to do this" but more "I choose to do this, but I will have to do it differently."

For example, if summer reminds us of canning forty quarts of tomato juice, freezing volumes of sweet corn, and picking buckets of green beans but pain now prevents us from gardening, perhaps there is still a way to enjoy fresh vegetables.

Perhaps we can shop at a farmers' market or plant a garden on a very small scale. If stooping or bending is a problem, we could raise beans that grow on poles so we can stand as we pick.

There was once a man who could no longer fish from mountain streams because the climb caused him severe pain. At first he was angry and refused to go fishing anywhere. Missing the sport he enjoyed so much, he finally decided to change his mountain fishing location to a lake in the woods. Finding pleasure and relaxation there, he was glad that he'd adjusted to his limitations and returned to his favorite pastime.

Choices reduce my struggle. They can lessen and sometimes eliminate my feelings of deprivation.

FOR TODAY: **I'll be honest about my abilities, open to new choices, and willing to try a different way.**

July 20 ∾ Forgiveness

He jests at scars who never felt a wound.
—*William Shakespeare*

I have had to forgive those whom I thought were determined to hurt me. There have been times when I expected understanding and support and received a minimizing of my complaints or even the denial that my problem was real.

It is peace that I am after, and I can't have peace when I harbor hatred. Sometimes I am more forgiving as time passes, and sometimes I feel sorry for the person who may feel the need to judge me wrongly.

Misunderstanding and ignorance still abound regarding chronic pain. We feel especially disappointed and betrayed when we encounter doctors, nurses, and other health professionals who think that our pain is completely psychogenic. One person with chronic pain remarked, ''One of my doctors thought that my pain was not unusual. He attributed it to family stress since my son has a chronic disease.'' She was bitter and had not yet forgiven the doctor. The resentment was causing her much distress.

Resentment and conceit on our part will only do further harm. We can forgive others as people who don't realize what they are saying or who lack the understanding we have gained through experience.

We can forgive others for the sake of our own peace of mind.

FOR TODAY: **My emotional wounds can be healed through forgiveness of those who don't understand. I was once ignorant of chronic pain, too. With tolerance and patience toward others, I can focus on my own actions.**

July 21 ❧ The Past

*Someone said that God gave us memory so
that we might have roses in December.*
—Sir J. M. Barrie

We're tempted to shut the door on the past when we recall how much better we felt. We don't want to remember for fear that the old angers and resentments we have had about our pain will come back.

However, there comes a time when we want to look. We find that remembering the good things affirms that we once were more happy and carefree. It prompts us to regain some of those characteristics. Maybe an old song on the radio reminds us of happy times and we remember the people, parties, and fun we had.

It is good to remember what happy people we were during those good times. The more we allow our past and present to meet, the sooner we can regain the positive qualities that were and still are ours.

FOR TODAY: **What can help me recapture the past—music, old photos, old friends? It's time to integrate my past self into the person I am today and let nostalgia help me be more carefree. I've delayed doing this too long.**

All paths lead to the same goal: to convey
to others what we are.
—*Pablo Neruda*

Friendships can be tipped off balance on the scale of give and take when we first experience chronic pain. It is natural to want compassion, sympathy, and understanding, and at first, it seems that we can't *not* talk about our pain. After friends have been given a detailed account of how we feel, however, usually little more can be said. We yearn for the times when pain was not the foremost subject in our conversations, and we feel guilty that friends are giving us their time and attention, while we are less able to give back to them.

Sometimes we tip the scales the other way. We become so involved in trying to return to an active social life that we prepare, clean, fix, and ready our surroundings to the point of being too tired to enjoy our guests. We can't listen well or participate fully when our thoughts revolve around increased pain and when we are so tired that we want our guests to leave.

Pacing ourselves and lessening our expectations of an ideal social engagement (such as, "The house, food, and conversation will be perfect") does help. We can enjoy laughter and gaiety more when we haven't narrowed an occasion to perfection, but instead are completely involved with our guests.

FOR TODAY: **A few special friends enhance my life and well being. What can we do together, soon?**

> *The change of one simple behavior can*
> *affect other behaviors and thus*
> *change many things.*
> —*Joan Baez*

There are days when I really want to give up. I'm tired of making compromises because of pain. I'm tired of saying, "Can you help?" and I'm tired of saying, "No, I'm sorry, but I can't do that." Most of all, I'm tired of trying to maintain my self-esteem. I have been guilty of being self-deprecating when I am able to do less than I feel I should. Often I try too hard to be acceptable to myself.

This is not new. In the past, someone would tell me it couldn't be done, and I'd prove it could. I unconsciously thought that something was not worth doing if it was easy. The epitaph on my tombstone in those days would probably have read, "She tried hard," because I could not just let myself be acceptable as I was. After much struggle and affirmation by others who were kinder to me than I was to myself, I was led to believe that I did not have to try so hard to prove myself any longer. I only had to stop judging myself in such a condemning way.

There's nothing wrong with putting forth my best efforts to accomplish something, but it's not necessary to "try" to be a worthwhile person. Because I live, I'm worthwhile. People love me as I am, not as I was before chronic pain entered my life and not as I wish to be. They love me unconditionally. I can accept rather than fight this.

Because I have nothing to prove, I can relax.

For today: I have something to offer to others through love and acceptance of myself. Thank goodness that I can be myself.

> *We are all vulnerable. Suffering is not*
> *confined to those "who deserve it."*
> —Daniel J. Simundson

We sometimes believe that our chronic pain originated because we deserved it. We point to some wrong we committed or some act that we failed to do and tell ourselves, "Yes, it must be true. I am being punished because I have deserved it. I must have needed to be humbled."

How ironic that we should feel this way when we don't cast such judgment on the suffering people around us. We would be the last to tell a mother whose child died that she surely must have deserved the awful thing that happened.

There is such a thing as ownership. I own the fact that when I should have asked for help in lifting, I injured my back. But I can't own responsibility for a congenital problem that existed all my life, of which I was unaware.

The most destructive thing that happens from feeling that we deserve our pain is that it turns God into our enemy rather than our friend. If we have abused our bodies, we can ask for forgiveness, knowing that God loves us. Even when we have no answer as to why our acute pain turned chronic, God stands by, wanting to link us to His love. With spiritual help we also can ask to be freed from the mental torture we have put ourselves through.

FOR TODAY: If I am full of guilt, I cannot be of service to others. I will try to be more gentle with myself today and receive the love I need.

> *To be nobody but yourself—in a world which*
> *is doing its best, night and day, to make you*
> *everybody else—means to fight the hardest*
> *battle which any human being can fight, and*
> *never stop fighting.*
> *—e.e. cummings*

Are we pulled in so many directions that we feel we are losing our sense of self? This can be true at any time and for anyone. Other people want their opinions to be our own, expect us to like what they like, and demand that we have the same values as they do. It can, indeed, be a fight to maintain who we are, when others want us to be entirely different.

Those who are caught in the workers' compensation system can really get confused. The insurance company may approve or disapprove of medical expenditures, our employers may or may not want us back, a vocational rehabilitation counselor may have ideas for work that we are unsure we approve of, and a lawyer may or may not be looking out for our best long-term interests. Even our friends bring us news of the "latest treatment" or say, "I knew someone who tried this and he's feeling great." It's hard to keep our sanity and maintain our balance.

Through the confusion, I look into myself to ask whom I am meant to be and what steps I need to take. Eventually I find the way.

For today: **I feel pulled in many directions. I will strive to be myself and to do what I was meant to do by listening to my soft, inner voice.**

> *Grief: sorrow, sadness, regret, melancholy,*
> *mourning, misery, trouble, anguish,*
> *despondency, pain, worry, harassment,*
> *anxiety, woe, heartache, malaise, gloom,*
> *unhappiness, desolation, despair*
> —*From* Webster's New World Thesaurus

We with chronic pain have experienced grief. What was is not. Not now, and may never be. We have reason to grieve.

Grief, while common to all of us, will be different for everyone, depending on the severity and effects of pain and the personality of the individual.

We may first deny that the pain is chronic, become angry, bargain with God and doctors, and feel intense emotional upheaval. There may not be a set order to our grieving process, but it is vital that rather than deny it, we move through it. If we do not move forward, we run the danger of having grief define our new self. We may gain an identity of being "always angry" or "always depressed." We may be chronically unhappy.

We can live today and look again to the future with anticipation. We still need to define what we can do today, rather than project too far into the future. Looking past grief to the pleasures of today and the challenges of tomorrow, we can confidently proceed in those directions.

FOR TODAY: I have felt the emotions associated with grief. At my own speed, I will be able to move on.

> *It is healthier to see the good points of*
> *others than to analyze our own bad ones.*
> —Françoise Sagan

"I knew I'd suffer the consequences if I moved the big potted plant. There was no other choice than to ask for help. I hated it but I didn't hurt," my friend said. Listening to her, I thought about how often I had unconsciously chosen to hurt because I didn't want to ask for help. What amazed me the most was that, after twenty years of pain since a car accident, she admitted to still hating the need for help.

By her example, she was giving me permission to feel embarrassed to ask for assistance, but still she urged me to do it anyway. Knowing she had overcome those feelings, I felt that I could reach that point of swallowing my pride, too. What a relief to hear that, just like me, she didn't like appearing weak or different, either. The difference between us was that she stood up to the voices in her head that said "It won't hurt this time. I'll do it myself," while I plunged ahead and later paid the price.

It isn't that she perfectly walks the tightrope of managing her pain. I know something has happened to tip the balance when she occasionally lies on the floor or does some stretching during a meeting we attend. When I see her sitting with the group the following week, I know that she hasn't overextended herself.

Sometimes our actions have to precede our feelings, such as asking for help while our pride wants to hold us back. There are other things we can be proud of doing. Trying to do the impossible need not be one of them.

FOR TODAY: **I will be grateful if I don't need someone else's help with my duties and tasks, but if I do, I will value my well-being enough to ask for help.**

July 28 ❧ Pain, Acceptance

I believe . . . that all real suffering
contains an element of physical pain. We are
always too much inclined to emphasize the
suffering of the soul.
—Dietrich Bonhoeffer

Characters in movies bear pain nobly and become heroes. A child falls out of a swing, skins a knee, and after being briefly comforted (if at all), he or she is pushed back out to the playground to play. We are taught to be tough. Enduring pain is supposed to develop strong character.

But pain can have quite the opposite effect. Being unable to live a normal life can be humiliating and demeaning. Some do rise above their pain problem, while others succumb to it and become bitter. I ask myself which group I count myself a part of.

I don't have to be a hero every minute, but I don't have to let pain push me down to the ground, either. My "normal life" now includes the painful fact of its presence. I don't disregard this knowledge as if I have no pain, but rather I have an awareness that pain is with me and has put certain restrictions on me. Still, I insist that it has no right to interfere with my life in its entirety. Many times this takes strong character, hard work, and heroic efforts. When I tire, I remind myself that my life is worth it.

FOR TODAY: **I strive not to be beaten down by pain. Others in science can do the fighting for breakthroughs, while my efforts are directed at maintaining quality in my life. For fighting to live my life, I am a hero.**

July 29 ❧ Distraction

*My joys are great because they are very
simple and spring from the everlasting
elements: the pure air, the sun, the sea and
the wheaten loaf.*
—Nikos Kazantzakis

We want to turn our attention away from the pain so that
we can get involved in life again. The means of distraction
are as individual as the people who use them. A few examples are reading, having a conversation with someone, doing a minor household repair, playing chess, doing needle-
work, or talking on the phone.

We may be able to think of things that we once did to
distract our minds from problems but aren't able to do
now. Can we modify or change the distraction to get the
former benefit? For example, if we used to run five miles,
maybe a walk past interesting houses or in a natural setting
can help divert our attention from pain.

Talking to someone may be the last thing on our minds,
but listening to someone share life experiences can be very
effective in taking the focus off our pain.

Developing hobbies, engaging in tasks that require
problem solving, and sharing time with others can distract
us from the pain that grows with increased attention.

FOR TODAY: **Life contains more than pain. The more I
distract my mind from pain, the more living I'll enjoy.**

July 30 ∾ Single Life

Be what you are—that is the only thing one
can ask of anybody.
—Paul Tillich

Chronic pain knows no limits. It affects the young and old, male and female. I once thought that it ravaged only senior citizens with arthritis, construction men with back injuries, and women with migraines. I now know that all sorts of people can be its victims.

Not everyone is married; some are single. Dating can be a challenge for the single among us. We fear that we will be unattractive to our dates, once they know about our pain and limitations. We might try our hardest to deny our pain, attempting to hide it from the person to whom we feel attracted. But it is unrealistic to hope that we can hide the hidden part of us, chronic pain, for very long.

Our relationship with a person we admire can mature when we honestly explain that we have chronic pain, but that we are coping with it. Discussing our situation honestly, we can admit if we're unable to join this person in some activities, and we can suggest other options for things to do together.

We should remember that the other person is not perfect and has weaknesses, too, even though they may not be physical.

FOR TODAY: **I want to be honest, to do my best to cope with chronic pain, and to be the person someone wants to be with.**

July 31 ᴥ Future

> *As for the future, your task is not to foresee,*
> *but to enable it.*
> —Antoine de Saint-Exupéry

I believe in the now, but sometimes now isn't enough. I want "then" to happen again. But it won't. What will the new now of the future be like? Regarding the past and the future, it is only human to remember and to expect.

What I believe about the future is that I'll be there. I have a past and will have a future until I die. The pain may have changed everything else, but I still am myself—changed, but myself.

The person I am is the only one who sees as I see, knows what I know, feels as I feel, can do what I do, and values what I value. One person may briefly enter into and then leave my life, like the one whose name is written but barely remembered in my old yearbook. Another may move away, and another may stay until death takes one of us. People move in and out of my life constantly.

Alone, I live in my flesh and listen to my own thoughts. Sometimes the flesh frustrates me and my thoughts trouble me, but they are my possessions. The thoughts in my mind cause me to reflect on what was and to anticipate what will be.

I remember the way it was, I see the way it is, and I expect the good that can be. My past and present selves pause at the entryway of a new now and I long to go in. I long to see if it gets better.

FOR TODAY: Unhesitatingly, I can make a change today if one is needed. In the scenario of my life, I am the one who stays. Today is, at least partially, in my hands.

AUGUST

August 1 ❧ Humor

> *When we begin to take our failures*
> *nonseriously, it means we are ceasing to be*
> *afraid of them. It is of immense importance*
> *to learn to laugh at ourselves.*
> *—Katherine Mansfield*

I got together with friends and we laughed most of the evening. I don't recall what it was that was so funny, but I know that I felt better for seeing the humor in their lives and in mine. Finding humor in everyday circumstances is a good coping tool, and it establishes, for me, the aspect of my life that can survive amid the pain.

The irony of chronic pain is that it can create some comical situations of its own. One lady tells of being trapped in a bathroom with her panty hose down, unable to get up because she was suddenly disabled with pain and lack of control over her legs. In retrospect, she can look back and see how funny she must have looked to the person who finally came to find her.

A past event that seemed tragic in retrospect, such as "How We Got Lost on Vacation," was probably stress-filled at the time but humorous in remembrance.

We need to be open to experiencing humor in both the past and present, if for no other reason than that it makes us feel good.

FOR TODAY: I will be open to humor—the funny, witty, silly, and absurd. I feel relieved of care when I laugh.

August 2 ∾ Decisions

If life had a second edition, how I would correct the proofs.
—John Clare

With excessive focus on pain, decisions do not come easy. Perhaps we have made the wrong decisions in dealing with our pain, and that has shaken our self-confidence. Perhaps we've never learned to make decisions for ourselves. Perhaps we are afraid to risk failure or rejection. Perhaps we are overly concerned about what others will think of our plans.

Wavering from one decision to another robs us of our peace of mind. The more we struggle with a decision, the more difficult it becomes to make.

In weighing alternatives, let us be careful that our decision, especially a radical one, is not too heavily influenced by anger, bitterness, or fear. Constructive solutions come more easily when we can consider all factors calmly.

Since we can't foresee the outcome of everything we do, it is best to decide on a course of action and rest in the fact that we made a decision. Trusting that we have acted appropriately with the information that is available to us, we execute our decisions without regret. Soon peace comes over us. We are now free to attend to the here and now.

FOR TODAY: **Big and small decisions await me. I am glad that I have the competency and courage to make them.**

August 3 ❧ Limitations, Family

It takes two to speak truth—one to speak and another to hear.
—Henry David Thoreau

"I was having a very painful day," she told me. "My family should have been able to tell how I felt by the way I walked, but they didn't say anything. It was a real struggle to make supper, but I did it anyway. I was feeling worse and worse, getting angry about having to make the meal. Then, during the meal, one of my grown children had the nerve to ask if I'd get up and get something out of the cupboard. I wanted to explode! Couldn't any of them tell how much I was hurting?"

There may have been several reasons why none of her family sensed that she was in greater pain. Since her children no longer lived with her daily, they may have failed to recognize the signs of increased pain, such as her troubled gait. Her husband may not have observed her movement. She may have hidden her pain so well that it was impossible to tell how bad she felt.

Our families can't always read our minds. "I'm tired of talking about it, and they're tired of hearing about it," she said. Still, it will save us a lot of anger toward our families if we simply say in such a situation, "I'm having a rough day. Can you get it yourself?"

FOR TODAY: **There are days when I cannot give to others in the way that I usually can. Since others can't read my mind, I owe it to myself and them to say when I am having a bad day and ask for their cooperation.**

> *Resolve to find thyself; and know that he*
> *who finds himself loses his misery.*
> —Matthew Arnold

Chronic pain can force us to look, perhaps for the first time, at the relationship we have with ourselves. Can we love and trust, forgive, and be honest with ourselves? How do we feel about our right to happiness, about what we deserve in life, and about our self-worth? Do others know us better than we know ourselves?

Our reaction to pain can depend not only on the degree of pain and its effect on our ability to function, but also on what kind of a friend we are to ourselves. Are we gentle and understanding, or critical and judgmental? Our orientation to ourselves can make a world of difference.

Today we have what it takes to cope with chronic pain, even if it is only an ounce of strength. We have had it latently all along, through all the struggle, chaos, and drama of living with chronic pain. When we take time to know ourselves better and value ourselves, we release latent energies that undergird our health and our well-being. It is essential that we take time to get to know, befriend, and cherish ourselves.

FOR TODAY: **I'll treat myself, today, as my own best friend—someone worth relying on.**

August 5 ∾ Intuition

The intellect has little to do on the road to discovery. There comes a leap in consciousness, call it intuition or what you will, and the solution comes to you and you don't know how or why.
—*Albert Einstein*

Often we have to tackle several therapies and look at important issues simultaneously, in order to feel better. It's not enough to focus only on our physical pain, because our perspective on how pain affects us is based on many other factors. Sometimes we have a "gut feeling" or intuition that leads to solutions.

For some, there are no issues to deal with. For others, certain issues may be too difficult to face at a particular time. Pain may entice us into not dealing with important personal issues, but questions arise anyway. How happy have our relationships been, and how much does this influence how we feel around others? We may later judge some questions to be absurd, but they still need to be addressed. For example, do we feel we've done something to deserve our pain? Other questions may need probing. Have we felt like failures or victims in other areas of our lives? What has helped us cope with problems in the past?

We need to remember that our lives are too important to discount anything that may lead to an intuitive discovery of how we may feel even slightly better.

FOR TODAY: **I want to improve my response to pain. Addressing my reactions to difficult issues may be the place to start.**

August 6 ❧ Pain Cycle

> *A crust eaten in peace is better than a*
> *banquet partaken in anxiety.*
> *—Aesop*

I'm in pain, and it makes me anxious. Anxiety causes me
to tense up and cause more pain. Because I have more
pain, I feel more anxious, and the self-perpetuating circle
goes on and on.

What distraction, relaxation, and exercise therapies do
for me is to help me break out of this vicious cycle. When
I practice these therapies, I feel a semblance of control—
not of eradicating pain, but of keeping it from dominating
me. Because I have concrete things to do, I have a sense of
confidence that I am able to cope rather than panic.

In exercise, an improved physical fitness level induces a
feeling of well-being that was denied me by the pain-im-
posed inactivity.

I want to achieve everything that is possible. While I
once scoffed that these methods could affect my pain, I
now use them regularly for one reason: I know by experience that I feel better.

FOR TODAY: **I want to be open to any ideas that can help
me break out of the anxiety/pain cycle. Any method
that will help with pain reduction is welcome. After I
learn, I'll practice, just as I would a musical instrument.**

August 7 ∾ Patience

*Patience is the best remedy for every
trouble.*
—*Plautus*

Our recovery from the negative effects of chronic pain is
like a marathon race—a long-distance run that is both gru-
eling and exhilarating. It begins with the first step, continues with each successive one, and results in the satisfaction of a course pursued and an attitude sustained.

The pain weighs us down and we become faint and
weary. Though negativity may threaten to take the lead we
can move forward steadily by mentally and physically pacing ourselves in order to live each day confidently.

When slow progress discourages us, we must remember
that we are gradually moving in a positive direction. Like
the tortoise, we can be winners, too.

**FOR TODAY: I will be patient with myself. Learning to
persist in spite of the pain with its hills and valleys, I'll
keep moving forward, finding a certain happiness even
in my difficult course.**

August 8 ∽ Frustration, Family

Your children may see character flaws in
place of the physical ones.
—Cheri Register

When I realize how my self-centeredness has hurt others, I feel very sad. Often it has come as the result of my wanting to have some control in my life. If my pain and my life seem out of control, I strive to control something or someone else.

Of course, the person I try to push either retaliates or withdraws from me. In either case, not only have I been unable to control that person, but I am left either with a damaged relationship or alone.

I need to forgive myself for harsh words and rash actions, and apologize to others for what I have done. After this, I will work toward a more honest, open, and caring relationship by not exerting my will on others and by accepting them for who they are.

Force never works, to control pain or other people. My frustration over my pain has nothing to do with innocent bystanders. Others may see wrath or withdrawal rather than the underlying physical pain. Transferring this frustration to others will not ease my pain—it will only increase my guilt. I will find another way to express my frustration.

FOR TODAY: **I will seek other outlets for my frustration at being unable to control my pain completely. Whatever my outlet, I don't need to hurt others. Perhaps I need to take a walk, hit a punching bag, scream into a pillow, or I might need to let tears come.**

August 9 ❧ Denial, Future

*And should this not be of importance, since
not until a man is finished with the future
can he be entirely and undividedly
in the present?*
—Sören Kierkegaard

Sometimes I toy with the idea that pain relief is just around the corner. I hear of someone who has regained some of the function that he thought was lost forever, and I'm eager to hear what happened. I scan the medical literature, hoping to read good news.

Some people have a recurring type of pain. They feel cured until the pain comes back, like the surf that has steadily been increasing in height, then crashes with pounding impact. Whether our pain is daily or periodic, the pain comes back. We learn to expect it.

If I wait for a miracle, my life may be spent before one happens. Chronic pain is a part of my being now. I do best when I invite God to help me through only one day of pain rather than a lifetime of it.

Sometimes it helps to pretend that relief is just around the corner, but I can't practice my selective denial for long. Today's joys and challenges bid me to come back to the present. Complete pain relief may not be here, but here is where my life is lived, to the best of my ability.

For today: **I will walk through this day, and bring to mind thoughts of goodness and contentment to replace my fantasizing.**

August 10 ❧ Denial

The past is such a curious creature,
To look her in the face.
A transport may reward us
Or a disgrace.
         —Emily Dickinson

"I was moving forward, forward, forward," my friend said over the phone. "Where I once could only sit for fifteen minutes at a time, this month I sat two hours. I felt almost normal and started skipping my exercises. Then I overdid it one day and my pain stayed flared up for twenty-three days. It was awful!" she said. "I'm better now but July is half over and I haven't done one summerlike thing. I'm so tired of this pain that I'm tempted to go to bed and read romance novels until school starts again!" We laughed, not because what she said was so absurd, but because escapism sounded so tantalizing! She felt "almost normal" in the spring and now she felt as if she had to start over.

When I hung up the phone, I thought about something else she had asked me once. The question was, "Isn't it human to always want more?" Yes, I believed so, but I also recognized the big role that denial had played in contributing to her pain, because I had used it, too. Denial of my pain helped protect me from despair. It was a survival mechanism and, for a while, the only way that I could cope.

Finally denial became my enemy. I was acting like someone who denies it's cold outside and repeatedly goes out without a coat. One could imagine that after several bouts of frostbite, denial would give way to awareness of the cold and the action of putting on warm clothes would finally follow.

It's easy to feel "normal" when our pain is less and we're able to do more, but we must always be vigilant. Denial of what we need to do to take care of ourselves can carry a heavy price, a price that we're tired of paying.

FOR TODAY: **I'll keep in touch with how my body and mind feel today. I'm strong enough to face reality now.**

August 11 ❧ Asking for Help; Pacing

> *The first point of courtesy must always be the truth.*
> —Ralph Waldo Emerson

"What did you do this time? How did you overdo?" These questions came from a well-meaning person at a time when I was having a pain flare-up. I unintentionally snapped back, "Living is overdoing."

My answer voiced my frustration at not being able to do the things I wanted to do according to my timetable. I didn't like the idea of having to make modifications.

At times, it still bothers me, but I'm now less concerned about how and when tasks get done. I am willing to spread errands out over the week, rather than do everything in one day. Friends may need to be invited for coffee rather than for dinner. I am willing to change. But if someone has agreed to help me accomplish something by a certain day, I have the right to ask when the person will be available. The other person sometimes forgets my request, while I become more impatient and unwilling to ask a second or third time. As appointments offer certainty, so knowing when we can expect help alleviates a lot of stress and the work gets done.

FOR TODAY: **I can be flexible with my timetable today, but I can ask for help if I need it, even if it involves making an appointment with someone I live with.**

August 12 ❧ Pessimism

> *As for joy, I labeled it "aesthetic experience" and talked much about it under that name and said it was very "valuable." But it came very seldom and when it came it didn't amount to much.*
> —C. S. Lewis

"Yes, but . . ." can enter our thoughts, and, like a noose around our neck, it can wrap tighter and tighter, suffocating the happiness that we could be experiencing.

Still able to work? Yes, but not as much. Still able to swim? Yes, but I don't feel like it. Still able to have coffee with your friends? Yes, but I don't have much to say. Still able to enjoy a good movie? Yes, but there aren't any good ones out.

Too many "Yes, but . . ." statements can choke the good from our lives and sentence us to despair. There is a world of experiences left for us, and pain does not need to steal all the pleasurable ones from us.

We can loosen the rope, breathing easier until it relaxes completely and we are set free. Then we can throw the rope away. We can be done with "Yes, but . . ." and explore options, make choices, and take responsibility for ourselves. We can claim the good and rejoice about our freedom to be happy.

FOR TODAY: **I can be happy, in spite of the pain. I will look for pleasing options today.**

August 13 ❧ Pet Therapy, Affection

Oh, to throw my arms around the neck of a
creature, dog or man, a creature who
loves me!
—Colette

He's never angry with me, although I sometimes get per-
turbed with him. Always ready to give unconditional love,
he gives me a kiss when I return from vacations. It is
special because he saves it for only such times. He rejects
people that I don't invite in, such as the mailman. He's
brown, warm, and sleeps a lot. He'll never repeat what I
tell him because . . . he's my dog.

Pets can be good therapy for many people. They bring
cheer to both young and old. Dogs are especially good to
hug, and my dog shows me that we all need physical touch
and a reassuring presence. We like to have someone be
glad to see us, and we like to reciprocate the affection.

When there is no pet, we can be the instruments of affection. We can be the ones to warmly welcome a friend or
guest, greet a family member who comes home, and glad-
den another person's day by our tender or happy look.

And, if that's not enough, we can pet a puppy.

FOR TODAY: **I need to show love and I won't hold back
today.**

August 14 ∾ Problem Solving

> *God obligeth no man to more than He hath*
> *given him ability to perform.*
> *—From the Koran*

We have limits, but these very limits can help us bring what is important into finer focus. When a day of living with worse pain than we are accustomed to is hard to bear, we want each day that is less difficult to count by living rather than just preparing to live. And living includes working on problems.

I remember having a job on the night shift. I loved the job, but my body protested over the fatigue, never quite able to rearrange its biological clock. I put so much emphasis on my fatigue that I almost had myself convinced that everything would be all right once I left the job, implying that every other problem would be solved. It didn't work—everything was not magically "all right."

I have a more clear-cut idea of my problems today, knowing that chronic pain has complicated some of them. I don't waste time waiting for my pain to go away. As welcome as pain relief would be, it is unrealistic to think that it would solve all my problems. Today counts for both seeking solutions and for finding contentment. I won't wait to begin.

FOR TODAY: I can't postpone living until my pain goes away. Living includes working toward solutions for my problems and grasping whatever good comes my way.

August 15 ～ Patience

In my experience, nothing tortures us so
much as longing.
—Dietrich Bonhoffer

It seems as if I have a train schedule in my head. The trouble is, the train is never on time and there's nothing I can do about it, except to be patient and wait in the station of time.

This schedule has to do with my pain. During a pain flare-up, I think to myself, "Okay, it happened, but it will be better by Wednesday and I'll be back to where I was by Saturday."

Then something happens and my pain doesn't leave "on time." I wait with all of the extra baggage of discouragement and frustration. Patience is only a lost piece of luggage. I want to wave good-bye to all this accumulated baggage that surrounds me and my pain now.

Sometimes pain and problems have their own timetable, and it is I who need to set my clock differently. As frustrating as it is, acceptance of my pain and adjusting my actions to be in better synchrony with it takes time. I don't need to berate myself for being restless. It is difficult to be patient. I may simply need more time to change old habits and thought patterns, such as, "Forever is a long time. I can't stand this." It is hard, if not impossible, to force the virtue of patience on myself. Perhaps my experiences with pain are preparing me to be patient in some other areas of my life.

I wait for a flare-up to end. Sometimes I even let someone else carry my baggage for me. The load of pain is sometimes too heavy for me to manage alone. This, too, helps me to be patient.

FOR TODAY: I do what I can about pain and problems, but sometimes patience does more.

August 16 ∾ Pain Flare-up

> *Don't let life discourage you. Everyone who*
> *got where he is had to begin where he was.*
> —*Richard Evans*

If we were perfect human beings with perfect foresight and hindsight, we might not have a pain flare-up. Unfortunately, we are not perfect and often misjudge our abilities. Or things happen that are beyond our control.

One of the most helpful things I can do initially during a pain flare-up is to remove myself to a place that is dark and quiet. First I take a hot bath to relax. Then I breathe slowly and deeply while listening to calming music or a relaxation tape.

If the thought that this is wasting time enters my mind, I concentrate on erasing it by substituting words such as ''peace, soothing peace.''

We can be grateful that there is something that we can do during a pain flare-up, that we can feel actively involved in our recovery and not feel guilty about taking time to relax. Eventually the pain flare-up passes.

For today: **I will have a plan of what to do in times of a pain flare-up, and I will follow it during those times without feeling guilty over ''wasting time.''**

August 17 ❧ Depression

If what I feel were equally distributed to the whole human family, there would not be one cheerful face on earth.
—Abraham Lincoln

My friend says, "I've been battling depression again. You go along coping all right for a while and then one morning you wake up and say, 'I haven't made any progress for six months.' It really gets you down." She was depressed about her physical function as well as her inability to do what she thought a "good parent and spouse" should be able to do.

There are a lot of fits and starts in our dealing with chronic pain. Not being able to depend on our bodies to take us where we want to go causes us to feel depressed. Feeling inadequate because we're unable to meet the expectations of friends or family doubles our depression.

We can prevail through these discouraging periods by giving ourselves time, talking about our frustration with another person, and trying to focus on something besides the pain. One person says, "When I was very depressed, it seemed like everyone around me was in a play and I was on the outside watching, with little interest. It was hard for me to stay involved in the lives of others, but that involvement finally helped me break out of the depression."

The sooner we can take such steps, the better we will feel.

FOR TODAY: **I cling to my involvement with life when depressed, but deep depression can be life-threatening. Before it reaches this stage, I promise myself, even if I'm unwilling, to make a phone call to someone who can help.**

August 18 ❧ Love

The best portion of a good man's life,
His little, nameless, unremembered acts of
kindness and love.
—*William Wordsworth*

A few years before my injury, I was on vacation at a big lake in Minnesota. I was taking a break from swimming and just lying on the beach.

Suddenly I looked up and saw a beach ball being pushed across the water by the wind. Looking down the shore, I saw a little boy crying because his ball had gotten away from him.

At this time, I had great swimming endurance. Seeing in what direction the ball was headed, I started swimming after it. The wind continued to push it, but I was persistent. Finally, after swimming halfway across the lake, I retrieved the ball and, placing it in front of me, swam with it back to the beach.

It dawned on me while I was out there that this was a much different situation from swimming in the deep end of a swimming pool. I didn't know how deep the lake was. I wasn't able to touch ground, and I knew my husband couldn't swim that far if I got into trouble. I only knew that I had a basic trust that I would be able to get back.

I was able to use my swimming abilities to help the small child. For him it will probably be one of those ''unremembered acts of kindness'' that some stranger did for him.

My strength is not as great today, but I can still ex-

press love and kindness, no matter how small my gesture
is.

FOR TODAY: **An act of kindness may be the best part of
my day.**

August 19 ∾ Fear, Risk Taking

It's kind of fun to do the impossible.
—Walt Disney

It's hard to take risks when the fear of a pain flare-up or failure is great. Eventually we may end up excusing ourselves from doing so many things that all we have left is pain, fear, and depression.

Gently and carefully, we can take a risk, testing our abilities, even though we are afraid. Like a baby learning to walk or a child learning to ride a bike, we can try new things—both activities and attitudes. Whether it is trying to walk a little farther or initiating conversation with a new friend, we can practice new skills in our quest to be as whole as we can be.

Like riding the bicycle, we may fall from time to time, but after a while we may see progress and feel a sense of accomplishment, proving to ourselves that taking a risk was worth it.

Self-defeating fears, our worst enemies, need not engulf us. We can love life again and be willing to risk failure in order to feel better.

FOR TODAY: **I don't need to be afraid. I can't succeed unless I try. If I fail, I will know that I have put forth my best effort and feel good about that.**

The quality of mercy is not strained,
It droppeth as the gentle rain from heaven
Upon the place below; it is twice blessed
By him who giveth and him who takes.
—William Shakespeare

The circle goes around. Someone helps us; we help another person; someone helps us; and we help another person. It goes on and on.

After discussing some coping problems I was having with a spiritual advisor, I felt some relief. He said, "I don't know what part of what I've said will help you, just as you may not know you have helped someone until the person tells you or drops you a note."

Coincidentally, when I got home and looked at the mail, I saw a letter from a pen pal with chronic pain. She was a person whom I had only seen one picture of, but we had written many letters of encouragement to each other. I smiled as I read the first sentence: "Have I told you that you are my favorite person whom I've never met?" My spirits soared. "How wonderful that this should happen," I thought. "I have been helped and I have helped someone else."

Other people are waiting for our words of encouragement—family, friends, and strangers. The circle goes around.

FOR TODAY: **I open my heart to someone who needs my help today, by my example, compliment, or consolation. Just as I have been helped, so I am ready to help someone else.**

We must travel in the direction of our fear.
—John Berryman

We may be afraid of some activities when pain puts restrictions on it. We also may be self-conscious if our pain necessitates modifying an activity to give us a degree of comfort. Whether it is from the reluctance of needing to put forth extra effort or our embarrassment over not participating, we can lose out on happiness if we let pain be the dictator with absolute power over us. Some people find that thinking of pain as their normal condition helps free them from feeling different and ashamed of the necessary accommodations that they have to make.

One person says, "The pain is an inevitable fact of my life now. It makes me tired. I sometimes think that it's too exhausting to invite people over, but I do it anyway. My guests don't care if, because of pain, I have to get up and move around often. I find that I have more energy, because a stimulating conversation helps me connect with others. Having a good time motivates me to do the work I have to do."

Some people find that if their leisure activities are limited, they wrest as much fun as they can from the ones that they are able to participate in. One person says, "I can't play baseball with my children, but I'm a great spectator. It thrills me to see them having such a wonderful time."

There are people and events that add to the significance of our lives. If we live realistically and allow room for uncertainty, we can still join in a connectedness with others and construct a life that has room for joy.

FOR TODAY: **I don't have to huddle within the walls of fear and embarrassment. The joy of living is mine today.**

> *One doesn't recognize in one's life the really*
> *important moments—not until it's too late.*
> *—Agatha Christie*

One day I was looking through a photo album. There I was, standing on a ledge in the Rocky Mountains. My face looked tired from the long climb, but my body looked strong and firm as I posed with my backpack.

As I looked at the photo, it occurred to me that it represented the last vacation during which I was free of pain. I suddenly wanted to close the album—both on the pictures that reminded me of when I had felt good and on the subsequent ones where my smiles would veil the pain inside. When I wanted to close the album, it was as if to say that the rest didn't matter—that my life had become meaningless. In so many ways, I was not the person I had been because pain had affected me physically and emotionally. I was slow to realize that I was still myself, that I still had many of the same people in my life, and that I could do more than I thought.

As I look with longing on the past, I retain the memories that I need to connect myself to the life I knew before the pain started. Good memories lift my spirits. Sometimes I call or write an old friend who has celebrated good times with me, so that fond memories can be rekindled.

During this day, I can live in a way that promotes good experiences and happy relationships. Something that happens today might be a joyous memory tomorrow.

For today: **Though my before-pain life seems like a separate existence, I need to retain the connection to my former self. I want to welcome back my past and em-**

brace my present. Pain can temporarily embitter past memories and experiences, but it can't take all my pleasant memories away. It will not rob me of a good future, either, because I have worthwhile goals to accomplish along the way.

August 23 ∾ Problem Solving, Spirituality

> *Still, his soul stood in need, and as this*
> *need did not lie in external things, he was*
> *unable to seek consolation from men.*
> —Sören Kierkegaard

Things go well for us and then suddenly something happens that causes us to say "This isn't fair!" Perhaps it is an increase in the severity of the pain, or a feeling of pain that we haven't experienced for a while, or a spiritual longing to feel whole and content.

We may have consulted with others over a period of time, but eventually they had no new words of comfort or helpful suggestions to make. Perhaps we saw that our need for consolation was only bringing the other person down with us.

Instead of relying totally on ourselves or other people, we can tap spiritual resources that have been neglected or too little used. There is a creative, healing Spirit to call on in thanksgiving when things go well and in adversity when burdens become too great.

FOR TODAY: **I admit that I sometimes feel confused and like a prisoner in my body and my mind. Great Spirit, provide me with insights into my problems that point out new directions I should take.**

> *Whatever you can do, or dream you can,*
> *begin it.*
> —*Johann W. von Goethe*

What is the thing I have been procrastinating? If it increases my pain level, can I make any changes to prevent this? How successful can I be in cutting corners to accomplish what needs to be done?

On the other hand, pain may have no relation to what I delayed action on. Perhaps I have always put off writing an overdue letter, balancing the checkbook, or cleaning my desk. I may excuse myself by thinking that I will start when I "feel better." The danger is that in my mind, I may never feel well enough.

To deal with procrastination, I need to start and finish one specific task before starting the next one.

Procrastination due to pain may lead to people expecting less from us, taking away more of our responsibilities, and leaving us with lower self-esteem. However gradually, we will want to get our own work done.

What we have been putting off may seem overwhelming, but we can chip away at the task, starting today, feeling greater respect for ourselves and more motivation to continue.

FOR TODAY: **My pain need not keep me from accomplishing something I am capable of doing. I will start working on a neglected task today.**

August 25 ∿ Pain Management

> *It is not true that suffering ennobles the*
> *character; happiness does that sometimes,*
> *but suffering, for the most part, makes men*
> *petty and vindictive.*
> —W. Somerset Maugham

Sometimes we feel more compassionate toward others because of our experiences with pain, but often we either retreat from the world or show our worst side. Our sleep can be disturbed, we can be short-tempered, our appetites can be affected, and our families can suffer from social withdrawal. We can be so preoccupied with pain that we exclude the things that are important to us.

People have committed suicide and families have broken up due to the disruptive effects of chronic pain. Authorities on chronic pain suggest these as some ways to help us live effectively with pain: accept the fact of chronic pain, set goals for work, pursue hobbies and social activities, get angry at the pain if it gets the better of us, taper off pain pills until they are no longer needed, achieve the best possible physical shape, practice relaxation techniques, keep busy, pace activities, and encourage family and friends to support our efforts. Other suggestions include being open and direct with doctors, being empathetic with others having pain problems, and remaining hopeful.

Sometimes pain can be modified. We must do all we can to lessen the destructive effects.

FOR TODAY: **I'll check the list and see what areas I need help with. I'm grateful there are things I can do.**

August 26 ⌘ Emptiness

> *A believing love will relieve us of a vast*
> *load of care. Oh, my brothers, God exists!*
> —*Ralph Waldo Emerson*

During acute pain and illness, cards and flowers give us the love and encouragement we need. During this time, doctors reassure us that the pain is a necessary part of healing, and we accept it as a sign of getting well.

With chronic pain, cards and flowers stop coming and the doctors wear a worn expression and tell us, "There's nothing I can do." Friends quit asking how we are, even though we still hurt. We want to be relieved of our cares, and no help comes.

Chronic pain is a lonely condition that fills me with doubt, but God is there, especially when I come to the end of myself. He helps carry me through, replacing my "vast load of care" with a strength that only He can give. It is the inner strength that gives me the courage to go on. People will ultimately fail me, but spiritual love and strength go far beyond what the senders of the flowers can do.

FOR TODAY: **Thank You, God, for giving me the strength to go on.**

August 27 ❧ Assertiveness

> *If a person continues to see only giants, it*
> *means he is still looking at the world*
> *through the eyes of a child.*
> —Anaïs Nin

To be assertive is to encourage equality in our relations with others, whereby we are true to our interests and act according to our personal rights, without preventing others from acting on theirs.

How equal in our relationships do we feel? If we aren't as productive in terms of the amount of work we get done, do we feel less worthy than those around us? Do we give as much attention to our needs as we do to those of others? Do we get anxious when thinking about standing up for ourselves?

The benefits of assertiveness are a reduction in stress and an increased sense of worth. Some applications of assertiveness for us might be to trust our judgment, saying, "I really believe doing this is right," to ask for help when necessary, to take the initiative in organizing activities, to defend an opinion, to express feelings without anxiety, and to accomplish these things without manipulating someone else.

Assertiveness is not incompatible with politeness and compassion. We can still listen and respect the other person. It doesn't mean forcing others to see things our way, but instead, communicating more directly. Changes may not occur overnight, but we have laid the foundation for the building of equality and mutual respect.

FOR TODAY: **Assertiveness, not aggressiveness, is a skill for me to learn. I'll start today by making a decision and expressing how I feel about it.**

August 28 ❧ Sexuality

> *All things are possible until they are proved*
> *impossible—and even the impossible may*
> *only be so, as of now.*
> —*Pearl S. Buck*

Sexuality is a part of ourselves, a natural part of life, and one of the joys that two people can experience as a by-product of the closeness and love that they feel for one another.

Physical and emotional factors related to chronic pain can influence sexual expression. Physically, exhaustion, loss of muscle tone, or loss of range of motion can interfere. Emotionally, depression, fear of increased pain, anger, and unresolved conflicts can contribute to sexual dysfunction.

In spite of these barriers, it is possible to find a means of stimulation that will keep our focus off the pain and on finding enjoyment and satisfaction.

What may seem awkward at first, such as a position change during intercourse, may lead the way to bliss between us and our partner.

With communication, patience, and experimentation, the door to sexual fulfillment can be opened again.

FOR TODAY: **I have the same need to be touched as before. I can have a satisfying sex life, and I will gently explore it.**

August 29 ❧ Sorrows

When sorrows come, they come not in single
spies, but in battalions!
—*William Shakespeare*

A family member gets sick, unexpected guests drop in, a quarrel begins over something trivial, a major appliance breaks, the roof leaks, and then you get a speeding ticket for hurrying to keep up with it all. Sorrows indeed come in battalions!

We can feel so unique about having pain that when a multitude of troubles hit, we may feel that no one else is plagued with such problems. One person says, "I can deal with my pain better when things are happening in a routine way." A string of unfortunate circumstances can alter our pain and make us fatigued, lessening our ability to cope effectively. Our emotional reserves may be depleted when these sorrows come "in battalions."

Chronic pain will never be our only problem, unless we blame it for everything else that happens. Life goes on, and so do the challenges. We have experience in dealing with the problem of pain, and we can deal with our other problems, too.

During such times, we may need to prioritize what we need to do and, as much as possible, simplify our days to make room for work and rest. We can tell ourselves, "It won't always be like this," and be ready to look back and laugh at our circumstances long after the calamity is over.

For today: **I can deal with the challenge of living with chronic pain and have the ability to handle my other challenges, too.**

> *Life only demands from you the strength you*
> *possess. Only one feat is possible—not to*
> *have to run away.*
> *—Dag Hammarskjöld*

My nine-year-old nephew was diagnosed with brain cancer at the same time that I had the injury that led to my chronic pain. On one of my worst days of pain, I said to someone, ''At least my nephew can die. I have to live with this for the rest of my life.'' I needed to say those words in order to begin to face the fact that I felt no desire to embrace life. My nephew's chemotherapy treatments obliterated the tumor. He is now a five-year cancer survivor, busy with school and extracurricular activities. I am happy that his treatments worked, that he has gone beyond survival, and that he can now go on to experience adolescence and many fun-filled days ahead. Doors are open to him.

''Why live?'' is the question that most of us with chronic pain ask at some point when we find many doors closed to us. Most of us do continue living rather than choose to end our lives. Why do we make that choice? Basically, we want to live more than we want to die. We still want to feel the sunshine, to smell fragrances, to be touched, and to listen to the ones we love.

Something within us calls us to courage, no matter what our circumstances are, and we feel that life is good enough to partake of. We also play a part in someone else's life—someone who cares about us. We can't let go before it's time. There is a feeling of freedom in knowing that suicide exists as an option, but one that we choose not to use.

FOR TODAY: I am wanted and needed, perhaps by someone I haven't even met yet. There is a wonder to life that I can look at with awe today.

> *To put it another way: I began to*
> *understand that self-esteem isn't everything,*
> *it's just that there's nothing without it.*
> —Gloria Steinem

"Last year I went back to school for my master's degree, got all A's and many favorable comments from my instructors. It did a lot for my self-esteem. Yesterday I had an interview for a part-time job. The only problem is that a two-day training session is required and I know my body can't last that long. The interviewer saw me sit for two hours, so how was he to know I had pain? I certainly didn't show it and I just couldn't tell him," she said. "What I really wanted to say was 'I have a pain problem, but I would make an excellent counselor. During the training session, I will need some breaks for stretching.' I couldn't, though; I just couldn't," she said remorsefully.

The words didn't come because she didn't want to risk rejection and her insecurity kept her from stating her needs, the ones she herself had difficulty accepting.

Sometimes we need to appear self-assured, even when we're not, courageous when we feel threatened and fearful, and in perfect control of our pain, even when we're not. We are experts at hiding signs of pain; we can be masters at hiding how vulnerable we feel to obtain what we desire.

Our composure around others can speak louder than our words, and a calm attitude can help enhance the self-confident beliefs about ourselves that we long for. A simple statement, calmly spoken, such as "I have a pain problem, but I can work around it," may be all that's necessary.

Pain is not our only identity. Even if self-esteem lags

behind, we are worthy of so much more than its domination. We can act certain of ourselves, even if we are not yet convinced.

FOR TODAY: **Self-doubt is an obstacle to overcome when trying something new. I will believe in myself today and project self-confidence.**

SEPTEMBER

September 1 ❧ Autumn

> *Open your mouth,*
> *Always be busy*
> *And life is beyond hope.*
> *—Lao-tzu*

Autumn means colorful leaves, harvest time, the start of school, and cooler weather. It is a new season in the cycle of nature. It also ushers in a certain amount of predictability, in contrast to the more impulsive activity of summer.

Fall offers a slowing down and return to routine. Our summer vows to take more breaks and relax more can be repeated again next year.

Whatever the season, we need a time of reprieve from the busyness of our lives, a time for renewal and reflection. Whether we use solitude for meditation or to regenerate and reinvigorate ourselves, it is up to us periodically to set aside time to be alone, even for brief periods.

We can get to know the spiritual side of our nature when we still the physical, mental, and emotional ones. Sometimes, in solitude, we can get the glimpse of a clearer direction for the course of our lives.

FOR TODAY: **Insights come to me when I am less rushed and by myself. I'll claim time for myself, rather than waiting for permission to take it.**

September 2 ∾ Pain Management

No problem is solved when we idly wait for
God to undertake full responsibility.
—Martin Luther King, Jr.

I don't sit idly by, waiting for God to do all the work of coping with pain. I have a big part to play in its management. Pain clings to me, wraps itself around me, and wells up inside me, dictating that I give it my exclusive attention.

I want to run away as I would from a person who threatens to do me bodily harm, but I can't get away, and pain stalks me, moving faster until it has me cornered. I escape to a temporary hiding place, and there I rest and catch my breath. The attack is stalled, and my pursuer loses power.

My hiding place from pain takes many forms. I hide in distracting activities, deep breathing, prayer and meditation, and conversation. I also hide in humorous events and in the amusement I get from clever and funny people. Pain loses power when my mind is not fixated on it and when I try such alternatives.

Some with chronic pain hide in chemical or substance abuse, but theirs is an unstable shelter. In drug tolerance and addiction there is no rest.

FOR TODAY: **I am motivated to find healthy ways to cope with my pain.**

September 3 ❧ Affirmations, Feelings

> *Remember always that you have not only the*
> *right to be an individual, you have an*
> *obligation to be one.*
> —*Eleanor Roosevelt*

Affirmations should provide encouragement, not discouragement. Sometimes we try a particular affirmation and feel as if we've failed if it doesn't bring the desired result, such as optimism and confidence.

In those times, we need a somewhat different course of action. We might start the day with the affirmation "I have what I need today," but inside we want to scream "What I need is to get rid of this pain!" What do we do if we try to visualize ourselves happy in a group of people but we really can't picture any scene, other than wanting to stay alone in bed?

Those are times when we need to acknowledge our feelings that won't go away, no matter how positive we try to be. Maybe we need to be honest about our emotions and call someone, start a journal, or have coffee with a friend.

We can't ignore the feelings, but with the help of others, we can believe in ourselves and our worth again.

FOR TODAY: **If I feel like a hypocrite when I tell myself to think positively, it's not a failing. We all have times of struggle. I may first need to talk about what's bothering me with someone I trust.**

September 4 ❧ Problem Solving, Anger, Journal Writing

If anger is not restrained it is frequently more hurtful to us than the injury that provokes it.
—Seneca

Some of the things I put off doing are the things that help me the most. A problem-solving method I employ is to write my feelings down in a journal. It helps me center my thoughts regarding what my key concerns are. Sometimes these concerns and problems circle around my head like buzzing mosquitoes. Rather than actual harm, they are tenacious annoyances.

I can't swat a problem away, but I can write down an event that upset me and let my pen continue to explain what really triggered my troubled feelings. One time I wrote, ''Seeing all my relatives at the wedding reception bothered me. I'm jealous that everyone else could stand and talk to so many people, while I couldn't. I'm angry that I couldn't stay longer and enjoy a rare time to be together.''

In that situation, journal writing guided me into doing further work on what was bothering me. I learned that being unable to accept my limitation was preventing me from focusing on the positive remembrances. Gradually I became grateful for the amount of time I could stay and tried to focus on the happiness of the bride and groom.

Sometimes it feels good to confide our feelings to a piece of paper that we can keep or dispose of.

FOR TODAY: I need not write in my journal every day, but I'll consider it as a step toward understanding my problems and reactions and helping direct me toward changes I may have to make.

September 5 ❧ Gratitude, Envy

Every man has his own courage but is
betrayed because he seeks in himself the
courage of other persons.
—*Ralph Waldo Emerson*

Because chronic pain has accentuated our physical imperfections, we sometimes look at others who seem to have perfect lives, perfect houses, perfect jobs, and perfect relationships. Those "Joneses" don't really exist, except in our imaginations. Outward appearances don't reveal everything, and no one is perfect. All that envying of the "Joneses" does is to make us reach exhaustingly toward an ideal that is not real and to make us feel inadequate.

The "Joneses" have their own personal struggles of which I am unaware. They have their own challenges. But my focus must be on my own life and not theirs. We can't afford to become envious of others whose true condition we don't know. And self-pity and resentment keep us from appreciating our own special lives and homes.

Opening our eyes in thanks and being grateful for riches that have no monetary value is invaluable. The ability to love, have compassion, show understanding, and enjoy what reciprocity we may find is worth more than material goals. Envy can destroy us, but gratitude makes us more whole.

FOR TODAY: I will keep my focus off the fortunes of others and see the riches I already possess.

> *[Faith] instills us with the inner equilibrium*
> *needed to face strains, burdens and fears*
> *that inevitably come, and assures us that the*
> *universe is trustworthy and that God is*
> *concerned.*
> —*Martin Luther King, Jr.*

There are days when God's protection and guidance feel tangible. There are days when I stand in the middle of a spiritual desert and thirst for answers and comfort. On the dry, barren days I implore God to help me, even though His presence seems elusive.

I bring many requests. I need help to make time for both work and leisure, help in not being afraid to test my limitations gently, help in coping with pain, and help in dealing with negative emotions.

God understands me and I trust that, though I may not have all my desires, I will always have myself, and I will always have Him.

FOR TODAY: I need to let go of old beliefs about God, if they stand in the way of my relationship with Him today. I am free to bring my small and large problems to God and to try to find solutions to them with His help.

September 7 ❧ Prevention

*True miracles are created by men when they
use the courage and intelligence that God
gave them.*
—Jean Anouilh

The basketball crosses over the sideline. "Out of
bounds!" the referee calls, and the direction of the ball
changes. The game also changes. Something like this happens with pain, too.

If I must have pain, I want it to stay in a space where I
can engage in certain activities, perform certain tasks, and
experience certain pleasures. If it goes "out of bounds"
by not living within my limitations, my direction changes,
too. I have to restrict my activities, put tasks "on hold,"
and I am not able to enjoy many things. At its worst, pain
is agonizing and incapacitating. I have to work at preventing my pain from going "out of bounds" by knowing
what worsens the pain.

Prevention of more severe pain helps keep my emotional pain inside its confines, too. Depression, anxiety,
stress, and tension are kept on the edges while I experience pain that I am accustomed to but easily can go "out
of bounds" during severe pain.

FOR TODAY: **I'll do what I can to live with prevention in
mind, for my physical and emotional self.**

September 8 ❧ Patience, Marriage

Who can wait quietly while the mud settles?
—Lao-tzu

In the outside world, we may face misunderstanding as to the nature of chronic pain. Within marriage, we want the reassurance that our spouse cares. We want our partner to learn to adapt to changes brought on by the pain, as we are learning to do. When the other person offers resistance, we can become irritable.

Although I tire of hearing the admonition "Be patient," it is still good advice. Working out a marriage commitment always involves patience, and with the stress of chronic pain, it is a virtue badly needed.

There is much room for adjustment in a marriage affected by chronic pain. Whether it is through greater sharing of responsibilities, exploring a new interest to replace an activity that can no longer be done jointly, or learning to listen to one another, good changes can happen when each person is patient with the other.

Chronic pain affects every area of our lives, including marriage. Reaffirming the original commitment and being patient with each other can make the difference.

For today: **I'll accept my spouse and let gratitude come back to our marriage. Patience will follow.**

September 9 ∾ Time Management

I learned this at least by my experiment:
that if one advances confidently in the
direction of his dreams, and endeavors
to live the life which he has imagined,
he will meet with a success unexpected
in common hours.
—Henry David Thoreau

Thoreau said that lives are frittered away by detail and that, in simplifying, one gains success. In his day, he said that people had no time to be anything but machines. Despite technological progress, we can still feel the same way, particularly with the added demands and stress of chronic pain.

He said that, like delicate blossoms, we need to treat ourselves and others tenderly to preserve our fine qualities, which he felt were enhanced through simplicity.

Always a difficult question: How do we simplify our lives? A good place to start is to find a peaceful time and place that allows us to see our priorities more clearly. It is easy to run helter skelter from one responsibility to another, without thought of what is essential, how to save steps, what can be delegated, and what can wait.

To Thoreau, reflection was important, not only for its own sake, but for guidance in decision making. He even believed that daydreaming and building castles in the air were a valid use of one's time, as long as one eventually put the foundations under them. Reflect, simplify, and act. Putting these words into effect is worth our time.

FOR TODAY: **Demands on my time and myself can seem overwhelming. I'll find a way to reflect and simplify.**

September 10 ❧ Quiet

I have found that no exertion of the legs can bring two minds much nearer to one another.
—Henry David Thoreau

During his years at Walden Pond, Thoreau recalled that not only did life in the city not bring two minds together, but it did not always vanquish loneliness, either. He referred to himself as the most companionable of companions, and he considered natural objects to be sweet company. While living at Walden he listened to the pattering of raindrops and the hoot of an owl, and enjoyed watching the wary approaches of the red squirrels. Even in wild areas and in dreary weather he found identity and new avenues of thought. After two years of being alone, he left because he felt he had many more lives to live.

I yearn for a quiet place like Walden Pond, where uninterrupted thoughts could thrive, where I could discover what kind of companion I would be to myself, and where I could look only to myself and God to replace loneliness.

In any quiet place, there is a limit to the time I can spend there. Too much solitude makes it easier to notice my pain. Uninterrupted thoughts turn anxious and selfish, and I soon yearn for human contact.

I would not like to have two years to spend entirely alone, but I can snatch minutes here and there to reflect or to talk to God and bring together, rather than fragment, the various aspects of the life I live.

FOR TODAY: May time alone be a period of healing today.

> *Sometimes I feel as though my life is lasting*
> *just as long as there is something to live*
> *and work for.*
> —*Dietrich Bonhoeffer*

Facing chronic pain means facing questions I never thought I'd have to attempt to answer consciously. For each person, chronic pain poses different ones, but for me, some of them have been: What does quality of life mean? If my energy is precious, how can I best spend it? Where do I get my self-worth? Who needs me in their lives? Do I have honest, open relationships? And the ultimate question: Is living worth it?

Many of us have been so busy that we never have had to face such questions. Meeting the challenge of living with chronic pain forces us to. Just about the time I've worked the questions through, though, something happens to make me ask them anew. New questions crop up. Sometimes I can't answer them by myself and need help—professional, spiritual, or a friend's. It helps to have the reassurance that I have something to live and work for.

FOR TODAY: **What is life asking of me? Am I ready with an answer? If not, who can help me?**

> *All paths lead to the same goal: to convey*
> *to others what we are.*
> —Pablo Neruda

Self-esteem is made up of thoughts and feelings that we have about ourselves. High self-esteem can make us feel effective, productive, capable, and lovable. Low self-esteem can make us feel ineffective, worthless, incompetent, and unloved.

A failure at managing our pain can lower our self-esteem, but we don't have to give in to a poor self-image. There are things we can do. We can be the kind of people we want to be, we can enjoy others and offer more of ourselves to the world.

We can begin by asking ourselves questions, such as: Am I honest and open? Am I able to laugh at and learn from my mistakes? Do I look for and try new challenges? Do I give myself credit for trying?

With such information about ourselves, we can accept our strengths and weaknesses. We can take steps toward taking pride in our achievements, enjoying our own company, acting on what we think needs to be changed, and contributing to the world around us. Instead of overreacting to our mistakes, we can see what we can learn from them.

A helpful exercise is to draw a picture of ourselves doing something we enjoy or to cut out pictures from a magazine that convey our feelings about ourselves. First we start to know ourselves, and then we make any needed changes. Most of all, we refuse to think of pain as a personal failing that undermines our self-esteem.

FOR TODAY: I can have a healthy self-image in spite of the pain. I'll treat myself kindly today.

September 13 ❧ Focusing

As my suffering mounted, I soon realized
that there were two ways in which I could
respond to my situation—either to react with
bitterness or seek to transform the suffering
into a creative force. I decided to follow the
latter course.
—Martin Luther King, Jr.

A friend shows me the quilt blocks she has been working on. "It's my alternative to what I used to be able to do," she says, bringing out a beautiful old embroidered hanging. It is a huge counted cross-stitch picture with stitches so small that it resembles a painting.

"It would take me years to finish something like this now," she says, "because the position I use for doing it bothers me so much. Instead, I found something else I could do. I don't like doing it as well, but I'm learning to enjoy it. I've got to do something. Otherwise, I'll just sit in a chair and vegetate."

She sums it up so well. If we only look with longing and regret at what we used to be able to do, and we are afraid to try something new, we'll miss the opportunity to learn the art of accommodation and the chance to find another interest. Even if that one does not suit us, it can be the stepping-stone on the path that leads to finding our other creative aptitudes.

No, we can't vegetate. There are alternatives to explore, and focusing on what we can do helps point the way.

FOR TODAY: **It takes courage to change old ways of doing things, but I will keep an open mind to modifications of an old activity or be willing to try new alternatives.**

September 14 ¦ Assertiveness

Without discipline, there's no life at all.
—*Katharine Hepburn*

"May I have permission to take care of myself and do what I need to do to take charge of the pain?" We seldom verbalize our needs in such a way, but it is an important question to ask ourselves. Others often don't realize the significance of the actions we take to "stay on top" of our pain.

My friend says, "I've recently started driving separately to this weekly event that my spouse and I attend. After months of having my request to leave early ignored, I made this decision to depend only on myself to avoid a pain flare-up."

We are equals with others. If we meet resistance from another person, we firmly say, "This is what I need." Perhaps there are compromises, but if not, we stay on course and follow through with our plans. Doing what we need to do to take care of ourselves in a considerate but firm way —that's assertiveness.

For today: If I wait for others to give me permission to take care of myself, my needs may never be met. Aggression magnifies differences in a relationship, so I will favor an assertive style today.

September 15 ∾ Friends

A little girl was upset because she had an argument with her older brother, and, going to her room, she slammed the door behind her. In a few minutes, she sneaked into her mother's room and, too young to spell correctly, left a note that said, "Know oun likes me." When her mother saw the note, she hugged her daughter and reassured her that she was indeed loved.

If I isolate myself because of pain and negative emotions, such as anger, worry, frustration, or envy, I, too, can feel as if "no one likes me." I might convince myself that I have nothing positive to talk about, thereby justifying an excessive amount of time spent alone.

Once I am with friends, however, their positive feelings transfer over to me and become my own.

When I no longer take companionship for granted, it is a great feeling to be accepted and loved, to share and laugh with friends.

FOR TODAY: **I must take the initiative, sometimes, to be with friends.**

September 16 ❧ Problem Solving

> *Success is to be measured not so much by*
> *the position that one has reached in life as*
> *by the obstacles which he has overcome*
> *while trying to succeed.*
> —*Booker T. Washington*

Chronic pain brings us uncertainty and burden. We don't know what to deal with first—the problems it brings or the volatile emotions that are kindled.

First of all, we need to know that the center of our being is stable and able to adapt. In our humanness, we can ride out these moments of turmoil and manage both our problems and our emotions. Both elements come together to cause emotional pain.

Calmly, we can learn to clarify a particular problem, apart from the emotion that attends it, to see what action needs to be taken. We look at what resources we already have and what we might need to seek from the outside. Even when our emotions, such as fear or grief, are strong, we can problem-solve by breaking the problem into small pieces.

On another level, we can attend to our emotions by being mindful of what they are and telling ourselves that just as we learn to work with our physical pain, so we can work with our emotional pain. We can see negative emotions develop, accept the feelings, take a compassionate attitude toward ourselves, and learn what want or need they signify. We will gain confidence over our problems and cope with our emotions, rather than being blinded by them. Solutions will appear because uncertainty will not last forever.

FOR TODAY: **Problem solving begins with awareness of the situation and the emotions involved. An intuitive thought may open up new possibilities.**

September 17 ❧ Reaching Out

If you are reluctant to ask the way, you will
be lost.
—Malay proverb

Where are the answers to the questions that repeat themselves? Whom should I turn to, to "ask the way"? What kind of life am I after?

Many times, we don't stand still long enough even to know what the questions are. In a day with chronic pain we may be so busy keeping up with others that we may only act and react, taking little time to ask why we do what we do, and if we have a choice about it. This is a subtle form of denial, when we fail to take care of ourselves.

We might begin to know ourselves better and to consider our options regarding our time by asking questions such as: Do I say what I mean, and mean what I say? Do I let others make decisions for me that aren't in my best interest? Why do I allow this, and what options do I have? Can I let go of the embarrassment of asking for help?

"I don't want to bother anyone" is the attitude that can lead us into trouble. Lifting up the phone might seem to require the amount of strength needed to lift a car, but the relief of asking for help or guidance can be phenomenal. With practice, it often gets easier to do.

FOR TODAY: **It is so hard to call someone when I need it most but feel like exposing myself the least. Admitting my vulnerability will be worth the relief I feel after I contact someone I trust.**

September 18 ❧ Relationships

*So faith, hope, love abide, these three; but
the greatest of these is love.*
—*I Corinthians, 13:13*
The Bible, Revised Standard Version

The love that the passage describes talks about attitudes and actions, rather than emotions, which change from minute to minute. In my relationship with my spouse, if I choose to love, things will improve. It takes two committed individuals for the most satisfaction in marriage, but I can always improve the relationship with love.

I don't have to act negatively if I feel negative. For release, I can express my negativity to God, rather than impose it on others.

Love isn't always a warm feeling; sometimes it means demonstrating affection through loving acts, even when I don't feel loving. Simple courtesy may be all I can muster on a day when my pain is less tolerable.

Whether it is through my deeds or by complimenting my spouse, whether through asking his opinion or by accepting his faults (and, of course, the process is usually reciprocal), I can find a way to show love. Pain doesn't take away that ability.

FOR TODAY: **It is hard to be loving when we feel negative and in pain, but we can be courteous, or find other small ways to express affection. Such actions count.**

September 19 ∾ Solitude

> *A quiet mind cureth all.*
> *—Robert Burns*

In my quiet place, the CD player is off, as is the radio, the computer, and the TV. Everything is calm, quiet, and still. The only noise is the deep breathing of my sleeping dog. In my quiet place, my mind has a chance to pause and reflect, to contemplate the important things and not be frantic over the urgent things. It may be pressing that I meet deadlines, that the car is repaired, and that schedules run smoothly. But my quiet place gives me a chance to reflect on what is important and of most value.

It is important that I take care of myself through good nutrition, exercise, and rest. It is important that I have inner peace and that I realize that I have choices in the decisions I make. It is important that I realize that life and coping with chronic pain form a process and a journey, and that I must travel that journey as well as I can.

I love my quiet place, where important things are contemplated and the "how" is often revealed to me.

FOR TODAY: I will reserve my quiet place and retreat to it when I need to.

September 20   Depression, Goals

The prisoner who had lost faith in the future
—his future—was doomed.
—Viktor Frankl

When I am the most depressed, I feel no worth and I feel that I am a burden to others. I feel a sadness that shows no indication of leaving, a great lack of energy, and no motivation to get things done.

If we need professional help to break out of depression, we can seek it. Most of the time major depression can be treated successfully. Focusing on small goals has helped many. To achieve a simple goal is to feel capable and energized. In time, other goals can be accomplished.

A goal should be measurable, attainable, and, above all, realistic. For example, we can't expect to run a mile if we can't yet walk around the block. We can throw some enjoyment into a goal, such as, "I will call my brother once a month. I seldom see him and I always feel better after I call him." Goals can be as individual as we are.

For many, therapy and antidepressant medications are useful and important. For all of us, achieving goals can enhance self-worth and direct us toward a richer life.

FOR TODAY: Depression is a natural reaction to chronic pain, but there is hope for recovery. I will set a small goal today and work to reach it.

> *Isn't the whole problem of life the slow*
> *building up of an integral personality*
> *through the years? There's no point in a*
> *disintegrated life.*
> —D. H. Lawrence

Though according to the saying, time heals all wounds, time does not cure all pain. This is not to say that the nature of our pain never changes, but if we passively wait for the pain to leave, it may get worse.

That is the difference between acute and chronic pain. If we have a broken leg, we rest and immobilize the leg in a cast until it heals. If our appendix is removed, we can count on the incision healing in a specific amount of time.

Time may have healed our acute illness or injury but done nothing to change our pain levels. Rather than counting the days since the pain began or mindlessly watching calendar pages turn, time is used actively to recover from the negative effects of chronic pain. We all use time differently. For instance, it may take longer for some to finish the grieving process over their losses than others. It may take longer for some to form a new identity (for example, one separate from their work) in order to claim a new one. It may take longer for some to stop overprotecting the body part that hurts, in order to reach their highest activity level.

Time can work for all of us, no matter what our situation, the speed at which we progress in our physical, mental, emotional, and spiritual journey, or the type of support we have. It is never too late to begin to maximize our potential or to start to live.

FOR TODAY: Time is my gift. It gives me the opportunity to grow in courage and faith, and to live my life with conviction. I'll reflect on how dynamic time is to me and how it can help me build on what I have.

September 22 ❧ Love

She [Eleanor Roosevelt] would rather light a
candle than curse the darkness, and her
glow has warmed the world.
— *Adlai Stevenson*

Autumn leaves were falling during our camping excursion, and the forest was hushed by the stillness in the air. As the glowing sun set, dark shadows lengthened and coolness spread as quickly as the dark. When the campfire was lit, a small flame flickered like a birthday candle. A red spark ignited the small tepee of sticks and wood, and a glowing blaze warmed my face.

Whether it is lighting a candle or a campfire, a small flicker is all that is needed to create heat. What small flame can arise in a life plagued with pain?

Love is the flame that ignites the fire of joy and warmth, which spreads to others. Romantic love, parental love, mature love, the love of friends, of solitude, of nature, of God, of art, of music, and of literature can all serve as the flicker that ignites such a fire.

Love will come; it cannot be forced. Love can spread— that is our challenge.

FOR TODAY: **Love has great potential. I can light some-one's darkness with it today. It will spread, and the embers will warm the world.**

September 23 ∾ Open Mind

The truth often sounds paradoxical.
—*Lao-tzu*

Living with chronic pain has its paradoxes. Here are some:

- Taking care of ourselves may mean taking time to be alone, but paradoxically, when we're really hurting, we may still need to be around other people to keep our spirits up.
- A group of people with chronic pain have serious problems but they also have funny stories and like a good laugh.
- We accept our pain, but we don't give in to it.
- Honesty is a great virtue, but we use discretion in talking about our pain.
- We help others but observe our own needs.

So much of what we've learned about chronic pain is contrary to what we first thought. Instead of being good for us, resting all day can increase pain. When we're in a lot of pain, sometimes we need the company of others to avoid sinking into self-pity. People with chronic pain have been in funny circumstances that are worth laughing about, and humor helps. Honesty is good, but we don't need to tell everyone how bad our pain is, eliciting their pity but not their help. Finally, it's good to help others, but we're no good to someone else unless we first take care of ourselves.

Yes, the truth often sounds paradoxical, but in living it, it makes sense.

FOR TODAY: I will examine my old notions about living with chronic pain and be open to new ideas.

September 24 ❧ Pain Behavior

We all live with the objective of being
happy; our lives are all different
and yet the same.
—Anne Frank

Three-toed tracks of a bird ran beside a river where a young girl and her mother walked along the sand. "Look, Mommy," the little girl said, "it must be chicken tracks!"

Things are not always as they seem. Sometimes, as with the child's experience, this is due to limited knowledge. Sometimes it is because of the way we look at things.

For example, families do not understand our situation, and we think they're uncaring if they don't ask us how we're feeling. They may, in fact, be doing the best thing possible for us and for themselves.

Families show a loving response when they take measures to resist being ensnared in, and help us be freed from, the chronic pain trap. This happens when they divert our attention off the subject of pain, when they include us in activities that help us stay physically active, when they make interesting plans in and out of the home, and when they encourage us when our efforts to participate waver.

A lessening of our preoccupation with pain is what we strive for. Our families can help. What looks like neglect may be love in disguise.

FOR TODAY: **Chronic pain can take its toll on family members. They can help me most by giving my pain the least attention and by encouraging me to stay involved in their lives.**

Too many activities and people and things.
Too many worthy activities, valuable things,
and interesting people. For it is not merely
the trivial which clutters our lives but the
important as well.
—Anne Morrow Lindbergh

I have muttered many a "Yes, but . . ." sentence in my experience with chronic pain. At many times, we have wanted to settle for nothing less than complete pain relief and a cure. A quick fix was all we could think about. Yet trying something new frightened us, and made us feel overwhelmed by the challenge and the risk of failure.

I silently replied, "Yes, but . . ." to most of the suggestions offered to me. Regarding exercise: "Yes, but it's a hassle; it's boring; and my problem is more serious." Today I feel better physically and mentally because of exercise. Regarding relaxation: "Yes, but I don't have time." Today I make time in order to conserve energy. Regarding being assertive, asking for help, and finding solutions that work for me: "Yes, but I don't think I can change." Today my flexibility and open-mindedness can make the difference between a good day and a severe pain flare-up.

Changing our attitudes can be hard, and we can be cynical because of past promises of relief that failed, but it's time to let the past go. What works for one may not help another, but we can be open to suggestions about anything that might help.

FOR TODAY: I'll consider trying something I've said "Yes, but . . ." to in the past. If needed, I'll take guidance from health professionals, a pain support group, or pain management specialists.

September 26 ❧ Peace

When men lack a sense of awe, there
will be disaster.
—*Lao-tzu*

The sun is bright, the park's green grass extends all around me, the bees pass from clover to clover, the turtles are lined up on the log by the lake, the water is clear, and the swans gracefully move across the still blue. Life is worth living, I tell myself.

All is right in my world. I'm not aware of the sound of traffic because it is not important here. My craving to return to this city park has been satisfied, and nothing can extinguish my delight.

Is there comfort to be found away from here? What will happen to me when the sun's rays fade, when I have to turn away from my company of friends and make room for the homeless? Will my burdens increase once I leave? The wind drops, and I go home. The memories remain, and for some time, all is still right in my world.

FOR TODAY: Life is worth living when I can hold on to something dear.

> *The first point of courtesy must always*
> *be truth.*
> —Ralph Waldo Emerson

"How are you?" is puzzling to us with chronic pain because a response of "Just fine" is not entirely honest. It once angered me that those who asked the question didn't seem to notice if my response was positive or negative. I wanted someone to listen to my pent-up frustration about the pain, but few would listen for very long. I finally realized that "How are you?" is used most often as a polite gesture to start a conversation.

Today when the question is offered in passing, I usually have no trouble saying "Fine." If people are concerned and really are asking me about how I feel on a day when I'm not doing well, I say, "I've been better" or "Not as good as last week." If they want to follow with other questions, I allow them to.

With a good friend I might even be very truthful and say, "I feel awful." It all depends on the closeness of the person.

FOR TODAY: **Not being truthful about my pain can, in fact, be more courteous than telling the truth. People closest to me can count on a more honest answer.**

September 28 ❧ Boredom

Somebody's boring me. I think it's me.
—Dylan Thomas

Chronic pain has a way of wanting to take control of our lives. It happens easily if we feel that our situation is hopeless. Apathy pervades our being, and we can't seem to look past the pain to anything else that might concern us.

All is not lost. There are people, organizations, communities, and things that need our attention. Involvement of any kind can seem overwhelming when we are fatigued or in great pain, so we must pace ourselves. But there is always, as long as we live, something that we can be interested in.

For one person, it may be employment; for another, a local pain support group; for another, school; and for another, a yard and garden. People and things need us; they need the sensitivity that only we can bring.

FOR TODAY: I don't need to be bored today. There is much that I can tend to in a meaningful, sensitive way.

September 29 ॐ Exercise

Live each day as if thy life were just begun.
—*Johann W. von Goethe*

We with chronic pain need to stretch our muscles every day. Stretching helps us with mobility, promotes good circulation, and reinforces for us the idea that there is something we can do to help ourselves. It not only can decrease our pain levels through better muscle tone, but it causes us to feel that we have done something helpful for ourselves.

Because not all exercises were created equal, some may be of great benefit, while others are not. Obtaining our doctors' approval is important before we begin. Walking for short distances may be most some are capable of. Others can do floor exercises, walk, swim, and work with weights and equipment at a health club.

In either case, we start slowly, exercise until we feel a gentle pull, and gradually make progress. We want to be as healthy as we can and have a degree of control over pain. Exercise can help.

FOR TODAY: **I'll put on some music and do stretching exercises today, setting up a program that will help me feel better.**

September 30 ❧ Pain Stories

Accept your own aloneness and stick to it,
all your life. And then accept the times
when the gap is filled in, when
they come. But they've got to come.
You can't force them.
—D. H. Lawrence

As an adult, I still enjoy collecting fall leaves to press between the pages of a book. Most often, if I have placed them in a dictionary and find them months later, while looking up a word, I discard them. When I first saw them in the park, though, I couldn't bear to leave the finest ones. I didn't want to see them curl up, turn brown, and blow away.

I used to think that the only pretty leaf was a red leaf, perhaps because I live in a part of the country where red ones are rare. Now I value a greater variety in my collection and appreciate each one's individuality.

Chronic pain affects rich and poor, young and old, the educated and the uneducated. Within this variety, each person has his or her own story to tell. Alike but different, we share a common bond of similar emotions and some of the same problems.

I used to long to talk to someone with an identical story, but I have not met such a person. We are the same, but different; alone, but part of a greater whole. Indeed, I now listen for more than symptoms and concentrate on how pain affects all of us. I don't need to keep searching for that rare red leaf, the person with the same story as mine. I appreciate the variety of experiences that people with chronic pain share.

FOR TODAY: **Other people's stories offer me the insight that others feel as I do. I'll let in the people who have stories to tell.**

OCTOBER

October 1 ❧ Honesty

I gave him [Rousseau] a written sketch of
my life. He studied it and he loved me with
all my failings.
—James Boswell

The sumac glows a fiery red, as does the poison ivy on the vine that winds up the tree in the nearby woods. They are alike, in that the color of each is so brilliant and passionate. I want to save the sumac's leaf, because its color is exceptional this year, but in the woods I recoil at the sight of the poison ivy vine that still clings to the barren tree.

Likening myself to the leaves, how am I adorned? Like the sumac, is my appearance and manner appealing and attractive, inviting approach? Or do I impress as an outward show only, like the radiant but misleading poison ivy?

It is substance that counts. I want to display an authentic self and not one of deceit. On any given day, I don't want to fool people close to me that my pain is not an issue when it is; I don't want to delude them into believing that I am accepting when I am not; and I don't want to fool them into believing that I don't have limitations when I do.

I want my attraction and appeal to be actual and not just a façade—my passion for life real and not just a show. My inner self needs refinement for my outer self to be authentic.

FOR TODAY: **Honesty and directness are what I need today. I won't pretend that I'm something I'm not to the ones nearest to me.**

October 2 ❧ Happiness

> *Flowers are like the pleasures of the world.*
> —*William Shakespeare*

When we plant a fall bulb, we don't expect to see a flower the next month. We are willing to wait until spring, knowing that after a long winter of cold and snow, our excitement will be even greater.

Sometimes happiness comes when we have forgotten about wanting it. When our minds are absorbed in a project or when we are engrossed in a good movie, our pain may fade from the forefront of our consciousness.

Still, we can't force it away, as many of us have tried to do. Some have spent large sums of money trying to find the most expert opinion, medical miracle, or cure. Self-determination falters when our attempts to force our way to pain relief fail.

We can't force happiness, either, but we can open our hearts to receive it. By letting go of the fantasy of a cure, we live today in quiet confidence that although the pain continues, there is much we can do to keep it in perspective of our whole being. Even as we experience emotional swings, we strive for emotional evenness and stability.

The flower of happiness may open today or it may wait for another season. Growth may be subtle until, finally, beauty appears. The thing that makes us smile may be the first flower in a garden of gladness.

FOR TODAY: **Happiness may come when I least expect it. I'll open my heart to receive it today.**

October 3 ❧ Procrastination

> *Say, shall my little bark attendant sail,*
> *pursue the triumph and partake of the goal?*
> —*Alexander Pope*

When I aim for perfection, I often feel so stressed that I quit and find a reason to procrastinate. If I lower my expectations, I can relax, be more creative, and get more done.

I first have to ask myself how important a goal is to me and if it is worth my commitment. I look at possible reasons for my procrastination. Some may include being unmotivated, not having the information I need to begin, being afraid of failure, blaming others for imposing on my time, and not having self-confidence.

If I've decided that an activity is right for me and that I will pursue it to the best of my ability, I can make plans to fight procrastination.

I may need a plan for handling distractions or for breaking the job into parts. Once I get started I'll find a way over the hurdle of procrastination.

FOR TODAY: **I can accomplish something I am working toward today. I can make a plan and start some action.**

October 4 ❧ Gentleness with Ourselves

But I want, first of all—in fact, as an end to
all these other desires—to be at peace
with myself.
—Anne Morrow Lindbergh

Our pain has wounded us and it seems that we will never heal. Our bodies know our wounds; so does our serenity, our self-worth, and our emotional lives. Peace may be unknown to us as we experience our wounds growing deeper and deeper. We may find ourselves powerless to stop the pain from eroding more of ourselves.

How do we begin to heal? The most fundamental action to take is to begin to think gently of ourselves, to treat ourselves as we would a best friend. Would we not have compassion toward him, should he be in pain? Of course we would. Would we remind her of repeated mistakes she's made that have increased her pain? We wouldn't unless it was in a spirit of love. Aren't we worthy of our own goodwill and kindness? Yes, we are.

Besides treating ourselves as friends, we can try to remove our core self from the pain and see our bodies as less of an enemy. Someone told me, "I pictured that a kitten was lying on my area of pain. I had a lot of compassion toward it because I saw that it, like me, was hurt and frightened. After that, I quit being so hard on myself for the things I did and how I felt. I discovered that I was capable of comforting myself."

As hard as it is, we can resist what is not good for us, even our own negative thoughts.

FOR TODAY: **I have a new friend and it is I. Though I am not perfect, when I see myself in a new light, emotional wounds will heal. Peace is near.**

October 5 ∾ Pain Flare-up

They also serve, who only stand and wait.
—John Milton

"Be good to your body and use your brain," a friend recommended. She knew how I was feeling. I'd gotten the idea of doing a form of exercise I hadn't been able to do in a long time. I had pushed my body into it, and the next day I was incapacitated. It took me days to recover, and I felt hopeless of ever changing my overdo-underdo pain cycle.

My chronic pain friend helped me understand that moving forward while recovering from a flare-up is important, even if it means having extremely slow increases in activity. Preventing a flare-up, when I can, involves using my brain and being good to my body. I can listen to an intuitive thought and recognize warning signals from my body. Learning to do these things also lessens my dependence on health professionals. My main accountability is to myself.

FOR TODAY: I am physically and emotionally fatigued by repeatedly pushing myself beyond my limitations. I don't have to do that today. I will practice patience and proceed slowly.

October 6 ✺ Love

> *Mother whispered, "See, you don't have to*
> *think about doing the right thing. If*
> *you're for the right thing, then*
> *you do it without thinking."*
> —Maya Angelou

"What is the best and most loving response I can make?" sounds like a good question to ask ourselves when someone has upset us, but it can be so difficult to follow.

The best and most loving response to others may be only a return to the basics of simple courtesy and kindness. It can be extremely difficult, when directed at those we tolerate least or when pain can create a desire to act selfishly.

From our relations with those we find especially annoying, we can learn the lesson of tolerance and how to act our best, in spite of our pain problems and attitude. These people, too, may have troubles that are unknown to us and are in need of our unconditional love.

FOR TODAY: I can always profit from my experiences with others. I have flaws and so do they. Through tolerance, I can learn about the love that asks nothing in return and discover many others in need of empathy.

October 7 ∾ Faith

*Inside myself is a place where I live all
alone, and that's where you renew your
springs that never dry up.*
—Pearl S. Buck

What if I lived near a river that constantly overflowed,
sweeping away house and possessions, leaving me sad and
frustrated? What if I rebuilt and bought new furniture,
only to have it happen again? I might move or build on
higher ground. Those actions wouldn't be foolish, but if I
thought that knowing the name of the river would stop the
flood, that would indeed be foolish. The name of the river
would be unimportant—its devastating effects are what
would make me take action.

That's how I feel about my diagnosis. Enough doctors
have agreed on a term or two, but it doesn't help me very
much to have that knowledge. It doesn't change the reality
of pain. That is, I still have it. Like identifying the river, I
need to do more than know about my condition. For me,
building on higher ground means to find an inner, spiritual
core where I am less devastated by pain's ravages. The
pain is there, but it does not engulf or overwhelm me. I am
not ruined, but safe and secure.

FOR TODAY: Seeking greater self-awareness can help me
tap into strengths I may not know I possess. It can renew my springs of peace.

October 8 ❧ Living in the Present Moment

There is a wholeness about the fully grown
man which makes him concentrate on the
present moment.
—Dietrich Bonhoeffer

Once, as a nurse, reviewing my patient's chart, I was shocked to learn that although she was ninety-six years old, this was only her second time in the hospital. This visit was necessitated by back pain.

I introduced myself, gave her her medications, and remarked, "It looks by your chart that you've been very healthy all your life." With a serious look (and one that I remember so well), she said, "Yes, but I have back pain *now.*"

It's important to concentrate on what's happening today. For a long time I denied I had chronic pain, as most of us do. It was something I could get rid of, if only I tried harder, spent more money, or found the cure.

Like the older lady, I can say to myself, "Yes, I rarely had a health problem before my injury, but I have chronic pain now."

Now the question is "What can I do about it today?" I never appreciated the suggestion to "learn to live with it," but live with it I will. Despite the pain, I will live this day to the fullest, not worrying about tomorrow and not regretting the past.

FOR TODAY: **The past is past. I have chronic pain today. Using tried and as of yet untried coping skills and means of support, I will choose healthy ways to respond to this changed life.**

Humor was another of the soul's weapons in
the fight for self-preservation.
—Viktor Frankl

We have many stories to tell: sad stories, frustrating stories, courageous stories, and, of course, serious stories.

Oh, but the funny stories we have! At the time, they seemed far from humorous, but looking back and sharing them, especially with someone with chronic pain, we find reason to laugh at ourselves.

One man told me that he once got angry at his dog and threw him out of his way, twisting his back. "He must have weighed eighty pounds, and I spent two weeks recovering from my stupidity," the man said. The man told me of how, after the incident, he needed to spend the next day in bed. He wanted his wife only to take food to the bedroom and to leave him alone otherwise because he was so angry at himself.

I laughed at the scene. I pictured the man being left food by his wife, like a prisoner. It wasn't funny that he hurt himself, that he could have hurt his dog, or that he made his bedroom his prison, but in looking back at my own past misfortunes, I remember thinking that I could only laugh or cry. Laughter can, indeed, be a great release.

FOR TODAY: **I'll learn to laugh at myself and not take myself so seriously today.**

October 10 ❧ Denial

What jailer so inexorable as one's self!
—*Nathaniel Hawthorne*

I have buried myself under layers of denial. Denying that
my condition was and would be a fact of life for me
seemed to protect me from its reality. Such a reality signi-
fied loss, and I didn't want to give up anything—especially
my freedom to do what I wanted, when I wanted to do it.
The longer I denied the pain, the more I was made a slave
to it.

Denial is the protective mechanism against the shock
that comes from admitting that we have chronic pain. It
keeps us from acknowledging reality until we are ready to
cope with it. Readiness comes when we feel secure and
strong enough to deal with it. For some, this takes a long
time, while for others, the acceptance comes more quickly.
All proceed at their individual pace, in their own time.

We also might deny that we need to make any changes
in order to work with our pain. This can enslave us to
rigidity, negativity, and the indignation of "I won't change
for the sake of pain or anyone who tells me what to do."
In this, denial slows us and our attitudes enslave us.
Changes takes time. We may not be able to force acceptance of the need to change, but we can be open to it and,
just as we accept pain's reality, move forward in our own
time.

FOR TODAY: **I want to move through denial, so that I can
get on with the job of living. I'm willing to take even
baby steps in a forward direction today.**

October 11 ❧ Gratitude, Suicidal Depression

I had to experience despair, thoughts of suicide, in order to experience grace.
—Herman Hesse

A doctor once told his patient that he didn't know how the man could cope with the cancerous skin disorder that affected him. The doctor remarked that he would surely kill himself if he were in the patient's position. The man had at one time considered suicide. In deciding against taking his life, the patient concluded that either he could lie in bed and turn his back against the wall or he could try to get from life what fun and enjoyment he could, considering his disease. He called the good things that happened "bonuses," and he began to see that many days had bonuses for him, found even in a good TV show or an interesting conversation.

People may have told us, too, that they "don't know how we do it." Chronic pain is not listed under the heading of "life-threatening illnesses," yet it does threaten everything of value to us if we let it.

We have all felt desperate at some point, not knowing how we could possibly live with chronic pain. We do, though, like the cancer patient, by looking for the good things—the little bonuses—and trying to live fully from day to day.

FOR TODAY: **Sometimes I surprise myself at how well I'm coping with my pain. That is a bonus, too.**

October 12 ❧ Feeling Abandoned by God; Grief, Healing

> *Then, when you failed in everything, when*
> *what you had slowly built up was blown*
> *away in a moment, and you must toilsomely*
> *begin again from the beginning; when your*
> *arm was weak, your step wavering, then you*
> *still held fast to your expectation of faith,*
> *which is victory.*
> —Sören Kierkegaard

Chronic pain can foster loneliness, and the most painful aloneness I can feel is that of being abandoned by God. I pray for relief of pain, and none comes. I ask to be shown some good result from the pain, and instead, all I can see before me is the vision of being without it. I ask to see meaning and all I see is brokenness, anger, guilt, and grief. The magnitude of my loss overwhelms and threatens to crush me.

At the point of being filled with bitterness and despair, my only recourse is to cry out to God. I cry in anger at Him for not demonstrating His power by removing my pain, and I cry in anguish to Him with guilt over my allowing the pain to consume me.

Anger and guilt give way to emptiness, and I feel as if I am falling. I fall away from people, and then I fall farther and farther from myself. I descend still further, unsure of my fate.

At last I fall into the waiting arms of God, who has heard me without judgment and is unmoved by my anger. Peace envelops me. I am held close, not abandoned. Through rage and remorse, through complaint and lament,

He has listened to me. Now the feelings fade, and grief has turned to healing.

When my world is falling apart, I bring Him the wasteland of my life. In my feelings of abandonment, He comes back to me, because my purposelessness has brought me to Him. I feel God's love and am no longer alone and forgotten.

FOR TODAY: **God, stay by me in my pain even though I may be oblivious of Your presence.**

October 13 ❧ Understanding

No soul is desolate as long as there is a
human being for whom it can feel
trust and reverence.
—George Eliot

My sister-in-law called to apologize for seeming insensitive to my pain. Surprised, I reassured her that I didn't note any such attitude. It was rare that I mentioned my pain around her, but I had that day. "I still feel bad," she said, "because I try, but I just don't have the understanding to be able to relate to what you go through."

"I know," I said. "Things happen to others and I want to feel what they feel in order to help, but I just can't."

"My whole concept of pain is that it's something that you have and you get over it. I have no idea of what it's like when it goes on and on," she said in a frustrated tone of voice. I felt glad that I'd gotten to the point of no longer demanding that others understand.

"It's okay. It's nice that you care," I said.

When I hung up the phone, I thought about how I hadn't opened up much to her about pain's personal effects on me. I'd never admitted her into my worst moments of despair, I'd kept many protective barriers up, and I'd not exposed my vulnerabilities. How could she be more sensitive when I showed only emotional stoicism?

I know now that it's safe to expose myself to her. She cares and that's important.

FOR TODAY: **There are people I can trust my intimate self with. It's time I let someone care about me.**

October 14 ∾ Pain Management

Let me listen to me and not them.
—*Gertrude Stein*

A study at a medical center concluded that a high "helplessness factor" was part of a formula that led to psychological distress and depression. It found that the degree of pain control and the quantity of negative self-statements affected the quality of coping attempts.

As we already know, the management of our pain can be complex. We do feel helpless at times and our self-esteem can suffer when our efforts fail to make an impact on our pain. A friend told me, "I did everything right, like pacing myself, and I still hurt more today." With the feeling of a loss of control comes distress and depression.

What is it that works nonmedically for us? If not every time, how about some or most of the time? One person's technique may work for another, or it may aggravate the next person's pain. Whether it is exercise, visualization and deep relaxation, distraction and humor, prayer and meditation, or writing in a journal and crying, we can experiment to find what it is that can help us impact our perception of pain and enable us to feel more in charge of our lives.

FOR TODAY: **I may find a technique that I can benefit from daily or maybe one that I'll use only occasionally. Some pain management techniques may not affect my pain to the degree that I'd like. I'm open to discovering for myself what works best for me.**

October 15 ❧ Self-pity

> *If we look beyond ourselves at that which is greater than we, then we can feel called to help others in just the moment when we ourselves need the help most urgently—we can help. A power works through us which is not of us.*
> —Paul Tillich

I can't afford a poor-me attitude for any great length of time. I may not deliberately choose a life of negativity and victimization, but it is easy to be drawn into it. A sort of darkness sweeps over me and prevents the light of hope from shining in. I have to guard against it, because the combination of pain and self-pity have the power to ruin everything that is important to me.

Pain is real, and anyone in pain sometime feels, "Don't I have a right to feel sorry for myself?" It's true that the recognition of pain is necessary and its complete denial is unhealthy, but self-pity turns the recognition of pain into a rehearsal of adversity, disappointment, and misfortune. Talk about feeling awful eventually makes us feel even worse.

When we are pitying ourselves, we complain and make more demands on others. Initially we may get a lot of attention, but then rebellions and conflicts result and we end up feeling that others don't care. We don't want to feel sorry for ourselves; we resolve not to; but we don't know how to change.

In self-pity and desperation I ask God to set me free from my prison, to help me accept my pain, and to show me the gifts and talents that, even yet, I possess.

With God's help, I have a chance of being sensitive to

others and to create harmony instead of confusion and turmoil. I receive a gift from my spiritual Guide and Helper: freedom from self-pity's bondage.

FOR TODAY: **God, free me from self-pity and enable me to be a blessing to others.**

October 16 ❧ Fun

> *You have reached the pinnacle of success as*
> *soon as you become uninterested in money,*
> *compliments, or publicity.*
> —Dr. O. A. Battista

"Go, and have fun," my friend said, when I was contemplating whether to join my family on a family vacation. "Fun—what's that?" I thought.

Fun is a word that some of us have practically removed from our vocabulary. We're overly serious; we're afraid of doing something that may cause us more pain; and we just don't have the energy. Self-pity and depression may be sapping so much of our strength that we don't have room for fun. Unless we can have fun and be pain-free at the same time, we may not think it worth trying.

Doing something that brings us pleasure is well worth the effort. We don't have to be serious all the time, and it is good to be around others who can and do have fun. Sometimes it is contagious, and we join in without even thinking about it. The pain will be there, but it might take a backseat. We won't mind. Without it to cloud our view, we might even enjoy the ride.

FOR TODAY: I'll let myself have fun, even for a short time, even if it takes effort and even if I'm self-conscious. It is worth it to rediscover how to have fun.

October 17 ❧ Weight Loss

> *Go easy on yourself along the way.*
> —Joan Borysenko

Many people with chronic pain have gained weight, and this lowers their self-esteem. Then they feel frustrated at being unable to lose the extra pounds.

Weight gain usually happens as a result of a lower level of activity, lower metabolism due to medication, or dieting. (The body thinks it is starved and slows the metabolism.) As we age, it seems harder to lose weight, too.

When this happens we need to set realistic goals about our weight loss. We need to lower our expectations and strive to be patient. The loss of even one pound a week is a reasonable goal. We are tempted to restrict our food intake severely, but this is neither healthy nor effective for lasting weight loss.

If we become discouraged at slow progress, the weight can come back because we revert to old eating habits. Slow and steady should be our aim.

While we are trying to lose weight, we need to be easy on ourselves and realize that we are beautiful inside, no matter what we weigh. We can congratulate ourselves for small successes while being patient during plateaus and slow progress. We also can strive to increase our activity in a slow and steady way. There is no magic, but we'll achieve better results by a slow but persistent program.

FOR TODAY: **So many things require patience. While I wait for the weight to come off, I'll accept how I look and not let it prevent me from being the person I want to be.**

October 18 ❧ Fear

He has not learned the lesson of life who
does not every day surmount a fear.
—Martin Luther King, Jr.

It is hard to face our fears and take risks. We tell ourselves we shouldn't be afraid, and like the child who fears the dark, we are haunted even more. We can have all sorts of fears—specific ones, such as "I'm afraid of going places because it might increase my pain"; general ones, such as "I have a lot of anxiety and I don't even know where it's coming from"; and future-oriented ones, such as "I'm afraid of what my pain will be like as I grow older." There is also the fear of rejection or abandonment: "I'm afraid everyone will leave me if I don't start to get better."

We need to walk through each of our fears, pass through them, and move on in courage. Fears aren't facts, but we won't know that until we face them. Sometimes we need the help of God or another person. Saying what we are afraid of out loud to another person can be humbling, but it can help to loosen the grip that fear has on us.

Taking risks is important in overcoming fear, as well. We can risk asking for help even though we fear being rejected, and we can try new things in order to improve our ability to succeed. Fear can be faced and mastered as we live purposefully, from moment to moment and day to day.

FOR TODAY: **I realize that fear does not need to paralyze me today. I trust that a power larger than I will walk with me through my fears.**

October 19 ❧ Courage

> *The hero is no braver than the ordinary*
> *man, but he is brave five minutes longer.*
> —*Ralph Waldo Emerson*

After some sessions with a caring professional, I was ready to cope with chronic pain, using the tools I had been given. I had learned how to get more deeply relaxed than I ever had before, how to be more assertive, and how to feel less guilty about taking care of myself first.

One of the last things he said to me before I left on the final day was, "Now comes the hard part." I didn't like the sound of those words. Hadn't I been through enough already? Wasn't it going to get easier and easier?

I am better equipped now, but this is the hard part—to keep coping after the initial surge of energy that comes from believing that "pain does not have ultimate control."

The hard part comes in reacquiring happiness and living meaningfully. It is hard to go beyond the persistent will to survive and on to the richness of experiences that await us every day, but we can do it. With practice and changed attitudes, life with pain does get easier in many ways.

We can go beyond prevailing and move on to living fully. It isn't easy, it takes courage, and it may be the struggle of our lives; but our efforts can be transformed into celebration.

FOR TODAY: **I am ready to meet the challenge of dealing with chronic pain. Although my condition may be long term, I need only to experience today's pain and delight in what goodness I find in this one day.**

October 20   Visualization, Depression

I have not become downhearted. Life is
everywhere. Life, life in ourselves, not in
what is outside us.
—Fyodor Dostoyevsky

By using visualization, I can, at times and to some degree, alter my perception of pain. I may picture my pain as a large red circle and, in my mind, visualize it turning into a pale pink, shrinking in size and in intensity. I recognize my pain but, rather than dwelling on it and thinking about how badly I hurt, my mind is focused on reducing it.

We also can use visualization to picture the kind of person we want to be or the things we might like to have in the future.

If depression is our problem, we picture ourselves as winners rather than losers. We picture that we put depression in a small box, lock it, and say, "I'm locking my depression away. I am free of it." We can visualize ourselves as happy and motivated. Perhaps we are working on something that, because of depression, we have not been able to do. We picture ourselves being in control of the pain, at peace and proud of something we have done.

Visualization helps us picture what we would like in such areas as relationships, education, leisure, and creativity. Although it may sound as if we are only fooling ourselves with our imagination, visualization can provide an opportunity to look at the goals we want to strive for and the direction we want to take. The chance to be confident and in control of the pain can start with a visualization.

FOR TODAY: Picturing changes in my mind and imagination can be helpful to me as I plan a course to take. Being a winner starts with visualizing myself as one today.

October 21   ❧   Acceptance, Powerlessness

Beginnings are apt to be shadowy.
—Rachel Carson

No one can see my pain, but nonetheless, I am rather powerless over it. I can affect it somewhat through my attitude and pain management techniques, but the bottom line is that I cannot make it go away. No one can.

A member of my chronic pain support group said she finally was relieved when she was told that there was nothing left to try. She was relieved because she didn't have to have her expectations elevated only to be let down, because she didn't have to chase after any more cures, because she could stop spending money on treatments that did her no good, and because she could attend to other things in her life.

For me, the pain is. It's a given, a fact. It's my biggest challenge, but it's not my only problem. Life needs to be taken care of, after being forsaken or "put on hold" for so long. I can attend to my life only when I realize my powerlessness over pain and use my energy to build on what is good in my life. This I am eager to do.

FOR TODAY: **How do I react to my chronic pain? Accepting my powerlessness leads me to find new approaches to living with pain and to expect that life can still be good, even with the pain.**

October 22 ❧ Medication

*It is no easy thing for a principle to become
a man's own unless each day he maintain it
and work it out in his life.*
—Epictetus

I remember being psychologically dependent on my medication. At the time, I was taking a narcotic because I could not imagine life with constant pain. I developed such tolerance to it that it did no more for me than an aspirin would. Still, I was not willing to surrender to the fact that it had lost its effectiveness. Since I knew that my doctor would not prescribe anything stronger, I clung to the idea that, somehow, it would regain its potency.

One holiday I found my prescription bottle empty. I panicked; how could I get through the day without my medication? My pain became severe, further reinforcing my desire for my pills. Eventually I visited the hospital and was given a few days' supply.

Yet before I had taken even one pill, my pain decreased dramatically. This forced me to face the truth about my reliance on the drug, despite its ineffectiveness. I also was able to see the direct effect of stress and fear on my pain.

Some people in pain need strong medication. My experience taught me the difference between my body's need for it and my mind's need of reassurance that I could cope with the pain. This was the starting point of a search for contentment outside medication.

FOR TODAY: **Before reaching for a pill, I might consider using heat or cold, relaxation, meditation, exercise, or a distracting activity. I'm learning to discover what other methods besides medication can help.**

> *I am larger than I thought, I did not know I*
> *held so much goodness.*
> —*Walt Whitman*

Sometimes it's hard for me to be honest. I'm so careful about not using my pain as an excuse that sometimes I fail to be truthful. Often I cause myself more pain by participating in an activity that I should refrain from or failing to plan an activity so that I don't exceed my limitations.

For example, I know that I cannot "shop till I drop," but I want to choose the perfect gift. How can I do that if I haven't seen everything in the mall? I may not enjoy catalog shopping, but it may be my best option for conserving my energy. Most often it is I who pressure myself.

Sometimes I feel pressured by what I think others want me to do. I respect myself when I say no to something that may harm me. It is not an excuse but a fact. No is a short word, but it is often the hardest one to say. Unless we're able to say it, we can cause our bodies more harm, and resentments may build until they damage our relationships.

When we say no at appropriate times, we are being true to ourselves. We need not have a long script planned. "No, not now" or "I have to quit now" is enough. There need be no apologies, no regrets—just honesty.

FOR TODAY: **I will say no when yes is not in my best interest. My capacity for being assertive is growing larger. Being true to my needs is vital. Taking care of myself first, I have enough energy for others in my life.**

October 24 ❧ Visualization

*Every event in the visible world is the effect
of an "image," that is, of an idea in the
unseen world.*
—I Ching

A friend once told me, "My pain is part of my life now.
From here on, it's a mind game." I didn't understand what
she meant at first. I thought, "My pain is real. I can't just
think it away." That is still true, but I can, at times, alter it
somewhat.

Visualization is a way of taking some of my attention
from the pain, relaxing tense muscles all over my body,
and helping me find personal images for my pain and pain
relief.

I lie down in a favorite, quiet place, close my eyes, and
picture that I am lying on the beach. The sun warms the
part of my body that has pain, the part that I can see in my
mind as knotted, twisted ropes. I see them untangling into
loose strands, shrinking until they fall off me. Next I picture myself in the future, standing on the beach with loved
ones, watching porpoises and feeling little pain. After relaxing and distracting my mind from the pain with visualization, I am better able to cope with the circumstances of
the day.

FOR TODAY: **Visualization makes me feel content. I can
create my own scene today.**

> *Few people can fail to generate a self-healing process when they become genuinely involved in healing others.*
> —Theodore Isaac Rubin

People annoy us. They make demands on our time. They anger us. They're not who we wish they were. They don't do what we'd like them to do. They make us unhappy. They even make our pain worse.

We lash out at them or we sulk with an I'll-show-you attitude. We balk at the accusation that we ourselves may be self-centered and difficult to get along with.

One of the first things we need to do is to examine what our objective is in dealing with people. Our main aim is to develop the best possible relations with each person we know, even to love each one. That may seem like a big order, but it is something we strive for.

We can start by being tolerant and even courteous, forgiving others for their flaws as we hope that they would do toward us. We can look to see if we have had a part in causing an angry exchange or a situation that brings about resentments. Because of chronic pain, our bodies may not seem to be working in harmony. This we can't change. We can, however, try to work and live in harmony with others.

Most of all, we can let go of harsh, cruel judgments of others and ourselves and work toward peace and partnership.

FOR TODAY: **Am I doing to others as I would have them do to me? If not, I ask for spiritual help to release me from anger and to assist me in promoting peace in my relationships.**

October 26 ❧ Time

> *In the carriages of the past, you can't go anywhere.*
> —Maxim Gorky

We can't make up for lost time. Whatever we have missed can't be regained in this present hour or day. It is past, so we can quit trying to make up for it in either remorse or overactivity. It is we who pay emotionally and physically for trying to compensate.

Compensation takes on a new meaning, though, when we use it to our advantage and for the benefit of others. Now that we're done looking in all parts of the country for the one doctor, surgery, medication, or treatment to cure us, we have time for other things.

We can find time for happiness in the present. Perhaps it is returning some small service to the community in volunteer work, focusing on activities we can still do with family and friends, or rediscovering the humorous side of existence by watching a funny movie.

Our energy level may be low and our limitations great, but we can use time today to foster quality in what we can do.

For today: It is easy to waste time, but I'll use this day in such a way that I can look back on it not with regret, but with fond memories.

October 27 ∾ Worry, Thought Stopping

By means of imagination I had obliterated
reality and I felt relieved.
—Nikos Kazantzakis

Whether due to our chronic pain we now have more or less time on our hands, worry can be a real problem for us. We may worry about our health, about being able to keep up with our duties, or about major decisions, perhaps financial ones.

Other unwanted thoughts might be ones of self-doubt, thinking about things that we can't have, or thinking about something we may lose.

When worry or unwanted thoughts come back again and again, they can make us preoccupied and we lose our effectiveness to take care of the present day's responsibilities. One technique behavior therapists teach is countering these thoughts by shouting "Stop!" when they come to mind. Gradually, through practice, we can change our tone from a shout to a normal voice, then to a whisper, and until finally we can say "Stop" to ourselves silently.

Techniques such as this can help rid us of thoughts that make us anxious, and with relaxation may come less pain.

FOR TODAY: **There is a thought I want to put out of my mind. When it comes back, I'll say "Stop!"**

It is in relationships and in totalities that
life's meaning is revealed.
—Reinhold Niebuhr

Chronic pain was never on my agenda. I would never have wanted to hear at my high school graduation: "She's going to develop chronic pain and spend the rest of her life dealing with it." I had other achievements and successes in mind. At times, I have given in to pain rather than be challenged by it. At one point, my whole focus was on pain. I was so centered on pain and my efforts to control it that I had little time to think about anything or anyone else.

Eventually I had to face the fact that if pain was going to be on the agenda of my life, it couldn't be the only item. I had always liked to converse and do things with other people, and after a considerable amount of time, I realized that pain didn't have to stop me. I wanted and needed to make time for them.

Pain is an insidious thief who demands much from me if I allow it. I work hard so that it does not steal people from me. My real achievements concern not letting pain push me into a corner where there is room only for one— my isolated, lonely self.

FOR TODAY: **I can't afford to let pain be the only thing on my agenda today. I have things to do and people to call or see. "Living with it" is all about living.**

There is a point at which everything becomes simple and there is no longer any question of choice, because all you have started will be lost if you look back. Life's point of no return.
—Dag Hammarskjöld

When pain makes life difficult, it is easy to feel victimized by it. Changing our attitudes and being responsible for our own happiness are hard, but both are worth the effort.

We have more power than we realize, including the power to change our perspectives, to work out our problems, and to take care of ourselves. A healthier, more realistic view of our lives may include a statement such as "My pain complicates what I do, but one day at a time, I live a good life."

A life with chronic pain need not be all deprivation. Sometimes we suffer needlessly by focusing on what we can't do rather than on what we can. Sometimes we neglect our needs and deprive ourselves of the basic necessities required for good health. Sometimes we depend on someone else too much for our own happiness.

Life with chronic pain contains difficult moments, which can stretch into hours and days, but we are not helpless victims. Joy is just around the corner, if we don't look back.

FOR TODAY: **In my power is the ability to look forward. I don't want to feel like a victim, and I refuse to be one today.**

October 30   Love

The great tragedy of life is not that men
perish, but that they cease to love.
—W. Somerset Maugham

Love is waking up within us. It may have been asleep, tired of the effort that it took to stay alive. Love takes regular maintenance work, an effort that we may not have been able to make while in the throes of pain. We know that love itself can be painful, so we may have let it slip away, subconsciously thinking we already had enough pain in our lives.

With the awareness that love can help us, heal our emotional wounds, and make us feel more alive, we welcome love back—back from the place where we abandoned it. We welcome it back to life from its anesthetized state, the place where we, too, were drugged by our preoccupation with ourselves and our pain.

Love is a comfort and a joy, but it needs nurturing and renewing, care and appreciation. We never again want to be so indifferent to it that we risk its disappearance.

FOR TODAY: **Love can slip away from disuse. I'll guard against that by telling someone I love them today.**

October 31 ∾ Giving, Tears

Crying can bring such relief.
—Anne Frank

Giving was the last thing on my mind one day when I felt miserable. I felt pressured by holidays I feared I couldn't be ready for, deadlines I feared I wouldn't meet, and complaints I already couldn't handle. I felt like a hamster in a cage on its exercise wheel. No matter how fast I ran, I didn't seem to be making any progress.

It was Halloween and my pain had escalated so much that, with only thirty minutes left, I couldn't imagine taking the children trick-or-treating. Pressure had mounted and I felt overwhelmed. I broke down and cried uncontrollably. What seemed like hours took only minutes.

After I composed myself, I took the children around the block in their costumes. Forgetting my sadness and some of my pain, I had a very good time. Afterward, we had a small birthday celebration for my father, and I was proud of being able to give of myself, as he beamed at the gift I had found for him.

Sometimes we forget that friends and family members have difficult days when they need our availability and concern, and special days that deserve our thoughtfulness.

FOR TODAY: **When my life is too crowded and overwhelming, tears can give me release. Then I can think about the people who matter most to me and make room for them by some small, loving gesture.**

NOVEMBER

November 1 ❧ Courage

In the universe, the difficult things are done
as if they are easy.
—Lao-tzu

The snow geese flew overhead last night. I could not see them because of the dark sky. Hearing them alerted me to their presence. This morning I saw a long, V-shaped formation. I looked up and smiled. "It's true; they're back, heading for the wildlife refuge.

"They have a singleness of purpose, and there's no question of where they should fly," I thought. I felt such excitement watching them cross the sky above my house, even though it happens every year.

I'm sure it's hard work for the geese to fly from northerly regions to my state. Something that's hard work for me is staying focused on my life and not just my pain. The comfort for me is that I don't have to do it alone. God encourages me, ever providing other people who can "break the wind" ahead for me if I'm not strong enough. At times the leader of the snow geese needs to fall back and take a position in the rear. In the same way, I need God and other people to take over for me when I lack strength. My life with chronic pain is hard work, and I don't do it alone. I am inspired by the flight of the snow geese.

FOR TODAY: **Coping with chronic pain is hard work but I am being taken care of. My spiritual power, whom I call God, and other people are there for me to fall back on today.**

November 2 ❧ Rest, Fatigue, Insomnia

Sleep, that knits up the ravell'd sleeve of care;
The death of each day's life, sore labor's bath,
Balm of hurt minds, great Nature's second cause,
Chief nourisher in life's feast.
            —*William Shakespeare*

I was awake before the birds started singing. I slept off and on during a restless night, and waking up at 4:30 A.M. seemed a cruel joke. The constant chirp and chatter of the bird's songs, seemed to be a mockery of me.

I finally got back to sleep again after reading a little, putting in a load of laundry, and turning on some music.

Being unable to sleep is bad enough, but the fatigue on the following day is worse. I am more irritable; the pain seems worse; and I feel as if I'm just going through the motions of living.

During times like these, all I can do is survive and trust that I'll catch up when it is possible. In the meantime, I try to lessen the demands on myself, find quiet, and relax when I can.

FOR TODAY: **Rest is vital. If I can't have as much as I want, I'll settle for as much as I can get, hoping that the next night will give me slumber and repose.**

November 3 ∿ Pain Management

> *Courage is not fighting back; it is the*
> *power to endure.*
> —Robert Frost

Endurance is essential, but I can go beyond enduring, if I want an active part in pain management. Selecting a pain management technique used to be something I forced myself to do. Now if I don't use one, I feel as if I've gone to bed hungry.

Much of the action I take comes without much thought, just as it may take only seconds to decide what to eat at a fast food restaurant.

At other times, I make a conscious decision, making deliberate choices as I would sitting down at a restaurant with a menu in my hand.

It might go like this:

"For an appetizer, I'd like some distraction. That's my first choice in keeping my mind off the pain.

"For the entree, I'll take the combination platter: relaxation, meditation, and visualization. I can't resist dessert, even though I'm feeling full, so I'll choose humor. There's always room for that."

Practicing pain management techniques helps take the focus off the pain. Although choices from the menu may change, I leave satisfied. And I never turn down dessert—humor.

FOR TODAY: **I can choose the technique that best suits my needs. Like a menu, not everything will be to my liking, but I am glad I am offered choices. I will seek humor to brighten my day.**

November 4 ∞ Usefulness

> *My condition at that time was a kind of*
> *madness. Amid the ordered peace of our*
> *house I lived shyly, in agony, like a ghost; I*
> *took no part in the lives of others, rarely*
> *forgot myself for an hour at a time.*
> —Herman Hesse

I must turn my attention beyond myself in order to live well in spite of pain. Students take many subjects in school, not only to acquire knowledge, but to find those particular ones that most engage and intrigue their minds. My chronic pain has coaxed me into making fresh starts and developing new interests.

Energy once devoted to solving my pain problem is now flung into the world of things, places, and people. I have cause to arise from bed each morning, instead of slipping into slothful self-centeredness. My causes are not lofty, but they liberate me from myself and give cohesiveness to my day. Routine work requires order and discipline, and even everyday tasks humble me into the gratitude of accomplishment or show me the glory of my attempt.

Having purpose in the world of people, places, and things, I am acquainted with the usefulness I possess, the good I am capable of, and the meaning and joy that can be mine.

FOR TODAY: **I will organize my day so I have strength and energy for my work and time to relax at the end of the day. If all I accomplish is routine duties, it will be a productive day.**

November 5 ❧ Pain

Life is much more than the life of the body;
it is an infinite expansion of energy, a
continuum of love in countless dimensions, a
psychological and spiritual experience
independent of physical form.
—Marianne Williamson

My parents cut wood every fall in order to have lower heating bills in winter. They also love the warmth given off by their old woodburning stove. Because they live by a creek that is lined with many trees, finding wood is not a problem. Every year they make a long woodpile of neatly stacked logs. They tell me that, no matter how many different shapes and sizes of logs they have, there is always a place for each one.

I don't always see such a natural order in my life. Some things don't fit because others take up too much space. Pain is an element of my life that frequently demands more space.

Because chronic pain insists on staying, there is room for it, but I'm trying not to let it crowd out more than it must. It sometimes takes up the space I save for happiness, contentment, and peace. At these times I take action, such as rearranging my priorities, and pain falls back into its place.

Like the woodpile, my life contains many things that "fit." Although pain crowds in, it gives me no energy or warmth. That is why I strive to find room for God and other people.

FOR TODAY: **I will hesitate less to ask for help in coping when pain crowds out my happiness.**

November 6 ∾ Wants and Needs

Be patient. Our Playwright may show in
some fifth act what this wild drama means.
—Robert Charles Winthrop

To have faith is to let go of the need for things to go my way and to trust that some form of good will come. My pain is not always predictable, so I need to let go of the illusion of always being able to affect it. I don't know what will happen, so I need to let go of the future promises of relief I would like to have. My emotions run a sporadic course, so I need to let go of always trying to control them and instead to listen to them and take appropriate action.

Letting go of worry and anxiety is the process of releasing to God my cares and concerns, trusting that I will always have what I need. The best solutions for coping with my pain and interacting with others come when I get out of the way.

Letting go of my obsession to know what life holds for me is as refreshing as a cool drink, once I break from the feverish pace of trying to control the future. I can make plans but I wait for the outcome to unfold.

FOR TODAY: **God, help me be content with what I need, as I ask for the things I desire from tomorrow.**

For at least a moment, a person who laughs
can forget his troubles.
—Norman Cousins

I love to hear a good joke. A hundred-year-old man was asked, "How do you feel when you wake up in the morning?" He replied, "Surprised." One can find comedy in many places and situations. The other day I was at a pharmacy and a customer asked, smiling, "Have you been working hard or have you been here all day?" Fortunately, the pharmacist laughed, rather than being offended.

Just a touch of humor can brighten our day. I heard once that being amused by something is evidence of our acceptance of the human condition. Such an explanation for being able to have a good laugh may sound too philosophical, but we who have chronic pain can relate to it easily. Before we accepted pain as part of our particular human condition, we found little to laugh at. But as we've learned to focus less on ourselves and our pain, we are free to discover the part of life that is humorous.

Like Cousins, we laugh and, for a moment, forget our troubles. The funny side of life is worth our awareness.

FOR TODAY: **I can be lighthearted today. It may be just what I need.**

November 8 ❧ Grief, Dreams

You see things and you say "Why?"; but I
dream things that never were and I say
"Why not?"
—George Bernard Shaw

Dreams that have been shattered by chronic pain are still hard to let go of. We may have lost a job and, with it, the dream of promotion. We may have lost financially and, with it, the dream of a new home. We may have lost physical abilities and, with it, the dream of participation in our favorite sports. We may have lost some unidentified dream of the person we'd like to become and, with it, a sustaining hope.

We wonder if life is now only a dead end with opportunities closed behind us. We need time to mourn our losses before we can dream again.

Whatever our dreams were, there are some that we can save and some that can be replaced by new ones. These new ones may be less ambitious but more meaningful to us.

Today we can meet our obligations and solve our problems. We have a place here, we matter, and we can still dream.

For today: **I am not a prisoner of pain, "doing time." My life includes my dreams.**

November 9 ❧ Relationships

> *What makes loneliness an anguish*
> *Is not that I have no one to share my*
> *burden,*
> *But this:*
> *I have only my own burden to share.*
> —Dag Hammarskjöld

If we become unbalanced in the way of work and play, motion and relaxation, and activity and inactivity, it is no wonder that pain can contribute to an imbalance in our relationships, too.

We may react to pain by withdrawing from some family members and overindulging attention on others. The majority of our time may be spent on the one who is most demanding, while inside, the silent one feels deprived of our love. This can happen with attention bestowed on one child over another child, a child over a spouse, a spouse over a child, or a friend over the family. Perhaps everyone is excluded when we are thinking about ourselves and the pain.

Maybe there was a time when we had to nurse our own wounds before we could divide our sympathies. For us, there is a time for grief and a time in which to move on. Loved ones wait through these passages of time for their share of our affection.

FOR TODAY: Have I neglected someone while favoring another person? If so, I will work at righting the imbalance I see. I will strive for wholeness in my relationships.

November 10 ❧ **Revenge**

> *There is no sport in hate when all the rage*
> *is on one side.*
> —*Percy Bysshe Shelley*

There are those of us who have chronic pain as a result of someone else's error. We may have a strong desire to seek revenge. It may take many forms: It may be an urge to get even with an individual, such as a drunken driver, or perhaps an institution, such as a corporation with an unsafe environment, or perhaps with a doctor, whose promise of treatment success did not materialize.

If we are in a blame-and-revenge mode of thinking, there is no peace. To deal with the situation, we can allow ourselves to feel the anger but not to act on it. If someone else is at fault, we can acknowledge this, but we cannot be the judge and jury, nor would we really want to be. We can say to ourselves, "If they only hurt for an hour like I do . . ." but in our hearts, we would not want anyone else, even our enemies, to have the pain we do.

Contemplating revenge will not help us. It only will keep us focused on what has been and what was. We need to put past circumstances behind us so we can move forward.

After experiencing the feelings of anger and revenge, we can accept the fact that the hurt inflicted on us, though perhaps due to negligence, was not intentional. With that awareness, we can forgive. We can use the time that used to be filled with thoughts of revenge to decide what we need to do in order to find our way and to move on.

FOR TODAY: **I forgive, so I can go forward in peace.**

> *But even then, this moment . . . was my*
> *first inkling that there is a healthier self*
> *within each of us, just waiting for*
> *encouragement.*
> —Gloria Steinem

Imagine the compassion we would feel toward a little boy or girl with chronic pain. Just for a few minutes, we can become that child. We imagine ourselves at the park, lying on a grassy knoll, watching the clouds to take our mind off the pain. After a while, we sit up to watch the other children playing on the swings, going down the slide, and climbing the jungle gym. Someone asks us to play, but we say sadly, "I'd like to but I hurt too much." They look at us oddly and say, "Sure you can. Just try it." Again we say, "I can't. I might hurt worse." They finally say, "How do you know until you try? Just come and play for a little while."

"Maybe I could if you'd help me up," we say. For a little while, until we hurt too much, we have fun. We weren't so different, so afraid, so alone. We did something we thought was impossible to do. Maybe next time we could play longer. Maybe someday we could play all day.

There is a hurt little child inside of us, a little boy or girl who wants to be held, loved, nurtured, and then encouraged to go join others in play. Let's love the child inside us who doesn't deserve to hurt as we hurt, who doesn't have to be better to be liked or forced to do more than he or she is able. The adult part of us can tell the child that we have time for love, time to listen, and time to wipe away tears. We won't be anxious about tomorrow. We are free to play today.

FOR TODAY: I am taking care of my wounded self. Inside me, the child's heart is comforted, even though the body still hurts. In some way, I will give my body, mind, and soul some caring today.

The better the day, the better the deed.
—Alice B. Toklas

"People who have chronic pain are under constant physical stress," a health professional once told me. I had known that the pain made me feel stressed, although I'd never thought about pain itself being a constant stressor to my body. Physical pain, accompanied by its partner, emotional pain, is indeed a powerful stressor. Stress management is as useful for us as for the overworked executive who is in danger of a heart attack.

A technique worth learning is "belly breathing." Paying attention to our breathing relaxes us and teaches us how to tune in to our bodies. Our ability to concentrate increases as we focus on our breathing rather than our pain and outside pressures.

Whether we call it abdominal, diaphragmatic, or belly breathing, enlarging our abdomens with inhalations enables us to deepen our breath far beyond what we can using our chests alone. Like a sleeping baby who breathes in this way, we will feel more calmness, peace, and balance.

Breathing in slowly through our nostrils and out more slowly through our mouths . . . breathing in deeply while feeling our abdomen rise . . . breathing out deeply and feeling it flatten . . . again and again we repeat breathing in and out. We allow tensions to recede and feelings of sedation to enter in.

Slowly and patiently, we breathe—peace and relaxation engulf us.

FOR TODAY: Wherever I am, I can focus on my breathing to decrease stress.

November 13 ∾ Living in the Present Moment

We frequently see those who in life
conquered in every battle; when it was a
future enemy they had to deal with, they
became powerless, their arms paralyzed.
—Sören Kierkegaard

In a job interview we're asked, "Where do you expect to be ten years from now?" Let's imagine that someone who was unaware of our pain asked us the question. For those who despair, the answer might be, "I plan to deteriorate physically, mentally, emotionally, and spiritually. I plan to spend those years in idleness, drag others into my distress, and drift into obscurity." The person listening would probably be speechless.

The person who has a hopeless attitude toward the future needs to change in three ways. First, one must change a consistently negative outlook by deciding that from now on, life does not need to take a downward spiral. In spite of inevitable disappointments, there will be possibilities for inner gratification, no matter what external events occur. Secondly, one must learn to look beyond physical comfort for happiness and contentment. Though in pain, it is still possible to enjoy time with others, celebrate special events, learn new things, and show love. Thirdly, one must let faith in the ultimate goodness of life and the virtue of each day conquer the fear of the future. We can do this by being willing to open ourselves to friendship, allowing spiritual power to give us courage for tomorrow, and by believing that the future can be looked forward to with loving expectation instead of gloom.

Today can be a new beginning, the day that is lived in

self-acceptance and usefulness. Today we can positively alter our outlook on life.

FOR TODAY: I want to realize which people, places, and things are important to me and to welcome, instead of fear, the future. Let this day be an exceptionally valuable one, a day of rising above my pain and concerns.

November 14 ❧ Escape

*Although the world is full of suffering, it is
also full of the overcoming of it.*
—Helen Keller

Some of us have tried to escape from chronic pain, but
we've discovered that substance abuse isn't the solution. It
has detoured our journey toward acceptance, made us feel
worse about ourselves, and led to an emotional dead end.
Some have died from their addiction.

Whether we have sedated ourselves with food, prescription drugs, or alcohol, the result was the same—lowered
self-esteem and despair.

For many of us, turning to a Higher Power has meant
freedom. With a source of strength greater than our own,
we need not turn to foods high in sugar, extra pills, or
more drinks—substances whose promises of relief are
empty and only cripple our conduct. With spiritual help as
our lifeline to security, we have freedom to live within our
limitations and rest in the assurance that, at all times, our
lives have meaning and purpose.

In facing rather than trying to escape from the reality of
our pain, we are rewarded with greater peace of mind and
self-esteem. Facing it, we are not ashamed to look in the
mirror because we see someone who is free from the enslavement of addiction and a person whose life makes a
difference.

FOR TODAY: **I am not alone. My spiritual resources sustain me. I'm grateful that I don't need to withdraw
from life.**

> *People with pain very rarely talk about their*
> *anger, may not even accept there is anger,*
> *and the unconscious attempts to suppress it*
> *are instrumental in creating a barrier*
> *between the person and those who may be*
> *in a position to offer help.*
> —Neville Shone

I never know when the emotions that I think I've worked through will come back. One day a twinge of anger, envy and sadness unexpectedly returned. My intention was to offer comfort and encouragement to an acquaintance who had been treated for a similar pain problem. How surprised I was to hear her say that she was getting along fine and that her worst symptoms had been removed entirely.

I was genuinely happy that the treatment had worked for her, but after hanging up the phone, I couldn't help but feel a bit sorry for myself and angry that similar treatments had not helped me. I had come a long way in not being jealous of those without a pain problem, but apparently I still had envious feelings toward those with pain who had been helped. I talked to a friend about the feelings that I wanted to suppress. Having denied anger before, I realized that it could eat away at my peace of mind if not discussed.

After our talk I reached the point of telling myself, "The treatment worked for someone else. Period. I'm glad it did. I've no choice but to continue to do the best I can."

That's all we can do; it's all we can expect from ourselves. We do the best we can and trust that our emotional wounds will be healed. On the day described, my envy and sadness reappeared, but the wound closed quickly. I had made progress on my journey into healing.

FOR TODAY: **I accept that certain treatments have not helped my pain. I am challenged to live well, despite limitations. Today I am ready to meet the challenge.**

November 16 ∽ Love

Just one sincere surrendered moment, when
love matters more than anything, and we
know that nothing else really matters at all.
—Marianne Williamson

There are times when I pay the price for expressing love with greater pain, but the consequences are worth it. One holiday, last-minute preparations seemed unending. I had meant for them to be done earlier, I had meant to care for my needs better, and I had meant to be less pressed for time. My intentions were good, but my plans did not turn out as I had wished.

That holiday, I had more pain but I enjoyed the festivities and people more than I had the year before. What made the difference?

I believe it was because I surrendered to love rather than pain. I wanted to give and receive love more than I wanted to protect myself from additional discomfort.

It took a fair amount of time to recover from the subsequent pain flare-up, but I could be satisfied in a mental, emotional, and spiritual way. I could not help but think that next year I might find a way to have more physical ease, too.

Relief of pain was once what I cared most about. I now realize that love matters most of all.

FOR TODAY: **I can be happy and loving during the hours of this day.**

November 17 ❧ Depression, Learning

*Few people think more than two or three
times a year. I've made an international
reputation for myself for thinking once or
twice a week.*
—George Bernard Shaw

At the lowest point in my pain experience, I did not care about learning anything new, nor did I care about thinking about anything besides my pain.

Today I am interested in learning about several things. I care about the outer world, so I enjoy reading the newspaper and listening to the news. I learn about dealing with chronic pain by reading and listening to others. Finally, I learn even more about God as He demonstrates His caring through the love of family and friends.

I'm learning and thinking again. The more I learn, the more enlightened I want to be. I can open that book, turn that page, write that letter, or make that phone call. Learning keeps my mind from focusing on the pain.

For today: **I will learn something new today because God has given me an intellect to use. I will think of something I would like to know more about and be so enticed by it that I want to explore its mystery.**

November 18 ∾ Relaxation

How shall we expect charity toward others
when we are uncharitable to ourselves?
—Sir Thomas Browne

My friend says, "When I have severe pain, it's like I'm in a room full of noisy people where I can hardly think or talk to others. Then, when my pain reduces to its maintenance level, it's like everyone in the room has quieted down to a whisper."

Because my pain can reach such proportions, I can relate exactly to what she says. I find that relaxation techniques are a must when the pain is severe. I need as few stimuli as possible and as much quiet as is feasible for both my body and mind to relax. My favorite tape is music and ocean waves, which serve as the background for a voice that instructs me to fill my lungs by inhaling slow, deep breaths and releasing the tension in my body as I exhale. In comes the breath, out goes the tension, over and over as I repeat to myself "Relax."

This "time out" is valuable. I come away with renewed inner resources and more peace.

FOR TODAY: **Whether I have severe pain or have the tensions of everyday living, relaxation can help. I'll make the time to use it.**

November 19 ∾ Acceptance, Worsened Condition

> *Time past and time future*
> *Allow but a little consciousness.*
> *To be conscious is not to be in time.*
> —T. S. Eliot

I have to face it. There are aspects of my pain problem that can't be changed, such as its continual nature. To some, this sounds like a submission to suffering. To me, after much struggle against the inescapable, this means peace.

Naturally, I want as little pain and as much function and mobility as I can have. Acceptance of my pain does not change those desires, nor does it change my determination to be as active as possible. What it does change is my relationship with pain.

I was once shown some diagnostic test results that indicated that a structural problem had worsened in just a few years. Earlier I had been told that such deterioration was possible, in years to come. I never believed it would happen to me, especially in such a short time. Was I only to look forward to a lifetime of progressive deterioration in that region of my body? Maybe. Did this spell despair? No.

It was a moment of new awareness. I realized that there was no benefit in looking back, nor any good result to be gained in trying to predict the future nature of my pain.

Remarkably, there was peace instead of panic. That day I could cope with the news of a worsened condition. That was all I needed to be concerned with. This less emotional response seemed like denial, but it was not. It was a simple acceptance of a condition that I could not change and evidence that my acceptance of pain had deepened.

FOR TODAY: **My spirit is alive and well. It can retaliate against bodily deterioration to maintain quality in my life.**

November 20 ❧ Stress, Relaxation

Adventure and retreat are the two parts of man's courage. The drawing back is as important as the moving in.
—Robert Frost

My pulse is low, my breathing is slow, and I feel heavy, relaxed, and warm. All is well and cares have fallen off me like kicked-off old shoes. The quiet is soothing, not empty, and my pain knocks gently but does not hammer incessantly at my door. I tell it to go away, for I am in a deep state of relaxation. It stays, but I don't notice its presence as much. I feel somehow detached from it. My mind is sedate, my body is restful, and they are one, as they have never been before. I have never felt such peaceful unity between my body and my mind, and I want these moments to last.

So it is with the relaxation response, a state that can be induced by therapeutic massage, progressive relaxation, or self-hypnosis. These techniques help to reconnect my body and mind so I can operate more efficiently, after I have experienced the feeling of well-being and calm.

In deep relaxation, I have a degree of release from pain.

FOR TODAY: **Chronic pain puts stress on my body and my mind. I can consider achieving a relaxation response today to reduce such stress.**

November 21 ❧ Perfectionism

> *(About Vincent van Gogh) The theme of*
> *"I'm a failure. I'm a failure. I'm a failure"*
> *gave way to "What shall I try now? What*
> *am I best fitted for? Where is my proper*
> *place in the world?"*
> —*Irving Stone*

Many get caught in the trap of perfectionism, and we with chronic pain are no different. When we become satisfied with nothing but perfection, we find ourselves stuck in an impossible situation. We are bound to fail if our expectations for ourselves are unrealistic and unattainable. We lament: "I never do anything right," instead of learning from mistakes and accepting our humanness.

When we give up perfectionism, we don't give up doing our best. Instead, we give up believing that everything has to be done perfectly in order for us to feel adequate.

Pain may help us learn to delegate work, even though we would prefer doing things ourselves. "They wouldn't do it right," we may think, but delegating can conserve our energy for the things we like to do. Having time for work and play builds balance into our lives that the perfectionist in us is too busy to appreciate.

FOR TODAY: **I need breaks that provide time for refueling my energy stores. I can let go of my need to be perfect in order to enjoy this day more.**

November 22 ❧ Humor

All the things I really like to do are
immoral, illegal or fattening.
—Alexander Woollcott

Humor helps keep our minds off the pain, but it also does something else—it brings us out of self-absorption to a connectedness with our culture and with what we have in common with others. We feel that we are learning about ourselves and also becoming part of the world around us when we can laugh at the witty and absurd within and around us.

Many people look forward to a daily dose of humor through the comics. Some remember with nostalgia the humor of vaudeville and radio. Mark Twain said that humor was mankind's supreme weapon, and during the Watergate scandal, jokes about Richard Nixon offered relief for a nation appalled by deceit.

In stand-up comedy, we get a chance to laugh at ourselves by seeing our own human weaknesses exaggerated. We forgive the comedian his defects as we sigh in relief that perhaps his weaknesses are greater than ours. We laugh at the coward, the egoist, and the weakling but embrace their failings, because in one way or another, we have been those characters, too.

We with chronic pain need humor, whether to feel part of our society and its idiosyncrasies or to sympathize and laugh at our own.

FOR TODAY: **Humor is good nourishment for my body, mind, and soul. I'll partake of some today.**

November 23 ∽ Empathy

> *Birds sing after a storm; why shouldn't*
> *people feel as free to delight in whatever*
> *remains to them?*
> *—Rose Fitzgerald Kennedy*

I cried when I watched a documentary about the tragedies in the Kennedy family and about the death of Martin Luther King, Jr. I felt at least a fraction of the grief carried by the surviving family members.

I was struck anew by the injustice of it all, of the lives taken in their prime. As the interviewees described the grief of the Kennedy parents, I felt empathy for them like I'd never experienced before.

My pain has put me in touch with the suffering of others. Compassion connects me with others who hurt. Even if someone else's pain is something foreign to me, I have, in some way, experienced a similar emotion. I go away from a conversation having a renewed conviction that we are one with the suffering of humanity.

If I compare myself only to people who "have it worse" (an individual judgment), I am not really in their pain, suffering with them. If I share my story and allow them to share theirs, we have a community of spirit.

We really are not alone, although it sometimes seems so. We are all survivors, with an enormous will to go beyond loss and into living.

FOR TODAY: **I can touch another life today. The compassion I show will affect me, too.**

November 24 ❧ Busyness

Bless your uneasiness as a sign that there is still life in you.
—Dag Hammarskjöld

There's a saying that goes, "If you want to get something done, ask a busy person." People who can handle a lot are alert to their abilities and their individual skills. They are grateful for the tasks they are privileged to do and grateful for the people who have trusted them to get things done.

Many times we thrive on having lots to do, but sometimes keeping busy can have a wrong motive. Busyness may be a substitute for acknowledging and coming to terms with our pain. Busyness can be a substitute for real intimacy and letting people get close to us. It also can be a substitute for a relationship with God, whom we blame, instead of seeing Him as the one who awakens us to our abilities and helps us see new possibilities.

On the other hand, we like to be in the middle of the action when we can be, because it makes us feel more fully alive. Meeting responsibilities also can provide opportunities for growth, but we must take care that too many demands do not cause us to lose our creative energy. Then our busyness is wasteful, and we lose the connectedness with others that we seek.

FOR TODAY: **I want to see how to use my gifts and refrain from making busyness my only aim.**

November 25 ❧ Pain Management

Surviving meant being born over and over.
—Erica Jong

I don't have perfect mastery of my pain. There are times when I want to delegate a task to someone else so that I can pace myself better, but no one is available. There are times when I want to distract my mind from the pain, but its intensity grabs my attention. There are times when I think humor and less stress would help, but the mailman has just brought the month's bills and I wonder how I will ever pay them. In the meantime, my pain level rises.

Through it all, I keep aware of how quickly the pain is escalating and ask myself if there is anything that can act as a release valve before it reaches unbearable severity. If I can't delegate a task, can it wait until tomorrow? If not, perhaps I can try to simplify my day in some other way. I ask God to show me how to prioritize when I can't do it all. When pain grabs my attention, I say "God, help me," taking slow, deep breaths to get through it. When finances cause stress, I pray that I will have enough to live on, but I also try to set up payment plans or make other arrangements.

During more painful days, I cling to the belief that better days will come. Sometimes even twenty-four hours can make a great difference. I realize that I can't have a perfectly pain-free life, but my ability to handle problems, from irritations to crises, is growing every day.

FOR TODAY: **God, help me to find You, my center, so that I won't feel hopeless and helpless. Show me what to do first.**

November 26 ∾ Feeling Abandoned by God, Gratitude

Is your disgust at your emptiness to be the
only life with which you fill it?
—Dag Hammarskjöld

Can our pain and emptiness bring us something positive? Can any good come from pain? And where do we go from here?

Early in our pain experience we were angered at the thought that God could work a greater good from our pain if He chose. The more acceptance we gained, the easier it was to at least open ourselves to the possibility of other kinds of good. Maybe it is the realization that our life is not all pain—that we do have things we love and care about, and things that excite us by the mere thought of them. Maybe we learn to not be concerned with how others see us but accept ourselves—pain, imperfection, limitations, and all. Maybe we learn new empathy for others.

We seek some benefit in order to make the pain more tolerable. In some small or more dramatic way, we come to terms with it. It can still be a relief to tell God about our anger, fear, and doubts, but finding something positive to hold on to can be tangible evidence that our experience is not all for naught. One person found comfort in the fact that since his children had to take on more of the tasks at home, they were less selfish as adults. Our pain can have meaning for others, too.

I could not suggest a benefit to someone else, especially in the midst of great suffering. We must each do it for ourselves—find the gift within the pain and clutch it. Some may never find a gift at all and will answer "no" to "Can any good come from this?" The important thing is that nothing, not even pain, can separate us from God's love. He does not abandon us, even when we can't feel the love or see the gift.

FOR TODAY: **God, I open my heart to see some gift that is good in my circumstances, realizing that I have not been abandoned by You even when I can't see or feel any gift.**

November 27 ∿ Gratitude

> *Back of tranquility lies conquered*
> *unhappiness.*
> —David Grayson

I have days of struggle, but I also have what's known as a "good day." It is a day when, for some little known reason, my pain is less. I have fewer conscious thoughts about the pain, and I can do more. The world interests me more because I have greater freedom to participate in it.

Emotionally, I'm more at ease. I look better because, indeed, I am feeling better. I'm satisfied with my role in life; I'm not so interested in changing people to my liking; and I'm not worried about the future.

Although my pain is still there, these are indeed wonderful days. I cherish them with gratitude. It's a great day when I say that I feel good, even if "good" is still a relative term.

FOR TODAY: **If I am having a good day, I have much to be thankful for. If it is a bad day, I can hold on to the memory of those good days I've had and hope that they return soon.**

November 28 ❧ Weight Loss

*Nothing is more desirable than to be
released from an affliction, but nothing is
more frightening than to be divested
of a crutch.*
—James Baldwin

Our focus regarding our weight should be on good nutrition. People of all walks of life are being encouraged to eat less meat, less fat, and more grains, fruits, and vegetables. But lack of knowledge about nutrition does not always explain our weight problem.

Sometimes the weight is only a symptom of a deeper inner problem, and dieting can be another setup for failure. We need to put the weight issue to one side and work on some of the real causes of the symptom, such as fear, repressed anger, and insecurity. Coping with pain through the abuse of food can have devastating physical and emotional effects. Many of us feel that if we cannot control our pain, we can at least control our weight, only to discover that we may have trouble in that area, too.

If abuse of food is my problem, I can ask my Higher Power to take away my fear and protect me from harm. I can include Him in my struggles with weight and ask to be guided to nutritious foods and emotional balance.

For today: I will concentrate on the mental and spiritual aspects of my life, and the weight will take care of itself.

November 29 ∾ Sabotaging Good Feelings

> *Go for the light and the darkness*
> *will disappear.*
> —Marianne Williamson

I want to stay clear of sabotaging good feelings. If I feel good, I can enjoy it, rather than immediately working to feel better. If it is not a hectic day, I don't have to make it one. If I find something that I like, within my price range, I don't have to tell myself I don't deserve it.

I can let the good feelings be there and not sabotage them. I used to unconsciously sabotage an exercise program by telling myself I could do just a little more, only to go too far and ruin how I felt.

I would sabotage a relaxing day by creating more to do, wearing myself out. And I would deprive myself of some material item because I felt I didn't deserve it, having already spent money on medical bills.

If we see such a pattern, we can stop repeating it. We already work hard. Instead of working harder, we can accept those times that are easier for us and just let them be.

Dealing with chronic pain is hard work. Let's not sabotage feeling good.

FOR TODAY: **Sometimes I need to force gratitude and sometimes it comes uninvited. On either kind of day, I can find something to be content with.**

November 30 ❧ Attitude, Limitations

Mother gave me her support with one of her usual terse asides: "That's what you want to do? Then nothing beats a trial but a failure. Give it everything you've got. I've told you many times, 'Can't Do is like Don't Care.' Neither of them have a home."
—Maya Angelou

"I can't" is an easy thing to say, an easy attitude to fall into, but one that should be resisted. A change in the wording to, "I've decided against it at this time" is the difference between "never" and "maybe, sometime." If we say, "I can't go tent camping," which used to be a favorite activity, we close the door on something that once gave us pleasure. If we say, "I've decided against it at this time," we leave room for options, such as having someone else do most of the packing, purchasing an air mattress so that the hard ground is more comfortable, or deciding to buy a camper.

Our limitations are real but not necessarily final. Some of them we will need to accept, others we can "work around" through pacing ourselves and finding new ways to do things, and some limitations may not exist after we challenge them. We can start by recognizing our abilities and, like building that childhood tower, add one small block of accomplishment at a time until we find out what we are capable of.

Living with chronic pain is filled with continuous learning, and "I can't" is an unnecessary roadblock in that process.

FOR TODAY: It may not be time for me to engage in some activities, but I can relax and tell myself that this fact is true only today.

DECEMBER

December 1 ❧ Risk Taking

> *Success is never final and failure never*
> *fatal. It's courage that counts.*
> —*George R. Tilton*

We all breathe a sigh of relief when our efforts show and when our accomplishments are recognized. Since success is ours, we may feel like stopping or coasting, rather than working and pressing on.

On the other hand, we may think of failure as being fatal, especially if we place great importance on what we have lost, such as a valued job or an important relationship.

Dealing with our pain also holds numerous successes and failures. We may succeed at understanding our limitations but fail at overcoming them by forcing changes too fast. We may succeed at stating our needs but fail at communicating them kindly. We may succeed at asking for advice but fail to follow it. Success and failure are part of growth, and that is what we strive for.

Tilton reminds us that our successes aren't final and our failures aren't fatal. We can handle the lofty, elevating times as well as the depressing, low times. Learning to handle success without being cocksure and learning to face mistakes without being ruined is our aim.

FOR TODAY: **I dare to take risks, knowing I will be able to handle both success and failure.**

December 2 ❧ Hope, Courage

He who has never hoped can never despair.
—*George Bernard Shaw*

On the radio, I heard that in a commencement address to a graduating class, Winston Churchill went to the podium and said in his loud, strong voice, "Never give up." He took his seat behind the podium, waited, and returned to the microphone. Looking at the class, he again said in his loud voice, "Never give up." Once again he sat down, waited briefly, and when he reached the podium, he leaned into the microphone, saying louder and more emphatically, "Never give up. Never, ever, ever give up!" Those were the last words of his address.

He must have believed that we need both hope and determination. We are all capable of something, and while hope motivates us to keep trying, determination tells us not to stop. Accepting our chronic pain, having the hope of a fulfilling life, and having the determination to meet the challenges of living with pain is not always easy, but it is possible nonetheless.

Taking care of today's business and taking pleasure in doing one necessary task at a time keep us from killing our hopes and determination. This, along with a great deal of patience, gives us conviction to never give up.

FOR TODAY: **I have hope or I wouldn't be here. I have the willingness to find gratification in this day and to be patient with small signs of progress.**

December 3 ❧ Eyes

*My eyes look so clean and deep, my cheeks
are pink . . . I look as if I am happy and
yet there is something so sad in my
expression and my smile slips away from my
lips as soon as it has come.*
—Anne Frank

I looked at her and thought, "My eyes used to look that way." Behind her words of "I'm tired of this pain," her eyes pleaded, "Help me. Tell me what to do to get rid of it. I can't go on like this."

My eyes still tell it all. Those who are close to me know by my eyes' strained look that I am having more pain. Others see the lack of luster, the absence of sparkle that betrays my smile, and the taut lines that pull at the corners of my eyes.

What's different today is that I'm not begging with my eyes for friends and family to suggest something that will fix my pain. Though I appreciate their support, I don't urge them to find me a way out. I know that they cannot manage my pain for me.

Chronic pain has no magic answers, but I can practice some methods that may help (distraction, relaxation, visualization, humor, exercise, prayer, meditation, and so on). I have learned many things, among them that a commitment to working with the pain is essential, that much enjoyment of life is still open to me, that I can be useful to at least one other person, and, above all, that I cannot allow pain to ravage me and devastate my life.

Though my eyes may not plead for help to others, they still plead to God. "Help me through this . . ." "Help me be able to . . ." "Help me be willing to . . ."

"Help me." I need so much of God's help, and He undoubtedly sees my straining eyes. But with His help, I can manage.

FOR TODAY: **God, help me, because pain affects every area of my life. Give me the peace of knowing that a good life is possible, even with the pain.**

December 4 ❧ Faith

> *Lord, make me an instrument of thy peace.*
> *—St. Francis of Assisi*

I have a castle of faith—the fortress that is my security and foundation. Sometimes it seems as strong as stone, and sometimes it seems to collapse as easily as a sand castle. Time and again the waves of discouragement urge its fall.

When my faith is imperiled, I read more, listen more, and talk to God more. My faith is in the most danger when I feel that I can't persevere—when severe pain seems relentless and unmerciful. At times like these, I have doubt whether my castle of faith will last.

I long for days when my faith doesn't topple from circumstances and doubt. At least I am still willing to trust in the rebuilding process to strengthen my faith. I long to be closer to this God who keeps me from giving up and provides me with refuge.

As my faith is repeatedly rebuilt, God is rebuilding me and equipping me to meet new challenges. He has brought order into what was once a life of chaos with chronic pain.

FOR TODAY: **When my castle of faith is strong, I can live in peace. God, secure it for me today.**

December 5 ❧ Limitations

> *The world is supposed to be full of*
> *possibilities, but they narrow down to pretty*
> *few in most personal experience.*
> —D. H. Lawrence

"If only I didn't have pain, I could . . ." I've thought, probably a hundred times. What I've noticed is that the words that follow "if only I could" include many things that I had no desire to do before my pain started! Some of my thoughts have followed a "grass is greener on the other side" theme.

Once, I decided that I wanted to sled down a snowy hill with the rest of my family. I'd never cared for sledding, even as a child! Still, because it was something I knew I shouldn't do and an activity with the family that I felt I was being deprived of, I felt an urge to do it. The snow was not soft and fluffy, and stopping was abrupt as I ran into a hard snowbank. The next day's pain was unbelievable and the self-criticism enormous.

All of us would like the freedom to go places and do things, even to have the freedom to try things that did not attract us before, things that are not in our best interest. Our most precious freedom, though, is to seek our own way, to live the lives we choose, within our limitations. We are free to fill in the sentence "I'm able to . . ." and use this freedom to realize that we are vital human beings.

FOR TODAY: **I am willing to exercise my freedom of choice today and find my place of usefulness.**

December 6 ∾ Inner Resources

> *Creativeness often consists of merely turning*
> *up what is already there.*
> —Bernice Fitzgibbon

One person says, "I once thought that if I knew where the pain was coming from, it could easily be fixed. Surgery completely relieved an acquaintance's pain, but made me no better, and caused a friend's pain to be much worse. Who can predict how things will turn out? One thing I do know is that I'm not going to sit by and wait for my condition to deteriorate. Even though I'm partially disabled, I'm going to make the most of each day."

Many of us have been on the roller coaster of tests, treatments, medications, and procedures—all aimed at relieving our pain. The trial-and-error method has been difficult. Emotionally, there have been high and low mood swings. Physically, there may have been more pain or unwanted side effects. Confused by medical choices, we may say, "I don't want to get my hopes up again for fear of disappointment, but I still don't believe that this is as far as I can get."

Questions need some thought before we try a new treatment. Is it intended to provide temporary or long-term pain relief? What can I reasonably expect? What time and money investment is needed? What are some possible negative consequences? Could I speak with someone who has already tried this?

Perhaps we need to give our inner selves more time. Learning to cope with stress in healthier ways, developing a patient, more positive attitude, trying to increase our exercise tolerance, or learning how to prioritize each day and pace ourselves may take a long time. Still, we always can strengthen and develop our inner resources.

We have within us the potential for learning how to best manage our lives, in spite of the pain. Living with pain still requires trial and error, but we can accept this as a necessary part of our pursuit of quality life. We may have lost trust in treatments and procedures, but we can learn how to trust ourselves.

FOR TODAY: **I will do at least one thing to make this day better by looking inside, rather than outside myself.**

December 7 ∾ Acceptance, Being Human, Expectations

There is a weak being in every strong one.
—Paul Tillich

I am human, but sometimes I'm not accepting of the fact that my particular humanness includes chronic pain. At times, I'm not open to finding the good around me, and I just want to sulk in aloneness with the rationale that if I can't be "normal," I don't want to be with those who are.

Those feelings are natural. Each day is different, and my conception of my strengths and weaknesses varies. Slowly I am coming to accept reality while striving to be stronger in my body, mind, and spirit. It doesn't mean that I'm a bad person because I am sometimes tempted to revert to old patterns of sulking in isolation. Maybe there's a need that's not being met—a need for rest or a need to admit my anger and rage at God, telling Him how unfair life is and how depressed it makes me feel.

Whatever the circumstances, it's okay to be human. We all feel as if life has overwhelmed us at times. The important thing is to grow beyond our old beliefs and find a way to transcend our pain.

Frequently I let God take over. My Higher Power says, "Let me take your cares." Then I let go of trying to be 100 percent accepting, 100 percent serene. I'm human and fallible, but God shows me how not to give in. With His help, I have more confidence and courage, more inspiration and integrity. I am grateful that the sulking reminds me that I need God's help to get out of my misery.

FOR TODAY: **I am a weak human in need of a strong God. I'll make contact and put my cares on Him today.**

December 8 ❧ Single Life

*Only on the surface of things have I ever
trod the beaten path. So long as I keep from
hurting anyone else, I have lived as
completely as it was possible, the life
of my choice.*
—Ellen Anderson Gholson Glasgow

The problems that singles face are unique in some ways and universal in others. Even the reasons for being alone vary, although some live with roommates in mutual friendship or love. Some single lives are self-chosen, while others are not. There may have been a marriage that didn't survive, family estrangement, the loss of a mate, or a romance that didn't deepen.

What are some of the problems of the single person with pain? One problem is that the responsibilities and duties cannot be shared with other family members, which adds frustration and strain. With no one else to depend on, we may be anxious that our present means of support may fail us. We may feel pressured to stay busy but wear ourselves out, trying to prove our worthiness to those who consider singleness a personal failing.

We need to keep ourselves in the perspective of the whole of human existence. We are individuals who face unique situations, solve problems, and deal with our pain, single or not. If it seems easy to slip into self-pity when we are alone or to be overwhelmed by pain's demands, we can allow room for others and reach out for companionship. At other times we may need the stillness of our private spaces for reflection, meditation, or the simple break from routine. We singles are not unique in our needs, but our choices are individual.

FOR TODAY: Riches are found in renewing friendships and in using quiet as a reprieve from the noisy world. Either one can help calm me today.

December 9 ❧ Attempt

Attempt. It is the only way for your efforts
to be rewarded.
—Patti Nielsen

What I've learned is that if I ask people who have had pain a long time about their condition, they comment briefly and then move on to the topic of what is currently happening in their lives. Pain may be either ever-present or recurring, but they have learned to enrich their lives in some way that puts less attention on their bodily distress.

I'm learning to accentuate the first part of the "*living* with pain" rather than the latter, as in "living with *pain*." My friend with a twelve-year history of pain tells me, "Sometimes when I do something that I know will cause my pain to flare up, I just take care of it afterward, knowing that what I did was worth doing."

How do we know what is worth doing? The answer is both individual and circumstantial. We constantly will have to learn by trial and error in order to make a choice. From experience, we learn about consequences. If the consequences are bad, we probably prefer to avoid such situations. On the other hand, we may be able to do something now that we could not have done a year ago, either because of changes we've made in the activity or changes in ourselves (such as greater strength).

The emphasis on the *living* part of "living with pain" gives us the opportunity to consider, do, and learn.

FOR TODAY: **I want the emphasis of "living with pain" to be on *living*. With experience, I'll gain the wisdom to make the right choices.**

December 10 ❧ Forgiveness

We must be careful not to make the intellect
our God.
—*Albert Einstein*

Imagine a quote like this from a person whom I think of as the master of the intellect. Even Einstein knew that there must be another dimension, another power that is greater than the wisest of minds.

There is no doubt that my thought processes are useful and necessary. In living with chronic pain, there are choices to make, conflicts to work out, attitudes to work on, and a myriad of problems to solve. The intellect can be one of my most helpful tools but also one of my deadliest weapons.

Even with a sharp mind, I can rationalize unkind behavior, inappropriate expressions of anger, or the placement of blame where it does not belong. I justify such actions because I feel that my pain is a natural cause of my behavior.

I am human. Just because I overcome much in living with chronic pain does not make me a saint. Even though I am doing the best I can, I sometimes act out of frustration and hurt others. The intellect can do little to mend relationships that I may have harmed. A change of heart is needed. God forgives me and though He understands my difficulty, He still expects me to make progress in being the most loving person I can be. While He beckons, my desire to be this person increases.

FOR TODAY: As God grants me forgiveness, so will I forgive myself. Today is full of promise and love will guide me.

December 11 ❧ Fear

We should not let our fears hold us back
from pursuing our hopes.
—John F. Kennedy

For some of us, chronic pain started for no particular reason. For some, it resulted from an accident or injury. For others, it stemmed from a particular disease.

All of us at some time or other experience the fear of it getting worse or, if we reinjure ourselves, of losing more function than we already have.

Fear can paralyze us and, like a parasite finding a home in us, drain us of energy. We become paralyzed in inaction, afraid that one false move will bring back the worst pain we have ever experienced or something even worse.

I picture a light in my mind flashing, "Don't shut down," at times like this. I can be afraid but still keep moving, acting on life by staying as involved as I can be, rather than overreacting to my pain in fear and isolation. I don't "shut down" when I more or less follow my daily routine, keep my thoughts on what needs to be done, and reach out in order to tell someone that I need to talk about the fear of getting worse. When fear begins, I try not to seclude myself for long because it only makes my pain worse.

FOR TODAY: **I will recognize that some of my fears are groundless. If I refuse to give them much power, they will not have such control over me and I won't "shut down."**

December 12 ❧ Music

The cause is hidden but the result is known.
—Ovid

Music affects us on several levels. It can be a bridge of communication between ourselves and others. Perhaps "Amazing Grace" makes us feel part of a caring, spiritual community, or "The Star Spangled Banner" played at a sporting event stirs a loyal pride within us as we stand alongside our countrymen.

Music has been called the language of the emotions because it communicates meaning to the listener, apart from what the composer may have intended. We don't consciously think about it, but music can influence moods and mental activities and arouse a variety of feelings. Music can evoke states of meditation and relaxation, helpful to us with chronic pain. Many of us know that listening to calming music helps soothe us. One scientific explanation is that it helps produce large molecules called peptides that relieve pain by interacting with specific receptors in the brain. But we don't need to know why in order to feel better!

Just as listening to ocean sounds can bring comfort, relaxation, and possible pain reduction, music may evoke pleasant memories that connect us with others. In many ways music can be affordable therapy for us.

For today: I'll find the song that suits my soul today.

December 13 ❧ Idealism

I am an idealist. I don't know where I'm going but I'm on my way.
—Carl Sandburg

Idealism can cause hopefulness, but it can cause great disappointment, too. We may expect people to be trustworthy, kind, and good. We may expect our days to go smoothly and our nights to be spent peacefully. We may expect ourselves not to overreact to minor irritations and frustrations. There's nothing like pain and life's problems to burst our bubble of idealism.

When people we trust betray us, when home problems, car repairs, and bills mount at every turn, and when our nights are interrupted with worry, tossing, and turning, pain may magnify itself and again we may cry out, "I've had enough of this pain!"

What bothers us is not only the pain, though. It is the context within which the pain forces itself upon us. Problems will leave or change; they always do. The pain may lessen or change; we have days when we experience this.

When idealism is strong we expect the best. Out of idealism may come actions on our part that allow the best to happen. Like Sandburg, we may not know where we're going but we're on our way.

FOR TODAY: **I'll use idealism not to shield me from reality but to give me motivation to find the best in all I see or do.**

December 14 ∾ **Holiday Stress, Self-pity**

> *Pain—has an element of Blank;*
> *It cannot recollect*
> *When it began, or if there were*
> *A day when it was not.*
> *—Emily Dickinson*

"Bah, humbug" was my attitude about gift-giving one year. There were too many people to buy for, and I didn't want to leave anyone out.

There were too many social events to attend, and I didn't want to miss any. There was not enough money, and I couldn't make more. There were many more cards to mail than happy words of greeting to send. Definitely, there was more tinsel than time.

It wasn't only the constraints of time, energy, and finances that made me feel pressured. It was upsetting to have to make compromises because of pain and to admit that I couldn't do it all.

Although self-pity doesn't cost anything, it robs us of both time and energy, and offers no solutions. Unless I am grateful for what I am able to do, self-pity grows. There are people we can care about and include in holiday preparations. To avoid fatigue we can choose what to attend and what to miss.

What an asset it is to be tired but happy, or to be poor in the pocket but rich in the spirit.

FOR TODAY: **Gratitude is a wonderful antidote for self-pity. I'm grateful that simplification can bring me peace during the holidays.**

December 15 ❧ December Holidays

Love is nine-tenths the lover and only
one-tenth the object loved.
—George Santayana

The special holidays in December give us symbols to attach meaning to and festive moods to enter. Ideally, we unreservedly celebrate the presence of others and fondly remember the richness of holidays past.

During such times, we may expect to spread love tangibly and lavishly, to have our tired hearts revived by song, and to have reinforced the belief that the good of the world is greater than the evil. There is the anticipation of new surprises, alongside the stability of tradition. We expect to experience harmony and accommodation, a lightening of the spirit and a restoring of the soul.

Such are the ideals, but everything will not meet this standard, no matter how much we romanticize it. Yet we can be inspired by the principle of love so that we may give and receive it graciously. If pain interferes with our ideals, we may need to use new methods of expressing affection, but these methods can be the most loving of all. We can commit ourselves to finding them.

FOR TODAY: **There is idealism in the holidays of the month. I am prompted to spread love in all the ways I can.**

December 16 ∾ Relaxation

Because the world is not going anywhere
there is no hurry.
—Alan Watts

Progressive relaxation helps me.

I tense the muscles of my abdomen, then release the tension and feel the relaxation. I take a deep breath, hold it in, feel the tension, and let the air out, feeling the relaxation as my chest slowly falls.

I tense the muscles in my face by making a scowling face. I feel the tension, then release the tension, and feel the relaxation.

I tense the muscles in my arm, feel the tension, release, and feel the relaxation. I tense and relax other body parts, a technique called progressive relaxation. I close my eyes and say the word "relax." My abdomen rises and falls as I relax, and if other thoughts come into my mind, I picture them being erased from the back of my mind.

I tense my hand to form a fist and, in my mind, place my fist over a painful body part. Then I relax my fist and imagine that the sore, aching muscle group relaxes, also. I feel the tension draining away.

Anytime that muscle tension happens, I think, "Relax, release."

FOR TODAY: **I can use relaxation techniques to reduce my stress and tension today. I look forward to relaxing my tight muscles.**

December 17 ∾ Children

> *How awful if your kids only remember Mom*
> *or Dad as a whimpering, decrepit, impotent*
> *figure. Thinking about that can sometimes be*
> *an effective means of pain control.*
> —*Cheri Register*

While we want to appear strong and healthy in public, it is best, at the appropriate time, to explain our pain to our children. If they aren't involved, they may not make the connection between our actions and the fact that we have chronic pain. Especially children who are at a rebellious and self-centered age can be given the opportunity to develop maturity if we explain both our limitations and our desire to be involved with them. Younger children need to know what's happening so that they don't think it is their fault if we become impatient and irritable, or that we are uncaring if we cannot go somewhere with them.

Sometimes we are overprotective and fearful that our children will blame us in later life for not being a more typical parent. We shouldn't be afraid because anxiety over this can drive us to try to be Superparent. We then overextend ourselves, causing us to be in more pain, to be more irritable, and to feel more guilt. What a vicious circle!

We can be content that we are being good parents in loving our children, teaching them responsibility and awareness, and balancing their wants and needs with ours. In this way, everyone wins.

FOR TODAY: **My children are a blessing to me. I don't have to be Superparent to ensure that their future will be happy.**

December 18 ❧ Independence

A tree that is unbending is easily broken.
—Lao-tzu

She sits erect in her chair and speaks with as little movement as possible. Every move seems to threaten what narrow comfort zone she has.

"I see something that needs to be done and I just do it, even though it is too hard for me," she says, "but now I'm paying for it. I grew up in an alcoholic home and I've had to fight to get where I am today—owning my own business and being my own person. My independence is so important to me that I can't seem to ask for help."

In her business, she maintained independence, but by hurting herself, she was reduced to helplessness at home.

We want to be done with feeling ashamed of having chronic pain. It is easy to let pride stand in the way of getting the help we need, because we want to stay as independent as possible. But like taking medicine, we can learn to accept help in the dosages that we need it.

FOR TODAY: **For my well-being, I am willing to accept help when I need it. Independence means so much to me and I want all I can have.**

December 19 ❧ Spirituality

> *It is just such an exceptionally difficult*
> *external situation which gives man*
> *the opportunity to grow spiritually*
> *beyond himself.*
> —*Viktor Frankl*

Spirituality is essentially the connection to a power and strength that is beyond ourselves, even if we profess no specific religion. In pain, I live with a difficult situation, but through spiritual strength I am able to do what I thought I could not do. For me, spiritual growth bears the fruits of courage and stability.

Spirituality gives me inner freedom when outward circumstances imperil me. Every day I am given the choice to let pain overpower me or to receive help in refusing to submit to its tyranny. It is precisely because of pain's potential negative effects that I need help beyond myself.

Day to day, what life requires of me differs. There are many times when I'd like to answer pain's challenge, living and growing unaided. Failing at this, I gratefully receive the help that spirituality freely gives.

For today: **I look to spiritual strength to enable me to carry the weight that often presses down on me.**

December 20 ❧ Holiday Stress

We can do no great things, only small things
with great love.
—Mother Teresa

Stress, even "good stress," can increase our pain. We're surprised at how it creeps up on us. Stress can build while we're scarcely aware of it, until we're overwhelmed and at risk of losing control of our pain.

During the holidays, demands are made on our energy, time, and money. We want to delegate activities such as shopping, cleaning, cooking, or baking to someone, but we think we should be able to handle it ourselves. We get caught up in other people's opinions. What would our families think if we asked for more help or omitted a "to do" from our list?

Dealing assertively with others' expectations and taking care of our needs will keep our stress and pain levels in the manageable range. If we can ask for help the first time, it may be easier the next time.

Our families and friends don't want to see us fatigued, having severe pain, and looking at them with a just-leave-me-alone look. They want to love us and be loved in return more than anything else.

FOR TODAY: Today I will simplify one activity and ask for help with another. I want to be available for love.

December 21 ❧ Love

One word frees us of all the weight and
pain of life: that word is love.
—Sophocles

Chronic pain can be disruptive to marital roles. The man
with chronic pain may feel guilty if his wife needs to bring
in more income, and the wife may demand more household help from her mate if she is the one who is afflicted.
There may be frustration, misunderstanding, and resentment over role changes. For the person with pain, there
also may be the fear of abandonment, especially if the
spouse has to assume more responsibilities.

We with chronic pain feel vulnerable, disliking our
sense of dependence. We fear that we bring less to the
marriage and feel insecure. We often exaggerate our inad-
equacies. How long will our spouse want to stay with us?
We don't want to admit the thought, but it is there.

We aren't responsible for our spouses' feelings about
our chronic pain. That is their business. What we can do is
to communicate, accept help without fear, and be ourselves, letting peace, trust, and love guide us.

FOR TODAY: I will accept my needs and know that I am
doing my best to move forward. I will let others' reactions be their own.

> *Shall we permit adverse winds to overwhelm*
> *us as we journey across life's Atlantic, or*
> *will our inner spiritual engines sustain us in*
> *spite of the winds?*
> —*Martin Luther King, Jr.*

I am assaulted by the violence of pain, but I am not defenseless. Pain strikes, stabs, cuts, and burns me during an acute flare-up, but I counter with nonviolence. I am not a passive victim, though.

Often I counter pain with intense concentration on a thought or image in meditation, thereby dulling the edges of my sensitivity. In meditation, I develop a dimension of mind into which I can retreat and sometimes formulate a prayer by which I can be uplifted.

I am spared from the clutches of pain's piercing effects as time joins my side and pain lessens. In utilizing this peaceful response, I have gained self-preservation. My inner spiritual engine has sustained me in spite of severe pain.

In times like these, I am not immune to the violence of pain, but through meditation I have succeeded in not inflicting harm upon others while defending myself against pain. The aftermath of the assault is quiet, not cruel.

FOR TODAY: **God, help me refrain from injuring others while I am in pain. One of my choices is to give my mind a retreat through meditation.**

December 23 ❧ Blaming Ourselves

> *I have never seen a person grow or change*
> *in a constructive direction when motivated*
> *by guilt, shame and/or hate.*
> —*William Goldberg*

I once read a wonderful book about a courageous man who had heart problems and repeatedly had episodes of congestive heart failure. His doctors kept asking each time what he had done to bring on the complication. Was it lack of exercise? Too much? Was it his diet? Over and over he would tell them that he had done nothing to bring on his condition. The effect of diet, exercise, and medication was limited.

"I've done nothing differently. It's not my fault!" he tried to say. Finally the doctors believed him after they did open heart surgery and saw, firsthand, his multiple heart abnormalities.

I cried tears of empathy when I read the many pages that told of his struggle. It isn't my fault that my pain went from acute to chronic, and it isn't always my fault when I hurt more one time than another.

As I read, I realized that I had found a freedom from blame and shame. Today I don't have to blame myself for not being able to make my pain cease, and I am not ashamed of it. I continue to work to alter my perception of it and to lessen its negative effects on me. I am happy when this works but don't blame myself harshly when it doesn't.

For today: Even if I played some part in my pain, I need to know I am human. It's not my fault that I haven't the power to rid myself of the pain once and for all. I can be done with blame and shame.

December 24 ❧ God's Love

God may love us—yes—but our response
is voluntary.
—Dag Hammarskjöld

What is our response to the gift of God's love? If we don't acknowledge it, we miss the comfort of great strength and goodness. If we acknowledge it but don't appreciate it, we may not benefit fully from it. And if we don't use it, our lives may become meaningless. God's love is meant for us, to use and to pass on as a gift to others.

It may be hard to see God's love when we are in pain. We, at some point, may shake our fists at God, rather than open our hands to receive His loving gifts. If we shake our fist for very long, we only get an ineffective, painful arm. That is useless for our purposes. Yet God's love awaits us.

When we have accepted it, a natural progression prompts us to want to give love to others in order to share the gift. Henry Drummond once wrote that he had seen almost all the beautiful things God had made and he had enjoyed almost every pleasure, but as he looked back he saw standing out four or five encounters when the love of God had been reflected in some poor imitation, some small act of love of his, and those seemed to be the things that, of all the remembrances of his life, touched him the most.

Let us be mirrors of God's love.

FOR TODAY: **God, first help me accept Your love and then let me be willing to pass it on.**

December 25 ❧ Spirituality, God's Love

> . . . *as the years have unfolded the*
> *eloquently simple words of Mother Pollard*
> *have come back again and again to give*
> *light and peace and guidance to my troubled*
> *soul. "God's gonna take care of you."*
> *This faith transforms the whirlwind of*
> *despair into a warm and reviving*
> *breeze of hope.*
> —Martin Luther King, Jr.

My mother tells me, "I don't know how you do it," and I myself am amazed. It helps me when she says that. How *do* I do it? How am I willing to get out of bed every day knowing I will be in pain? How do I keep from being a wretched, self-pitying person who drives all friends and family away? How do I get the courage to try to do better instead of giving up?

I think it's because, like Martin Luther King, I am comforted by the thought that "God's gonna take care of you." He's seen me through times of severe pain and despair. At times, it is only His light, peace, and guidance that have helped, not only my troubled soul but all of me.

To a great extent, that is how I "do it."

FOR TODAY: **God, stay close to me today. I sometimes don't think I can "do it" much longer.**

December 26 ❧ Exhaustion, Worry

And if there is not any such thing as a long
time, nor the rest of your lives, now from
now on, but there is only now, why the now
is the thing to praise and I am very happy
with it.
—*Ernest Hemingway*

I wear myself out. The fatigue and exhaustion I feel are both physical and emotional, because the demands of chronic pain are great.

Daily living can use up my energy stores, especially as I try to expand my physical capabilities. I also can be exhausted from trying to fight feelings of anger, fear, or depression. Being tired, I seem unable to think about anyone else's welfare but my own.

Exhaustion teaches me about some of my most basic desires: physical rest and emotional serenity. There are ways to obtain those desires. I can learn to energize my body with exercise, pace myself, take time for breaks, and avoid the foods and beverages that make me feel sluggish.

For my emotional pain, I can meet it, release it to God, and let my spirit be free. In the place of anger, fear, and depression, my spirit substitutes love, confidence, and creativity.

The extent that I let God into my life helps determine how much I worry about things that may not happen. God helps me to concentrate on living in today.

For today: **There are lessons I can learn from exhaustion. It can lead me to ask my Higher Power for physical rest and emotional serenity. I then find it easier to take care of myself this day.**

December 27 ❧ Bad Days

> *When it gets dark enough, you can see*
> *the stars.*
> —*Charles A. Beard*

Darkness can surround us in many ways. Perhaps it is a letdown after a holiday, a relapse into greater pain, or the return of an emotion over an issue that we thought was settled, such as the feeling of helplessness.

A friend with chronic pain keeps a journal so that during the dark days, she can look back to the times that have been brighter and more positive. She says, "It helps me to see that I have had better days, especially when the worse ones are relentless."

As the historian wrote, "When it gets dark enough, you can see the stars." When I look at the starry sky above me, I am filled with awe. As the stars point to the vastness of the universe, I feel connected to this grandeur. Even though clouds may block my view, I trust that they will be present on the next clear, dark night. Then, to see the wonder of the stars, I have only to tilt back my head and look upward.

During our darker days, it may take more than simply having an attitude of "looking up," but we can appreciate things we once took for granted and let them lead us, like the stars, to connectedness with all things.

FOR TODAY: **On my worst days, I concentrate on simple things I once took for granted and look forward to enjoying them more when brighter days come. Like the stars, things I am grateful for may not have been as apparent in the glow of a better day.**

December 28 ❧ Willingness

> *To say yes, you have to sweat and roll up*
> *your sleeves and plunge both hands into life*
> *up to the elbows. It is easy to say no, even*
> *if saying no means death.*
> —Jean Anouilh

Courage and perseverance aren't the only qualities that help me deal with pain. Often it is willingness.

It takes willingness to look at my old ways of doing things and ask myself what, against the background of pain, needs changing. It takes willingness to keep participating in the dance of life and to sway with what comes my way. It takes willingness for me to allow myself happiness and to trust that I will be guided through troubled times.

I stand in the middle of old habits and old answers, and ask myself if there is a better way. I'm receptive to being shown new ways of acting and thinking. Willingness unlatches the door to solutions that were previously locked for me.

FOR TODAY: **I'm willing to give up the safety of the old in exchange for the possibilities of the new.**

December 29 ∾ Self-pity

Let any man, or woman, look too much
upon his own life, and everything
becomes a mess.
—Sherwood Anderson

Self-pity is easy. Too easy.

I have a friend who is more limited than I, and another who is less so. The three of us are at different stations in our journey with pain. The first friend teaches me about avoiding excessive self-pity. ''I can always think of someone who is worse off than I am,'' she says. ''Besides, if I complain too much that life is awful, I start believing it!''

I can depend on her to tell me, ''Don't give up!'' during days when self-pity invades my thoughts. Because I've listened to her during her own more painful days, I know she speaks from the heart, as someone who intimately knows my experiences.

When self-pity approaches, I try to resist coddling and encouraging it. I am not entirely successful, but it is getting easier to do. For me, I can break free of self-pity by picking up a book, getting some fresh air, calling someone, or writing about what's bothering me. It is easy to be taken in by self-pity, but I can think of ways to block it.

FOR TODAY: **I can be attracted to self-pity, but it only makes me feel worse. I don't need it today.**

December 30 ❧ Courage

You gain strength, courage and confidence
by every experience in which you really stop
to look fear in the face. You are able to say,
"I lived through this horror. I can take the
next thing that comes along." You must do
the one thing that you think you cannot do.
—Eleanor Roosevelt

At some point, when we realized that our pain was chronic, we cried out, "I can't live with this!" Like Eleanor Roosevelt, we must stop and look fear in the face. It is true that we have lived through horrors—painful medical procedures, the pain of loss, the pain of alienation, the pain of prejudice, the pain of futile efforts, the pain of guilt, and the pain of fallen expectations.

We have lived through it all and have not succumbed. We have gained the strength, courage, and confidence that Eleanor Roosevelt speaks about. There still may be things we think we cannot do. They may have to do with setting goals and establishing boundaries, asking the God of our understanding for help, or challenging our physical limitations.

Despite fears and disappointments, we must go on, even if it means doing the things we think we cannot do.

FOR TODAY: I look back and see my victories over fear. My spirit has the strength to do what needs to be done.

*Time carries you along, like a river, but
never flows out of the present; the more it
goes, the more it stays, and you no longer
have to fight it or kill it.*
—Alan Watts

The first day of the new year may find us making resolutions, setting goals, and looking with anticipation to a better year than the last. On the other hand, the new year may usher in feelings of failure and defeatism, as we review the past year with feelings of frustration and disappointment. Whether looking forward or backward, we can live well today.

This last year is drawing to a close. A fresh start can be made, but our progress in coping effectively with chronic pain will not be as simple as putting up a new calendar. The answers will not be as automatic as knowing how to write a new date.

Recovery from the negative effects of chronic pain is a process. It takes time to change our misconceptions, such as: "I can't live with pain," "My pain affects no one but me," or "If a cause for my pain can be found, the pain can be cured." It takes time to learn how to distract our minds from the pain, to stop negative self-talk, to learn how to control anxiety, and to concentrate on our abilities rather than our disabilities. It takes time to reflect on what is important to us and to take the steps toward achievement. It takes time to establish a relationship with a God whom we feel has let us down.

The first day of a new year approaches, and it has much potential. This may be the year when we accept our pain on a deeper level, better our relationships with others, learn to be gentle with our emotions, become more active, be thankful for what we can do, and feel good about the goals we accomplish. This may describe the new year, but all we have is today.

FOR TODAY: **I don't need to make impossible resolutions. I need only to take that first hesitant step in the direction of recovery.**

Index